YES, YOU ARE
TRANS ENOUGH

D0139934

of related interest

He's Always Been My Son
A Mother's Story about Raising Her Transgender Son
Janna Barkin
ISBN 978 1 78592 747 8
eISBN 978 1 78450 525 7

Trans Voices
Becoming Who You Are
Declan Henry
Foreword by Professor Stephen Whittle, OBE
Afterword by Jane Fae
ISBN 978 1 78592 240 4
eISBN 978 1 78450 520 2

To My Trans Sisters
Edited by Charlie Craggs
ISBN 978 1 78592 343 2
eISBN 978 1 78450 668 1

How to Understand Your Gender
A Practical Guide for Exploring Who You Are
Alex Iantaffi and Meg-John Barker
Foreword by S. Bear Bergman
ISBN 978 1 78592 746 1
eISBN 978 1 78450 517 2

YES, YOU ARE TRANS ENOUGH

MY TRANSITION FROM SELF-LOATHING TO SELF-LOVE

MIA VIOLET

Jessica Kingsley *Publishers*
London and Philadelphia

First published in 2018
by Jessica Kingsley Publishers
73 Collier Street
London N1 9BE, UK
and
400 Market Street, Suite 400
Philadelphia, PA 19106, USA

www.jkp.com

Copyright © Mia Violet 2018

All rights reserved. No part of this publication may be reproduced in any
material form (including photocopying, storing in any medium by electronic
means or transmitting) without the written permission of the copyright owner
except in accordance with the provisions of the law or under terms of a licence
issued in the UK by the Copyright Licensing Agency Ltd. www.cla.co.uk or in
overseas territories by the relevant reproduction rights organisation, for details
see www.ifrro.org. Applications for the copyright owner's written permission to
reproduce any part of this publication should be addressed to the publisher.

Warning: The doing of an unauthorised act in relation to a copyright work
may result in both a civil claim for damages and criminal prosecution.

Library of Congress Cataloging in Publication Data
Names: Violet, Mia, author.
Title: Yes, you are trans enough : my transition from self-loathing to
    self-love / Mia Violet.
Description: London ; Philadelphia : Jessica Kingsley Publishers, 2018.
Identifiers: LCCN 2018001666 | ISBN 9781785923159
Subjects: LCSH: Violet, Mia. | Transgender people--Great Britain--Biography.
    | Transgender people--Identity.
Classification: LCC HQ77.8.V56 A3 2018 | DDC 306.76/8092 [B]
--dc23 LC record available at https://lccn.loc.gov/2018001666

British Library Cataloguing in Publication Data
A CIP catalogue record for this book is available from the British Library

ISBN 978 1 78592 315 9
eISBN 978 1 78450 628 5

Printed and bound in the United States

To Loretta, because without you I wouldn't be me.

And to my friends and followers on Twitter, for being a support group, a cheerleading squad, and a family.

CONTENTS

INTRODUCTION

My name is Mia Violet, I'm a transgender woman, and I originally started writing this book because I was sick of seeing so much misinformation and lies about my community. I wanted to do something to help, to straighten out misconceptions and share my own story so that others could read a detailed tale of what it's like to be transgender without the stereotypes and lies. Meanwhile, I admittedly love talking about myself and this seemed like a great excuse to ramble endlessly about my history and varied opinions. But it was mainly the misinformation and helping people thing that drove me to do this. Honest.

When I originally pitched this book, I set my projected word count at what I imagined was a reasonable and realistic size for what I wanted to do. The goal was simple: recount my history of growing up as a transgender person by regaling the struggles and misadventures I had in coming to terms with the truth. Along the way I planned to pepper in discussions and elaborations of relevant topics, such as the facts on the tiresome bathroom debate and the truth about the existence and experiences of transgender children. My hope was that the result would be a book with multiple purposes and wide appeal, while being a light and entertaining memoir regardless of the reader's prior understanding and interest in trans issues.

When I came to write the book I found I had a lot more to say than I thought. Delving into extra concepts, such as questioning whether gender is performative and what the state of trans healthcare is, seemed necessary both to bring context to my life and to elaborate on the wider state of contemporary trans rights. Meanwhile, with the help of old diaries and dusty blogs, I revisited forgotten parts of my life and unearthed memories that were vital to understanding my complicated relationship with gender. Amusingly, while writing the book I then began a new transformation altogether, as my transition led to an opportunity to shed negative thinking and pessimistic thought patterns that I had picked up as survival techniques. This felt too relevant and intertwined with my transition to gloss over or exclude. Thus the final result you're currently reading is a book much meatier and more densely packed than I had ever expected it to be. The final length is double the size of my initial projection. Luckily my editor agreed that all of the extra material was well worth including and I'm happy nothing unexpected had to be sacrificed to create a breezier read.

So what is this book? At its core it's still a memoir, an unflinching account of the ups and downs of being trans; one that begins with my childhood, runs through my messy teenage years, and into my adulthood where my transition finally took place. But along the way the story makes frequent detours, to elaborate about the bigger issues at play in each chapter. There I untangle common falsehoods and explain concepts that are too often missing from mainstream discourse of transgender rights.

The reason for the title is something that will become increasingly clear as the book goes on, but if you're browsing this introduction because you've been wondering if you yourself are trans enough to be transgender, then I'm going to give you a big spoiler right now: yes, you are. Despite what you've heard, there are no rigid criteria of clichés that you have to exhibit or a measured level of misery that you need to profess to feel first. Likewise, you don't have to detest your body or weep at the sight of your genitals. To be transgender all you need is to have an inkling that the gender on your birth certificate is not quite right. That's it.

If that criterion includes you, that's not to say you should absolutely run out and start your own transition right now. But I do want to gently reassure you that if you've been looking for an excuse to identify as transgender, this is it. This is your permission to explore these feelings and work out what gender you really are. However, I also know that a nudge like this is rarely enough to put confusing feelings at ease, nor is coming out as transgender a choice you generally make because the opening few paragraphs of a book told you to. But it's my hope that if you stick with me, then the rest of this book can help you reach a conclusion about what's best for you.

As a transgender woman who often encourages people to reach out to her if they're anxious or questioning their gender, I'm used to inviting people to try out any label that feels fitting. When I say this, the person's response is usually to exclaim with horror that they can't call themselves transgender because they'd be co-opting the 'trans experience' of suffering and resilience. They're wrong. That identity belongs to them just as much as it belongs to me. But I know exactly why they hesitate to call themselves transgender, because I did too. I was in that same position for a very long time. I used to feel that the transgender label was something that couldn't be taken unless it was bestowed upon you, or earned through a fiery trial of harassment and mental anguish. I spent years absolutely convinced that I wasn't trans enough. The entire reason why I was so averse to that descriptor is complicated and multifaceted (and included in this book) but a simple explanation is that the media had done such a shoddy job of illustrating what it's like to be transgender, I didn't think I could possibly belong to that same group.

Instead of portraying the nuance and the variety of the trans community, documentaries and editorials often reduce us to sensationalist one-note characters. Our lives are routinely repackaged in a straightforward narrative that begins with a painful gender nonconforming childhood, and ends with us on an operating table to receive elective surgery. It's an overplayed and well-known story but it only rings true for a fraction of us. When I engaged with these stories I didn't see anyone like me. I was assigned male at birth, thanks to my genitals, and unlike the trans women I saw on TV I never played with dolls, I didn't want surgery, and I didn't think I was that upset about being raised as male. Clearly I wasn't trans enough. Except that I was, because there's no such thing as not being trans enough.

That may all sound like I abandoned my old life and transitioned for no reason, as if I wanted an excuse to wear dresses and I thought it might be fun to grow a pair of boobs (it is fun by the way). But I can assure you that's not the case either. Only trans people transition. Nobody who isn't trans looks at the loss of personal safety, the probability of abandonment, the employability issues, the health risks, the large financial cost and the fact we're constantly a target of ridicule and harassment, and then decides that they're going to transition anyway just for kicks. But the idea that we're all born with a sense of what gender we are and leap at the first chance to tell someone is completely wrong too.

You rarely see it in the media, but many trans people agonise over whether to transition or not. We analyse our histories, we panic about the future, we blame other factors for our problems, and we even concoct ridiculous scenarios to frame the decision in a way that might illuminate the answer. When worrying about whether to transition or not we often ponder about a 'magic button' that instantly transforms our body, or a reality-altering wish that could mean nobody ever knew us as the gender we were assigned at birth. Although this has become a bit of a cliché, it helps us to focus on the end result, to question if a guaranteed fast and painless transition would be any more enticing. We almost have to trick ourselves into seeing the truth by stripping out all the baggage that we've been taught about trans people, because so much of it is rooted in sensationalism. When most of us begin our own transition, making the change from one gendered presentation to another, we have no idea if it's going to work out. We just know that we have to try.

Before jumping into the first chapter, there are a couple of things that must be said. The first is that language is forever evolving. Although 'transgender' as a term is fairly well known now, in the 'ancient past' of the 1990s it wasn't used so much. Instead, 'transsexual' was the common term used to describe people like me – those of us who transition by changing our bodies as well as our names and outward presentation. Thankfully, this term is mostly retired due to its misplaced focus on sexual characteristics, meaning it awkwardly described someone's nether regions rather than their gender. For the sake of not perpetuating such an outdated term, I won't be using it in the book at all. Instead

I'll be using 'transgender', or 'trans' as an abbreviation. I'll also be using it as an umbrella term, to include people like me who transition, as well as those who do not transition in any traditional sense, and those whose gender doesn't fall on a binary male/female spectrum like mine does, but still belong to this community. For the specific type of trans person that I am, I'll be using 'trans woman'. It simply means a woman who is trans. The connotations of trans woman imply a woman who was assigned male at birth. That itself is another modern phrase to replace tired tropes like 'born a man', which sounds very messy and uncomfortable, as well as being rife with incorrect and problematic implications. I mention this not just to clear up some confusion but because although these are the understood respectful terms at the time of writing, they might not be at the time of reading. If things have moved on by the time you're reading this book, please note that these expressions are a reflection of the times and are not being presented as eternally correct.

It's also vital that I enthusiastically stress that a unified trans experience does not exist. Our community is vast, with countless alternative experiences and stories that are all equally valid and authentic. This book is my own personal account and, although it will certainly cover experiences that various other trans people have had, it will entirely clash with the escapades of many others. Furthermore, I am a bisexual, able-bodied, white woman of a relatively young age. Certain privileges and intersections of identity have played a part in my life and it's imperative that it's understood that being transgender is not an identity that overrides any other. Trans women of colour, who are the pioneers and founders of the queer movement, are disproportionately targeted with harassment and violence, while disabled trans people are forced to navigate unique challenges that I have never had to endure. I am also a dyadic trans woman, meaning I'm not intersex. Thus the book has nothing on the problems that the intersex community has to endure, which includes trans people who struggle with their own representational issues surrounding gender identity and sexuality. It would be grossly inappropriate for me to speak for any of these groups. This is not some sort of ultimate detailed catch-all explanation of what all trans people go through, as no such book can exist.

Finally, I owe a debt to every trans person who has come before me, not just for laying the groundwork I needed to understand these topics, but for fighting for a society where I have the right and ability to transition and live as myself. Without their work and courage, I wouldn't be here and this book certainly wouldn't exist. There's a responsibility that comes with occupying this podium, a space earned by people far more courageous than me. Therefore, I've done my very best to be as respectful and careful as possible when discussing everything within, as I know the impact and power that my words can have, even incidentally. But ultimately, I have to stress again that I can only speak for myself. These are my own thoughts and opinions, grounded in my own experience of the last 28 years. This is the story of one millennial trans woman, and the weird, embarrassing, funny, tragic and uplifting things that have happened to mould me into the woman I am today.

Chapter 1

EXPECTATIONS

I was born in Northern England at the close of the 80s, the first child in a fairly conventional family. My dad was working in the emerging IT industry, while my mother left the financial sector to raise me. Throw in our dog, who arrived later, and from the outside we looked like a stereotypical heteronormative nuclear family. Later I ruined this image and queered everything to pieces, but I'm getting ahead of myself.

As a child I lived in a sleepy suburb tucked out of the way of a busy main road. Beyond the road lay a prim Catholic church and its accompanying primary school, which I begrudgingly attended. In the opposite direction were a handful of shops and a line of hairdressers. If there was one thing my town had an abundance of, it was independent hairdressers. Otherwise it was a heavily residential area, mostly populated by new families and retired couples. For the first decade of my life, that small slice of a bigger city was my entire world.

One memory that beautifully sums up my childhood took place during my first winter at school. Overnight the region had been battered by relentless blizzards, turning my walk that morning into a picturesque obstacle course of snow drifts and frozen puddles. When I arrived at the school, it was deserted. Most kids had used the weather as an excuse to stay home. I wasn't that lucky. With both of my parents busy, I was left under the supervising eye of one of the teachers, who had little to do but babysit the handful of children who'd been dropped into their care. My morning was filled by sitting happily in a quiet classroom and building a sprawling house out of handheld blocks. Once satisfied, I sat back and proclaimed that I was finished, the house was complete. I remember being particularly proud that the house also had its own garden, carefully partitioned with a wall of coloured bricks. With that encouragingly bemused tone often used by adults to appease children, the teacher asked who was going to live in the house now that it was complete. I paused for a moment, considering who this quaint multi-coloured home could belong to. 'Batman!' I yelled with enthusiasm, producing a small toy Batmobile I had brought in my pocket. I then proceeded to help Batman dramatically drive around his new unorthodox home, on the prowl for criminals who might threaten his new garden. Left to amuse myself using my own imagination, I was thrilled to continue playing out superhero stories for the rest of the day.

To give more context to that scene, back in 1992 *Batman Returns* was released in cinemas. At just three years old, I can confidently say it's unlikely anyone took me to see it, or that I would have comprehended the plot. But once I later discovered it on VHS, I fell in love with it. The costumes, dramatic action scenes, and spooky gothic tone mesmerised me. Capturing my attention even more was the video game tie-in released for the Mega Drive console, a linear adventure where you played as Batman, punching your way through a silent and incredibly loose interpretation of the movie's storyline. Do you remember that part of the movie where two huge statues come to life and decide to belch fireballs at Batman for no reason? Nor does anybody else, but it was my favourite part of the video game amongst its other bizarre and violent changes to the plot. This enthusiasm also led to me buying my first Batman action figure, a second-hand well-worn model of Michael Keaton, complete with a stern, steely expression. Dolls never really entered my toybox or my imagination – as far as I was concerned, being left with Batman was far better than playing with Barbie.

I want to interject here and assure you that I am a trans woman, and therefore I was a trans kid back then. But had my gender been debated by concerned adults, my interests would have led them to declare me a cisgender boy. If you're not aware of the term, 'cisgender' means the opposite of 'transgender'. A cisgender person is someone who feels their gender aligns with the one they were assigned at birth, the one the doctor proclaimed when they got their first look at what genitals that person arrived with. Meanwhile, 'transgender' is an umbrella term that essentially encompasses everybody else, so those of us who later disagree with that doctor's assessment. There's been some pushback in the last year or so against the term 'cisgender', with many claiming that it's pointless and part of some agenda to force unnecessary labels onto people. In reality, the term 'cis' is Latin and is also used in chemistry. It exists because the English language works by labelling people by what they are, rather than what they are not. For instance, I could describe myself as 'a white, bisexual trans woman'. I wouldn't call myself 'a not-black, not-straight, not-cisgender, not-man'. Therefore, 'cisgender' is just a simple label to indicate what team you belong to – it doesn't carry any other connotations than that.

Returning to the previous point, toys, childhood interests, and even favourite colours are still considered a huge indication of what gender a child really is, despite the fact that attaching undue significance to these things is actively harmful. This can be unmasked as even more ridiculous when you consider how much of the children's market is influenced by simple marketing decisions. Although blue is considered the favourite of boys, and pink the choice of girls, the reverse was often true until clothing manufacturers decided otherwise. What our society considers masculine and feminine shouldn't be the basis for judging anyone's identity, yet it often is. There was a court case in 2016 where a judge ruled that a child must be cisgender due to their interests. The child, who the mother claimed was a happy transgender girl, also had an interest in traditionally masculine pursuits, specifically superheroes. That alone was enough to raise the alarm. This is a line of thinking which only gets produced when it comes to transgender children. We have playful terms like 'tomboy' to describe a girl who enjoys 'boyish' activities, but nobody is rushing to claim that all tomboys are actually transgender boys. Yet should a self-defined transgender girl also claim to enjoy boyish activities, her identity is invalidated and debated by armchair psychologists. It goes back to the big problem surrounding transgender children, one that affects the kids just as much as the adults: there is stunningly low awareness and very little understanding of what being transgender as a child even means.

If you could have seen me as a child, then I wouldn't blame you for having a hard time imagining that I was actually a girl. With a Sonic the Hedgehog t-shirt, fistful of Star Wars toys and a Mighty Max skateboard, on the surface I looked no different from a random boy raised on video games and 90s cartoons. If you asked six-year-old me if she was a boy or a girl, she'd wrinkle up her face and tell you she's a boy, duh. She wouldn't understand why you'd asked such an obvious and silly question. How could I have been a girl when literally everybody in my entire life had told me I was a boy and treated me as such? Well, I can tell you with the power of hindsight that I was a girl, even if nobody ever figured it out, even if *I* hadn't yet figured it out. If there had been wider awareness and education about gender identity, then I could perhaps have puzzled out the truth, but instead I was left to fumble on, ignorant as to what it was that made me feel increasingly out of place.

Prior to attending school, I put little thought into the concept of gender. My first friend was Sarah, a girl who lived with her grandmother next door. Most of my earliest memories are of running around her overgrown garden, drawing pictures together on huge reams of hole-punched printer paper, or playing with her trio of energetic black cats. We didn't think anything of what made us different; we were just two happy kids with a lot in common.

Just like when I was alone with my action figures, my imagination played a large part in keeping me entertained when with Sarah. For a time we became convinced that one of our neighbours, an unassuming man who lived alone and kept to himself, was actually a criminal working on a nefarious scheme. This idea started when he had glared at us from his car one afternoon. Thanks to our unburdened creativity, and childishly innocent lack of common sense, we had deducted that his expression was evidence of his diabolically evil nature. What other reason could he possibly have had to look disapprovingly upon us? Villainy was the only plausible explanation. Over the following weeks we continued this narrative, discreetly sharing with each other any strange details we had noticed about him, such as times he had gone missing in the morning for an unknown reason and only returned late in the afternoon, or when he'd spoken to another neighbour about what could have been his mysterious motive. We never actually developed any suggestions for what insidious plan he could be working on behind his net curtains as we weren't quite creative enough for specifics. Inevitably, in time we forgot about him and moved onto our next obsession, but for a while he was an exciting villain and unknowingly helped two excitable kids feel like shrewd investigative partners.

When I joined the local school, that's when the gendered differences between myself and my peers were rudely pointed out. Boys and girls were dressed differently, grouped together by their gender, and had different expectations thrust upon them. This wasn't helped by the fact that I attended a Catholic school with a long history of awkwardly traditional thinking. One example of this is that in my first year of attendance there was a school-wide costume contest which had two prizes to choose from: a rugby ball for the boys and a set of sewing supplies for the girls. I distinctly remember at the time finding both prizes completely unappealing, yet our head teacher was quite excited to unveil them. Naturally, I went as Batman (thanks to my mother's own sewing ability, a costume was produced at short notice). Since I failed to win the contest, I was spared the trouble of having to choose between each patronisingly gendered prize. As for the Batman costume, the lengthy black cape was repurposed as a hairdressing cloak and used in the family for many years.

When not dressed as Batman, I of course wore my school uniform. Being bundled with boys meant donning grey itchy trousers and a blue-collared shirt. Meanwhile, the other girls wore long dresses and were allowed to wear colourful headbands and accessories. There's a whole separate discussion to be had about the benefits and detriments of school uniforms, but you cannot deny that dressing children by gender encourages them to see the differences between themselves right away. Divisions formed very quickly, as boys and girls grouped together in large packs which seldom crossed over. If a boy was seen to be socialising with girls, or a girl dared to play football with the boys, then they'd each be teased by their peers for failing to conform. As far as us kids were concerned, there was a big difference between boys and girls because that's what all the adults were now drilling into us.

This division bled into my home life too. I lost my first friend when Sarah moved away to another city, a distance that seemed so impossibly far away in my tiny world that she may as well have left for another dimension. Seeking a new companion to spend my weekends with, I didn't approach nearby girls but instead made an effort to get to know two brothers who lived close by. In the way that kids do, we formed a friendship based on nothing more than the fact we weren't adults. Once I began talking to them I was introduced to their male cousin and soon we were our own little inseparable band. None of us went to the same school, which split my life between school friends and home friends, all of whom were boys.

The only female friend I retained was my cousin, Lydia. Often we would meet at my grandmother's house, a small terraced home in a quiet cul-de-sac at the other side of the city. We'd regularly be dropped off there during school holidays, while our respective mothers ran errands. Although the two of us got along well, our personalities were inverted. Lydia would confidently chat to our grandmother's neighbours with uncanny wit for her age, while I always hung back feeling too sheepish to talk to an adult so openly. If we were in the garden and spotted somebody walking a dog, Lydia would skip over to quiz the owner and excitedly play with their pet, even if they were a complete stranger. As there were no other children around, with the street occupied almost exclusively by retirees, we were usually left to make our own entertainment in the house. This involved everything from hunting ghosts in the bathroom, to playing hide-and-seek, and even seeing who could eat a plate of beans on toast the fastest. By virtue of being family, we had a free pass to ignore what would have kept us divided back at my school.

When a new year of school began, I became consciously conflicted about my gender for the first time in my life. One morning I was in the corridor hastily taking off my coat, with registration about to begin any moment. Meanwhile another group of kids from another class was at the end of the corridor doing the same. Before I stepped into my classroom, I saw their teacher direct them to queue into two lines, one for the boys and one for the girls. *I should be with the girls.* The thought surprised me, coming out of nowhere. I didn't understand why, but I felt a powerful desire to be grouped with the girls in my year group and no longer ushered in with the boys. I wanted to ditch my shirt, pull on a dress, and line up next to the other girls as if it were no big deal at all. Due to the lack of any sort of context, or an awareness that trans people even existed, I buried the thought and continued with my day. I didn't know what it meant, but I did know it was a thought that I wasn't supposed to have. I chose to keep that moment a secret, trusting that nothing good would come from revealing it.

Up until that age, and especially beyond (but we'll get to that in time), I was a kid who didn't fit in well at school. However, I was considered smart, though not exceptionally so, and successfully stayed out of trouble. But where the boys were loud, energetic, and all happily played sports at lunchtime, I was quieter and preferred to read or simply swap stories and gossip. This troubled my teachers for years. Every school report and every parents evening gave the same assessment: this kid is too quiet. This feedback then got back to me via my parents and through the nosey glimpses I took of my own report. A number of times I was even approached by teachers in private, who urged me to join in with my peers and be more noisy and outgoing. This criticism baffled me as I knew particular students who behaved the same way as me in and out of the classroom without critique. Of course, I missed the significance of the fact that the students I had in mind were girls. Over time these repetitive admonishments left me feeling more and more like the black sheep of the school.

This chasm between my personality and that of my male peers was awkwardly highlighted in other memorable ways too. At the start of another year I was drafted into a performance piece in a school assembly all about football. The entire point of the piece was to show how so many boys loved playing football at lunchtime, yet I didn't. This was demonstrated by having every boy in the class recite a pre-written ode to the alluring and electrifying sport in unison, while I stood at the other end of the hall and squeaked out my response as to why I didn't like it. The message was clear: Behold the strange outcast's peculiar resistance to the power of lunchtime football. During this, the girls in the class played no part whatsoever and were merely sent to sit quietly, despite the fact that at least one of them was as big a fan of the sport as even the most devoted of the boys. My best friend at the time was someone with just as much disinterest in sports as me, but when presented with the concept of the performance, he happily chose to chant along with the boys. Meanwhile I may have been terrified of public speaking, but not so much that I was prepared to stand shoulder to shoulder with boys, reciting an allegiance to something so symbolic of the uncomfortable expectations placed on me. I didn't want to become someone who people finally liked by faking an interest in something; instead I was hoping people would start liking me for who I already was.

Football eventually split me from my friends at home too. Although in the beginning we didn't play any sports, preferring to sit chatting or playing video games, the two brothers I spent my weekends with gained a sudden interest in football. I remember the day we all marched to the local park, a spacious haven of fields and playgrounds that I had perpetually ignored in favour of staying indoors. The brothers and their dad took the lead, while I lagged behind and secretly hoped my friends would find this as dreary and dull as I expected to. For the next hour, we ran around chasing the ball and practising penalties. The brothers left their dad beaming with pride at how immersed they had become in their new hobby. I recall thinking that perhaps he was delighted his sons were now going to be as enthusiastic about sports as he was, instead of hanging around with me inside. Although the other kids seemed to have a great time playing this sport, I felt rotten and bored. As expected, my friends began to grow more distant after that, preferring to head back to the football field without me.

Luckily, I was still adept at keeping myself occupied. One of my favourite pastimes was making pictures and primitive art. I had an extensive collection of paint, felt tips, glitter, colourful card, and other craft supplies. I could lose hours sat at the dinner table sticking bits on paper and making my own world of patchwork pictures. Elsewhere video games were another time-sink that didn't require friends, with the Sonic the Hedgehog series being my absolute favourite. Batman was eventually abandoned as I became obsessed with Sonic instead, finding his effortlessly cool attitude and confident demeanour worthy of idolisation. Religiously, I would wake up at 6 am and replay my collection of Sonic video games until the rest of the house awoke. He was a character that I wanted to emulate. I would watch his cartoons over and over, respecting how he was never overlooked or ignored. He was always the centre of attention, self-assured and unfazed by anyone who tried to stop him. I thought that if I wished hard enough, I could be more like that at school. Maybe I'd stop feeling so vulnerable all the time and afraid of attention.

To try and acquire more video games, I hoarded my weekly pocket money for months at a time. However, I would occasionally falter to treat myself to a new LEGO® set or whatever the newest playground craze was, such as Tamagotchis or yo-yos. A significant moment in the formation of my hobbies came when my dad offered to buy me an occasional book of my choosing for free, without it depleting my precious video game fund. I had enjoyed reading, but was often bored by the painfully limited selection in my tiny local library, and the dull mandatory reading books in school. With free rein to browse bookshops with my parents for anything I desired, I started to build up a collection of fiction spanning sci-fi, fantasy, and wholesome horror. Anything involving aliens was especially an instant favourite. Thanks to *The X-Files*, UFO culture was prevalent at the time, with plenty of allegedly non-fiction supernatural books on offer too. I found the whole topic simultaneously exhilarating and terrifying. There was something deeply alluring about the idea of there being much more to life than I could currently comprehend, like there was something fantastically strange and dangerous out there, something shrouded in secrets and mystery.

Despite how easy I found it to entertain myself with games and books, I still wanted to find more friends like myself. Yet I always felt like I wasn't on the same wavelength as everybody else my age. Privately I felt like a failure and a disappointment. I always seemed to fall short of what people expected of me. What came naturally to me, such as quietly getting on with my work or trying to be kind and patient with other students, was routinely highlighted as a flaw. This became even more blatant when I joined the class of an utterly petrifying teacher in my final year of primary school. In the presence of other teachers or visiting parents, she became all smiles and warmth, seeming to everyone involved like a wonderful and engaging role model. But when alone with children she was strict and angry, and even craftily alienated students from one another. Whispered playground rumours often told horror stories of how she'd treated certain pupils, which inspired outright terror at the prospect of being placed in her class. When other teachers heard these tales, they'd always laugh and reassure us that she was a lovely woman and such stories were overblown nonsense. That year I personally found out she lived up to every bit of her reputation.

I vividly remember in the first month her telling the class that my handwriting looked impossibly illegible: 'It's like a spider threw up on the page and walked all over it.' The other students sniggered at her quip as they'd quickly learnt to play along with her cruel humour, but they were all equally frightened of being the next target. Another humiliation came when she read my work aloud to the class and deliberately mispronounced what I'd written, mocking me for not writing more clearly. 'I live in a three-bedroom nose?' she theatrically recited with a feigned expression of befuddlement. 'It says "house",' I shyly corrected, but she ignored me and continued mining my essay for laughs. My handwriting was poor because I struggled to write in cursive, which the school insisted that we all did. Not only were we forced to write in it, but we had to adhere to a very strict form of cursive and loop our letters together just so. This was made even more difficult by the fact we were given cheap, blotchy pens which could only draw lumpy, black lines that smudged at the slightest touch. At home I relished writing, filling up notebooks with my own fantasy stories and private thoughts. Writing was my chance to create something precious and personal. But at school any writing task made me deeply self-conscious because I knew it was another opportunity to be twisted into a punchline.

Outside of my handwriting, I was once singled out by the same teacher for allegedly being a pathetic pushover. In actuality, I never felt pressured or bulldozed by my peers. Growing up on a diet of superheroes, I revered the idea of being helpful and selfless. I was proud of the fact that I would always try to be polite and help anyone in need. My kindness felt like the only part of my personality that wasn't criticised on a regular basis. During a school field trip to a local village, I was once sat with a group of girls at a picnic table. The makeup of the group was a rare occurrence in our highly gender-conscious year group, so it was unusual for us to talk together. While chatting amongst ourselves, the girls admitted that they all found me noticeably kind and considerate compared to 'other boys' who were crude and thoughtless. It felt wonderful to have my personality acknowledged positively. How much it meant to me is evident from the fact I still clearly remember that conversation 20 years later!

As I mostly felt ignored or disparaged by teachers, the particular instances where they praised me burnt into my memory as miraculous moments. I was proud when a charming elderly teacher jovially proclaimed how another girl and I were her favourite pupils in the school. When it came to assembling for any outdoor excursions or school assemblies, I was always one of the first to congregate in line. When I later told my mother what the teacher had said, she inadvertently took away my prestige by explaining that the teacher must have just meant that I was very quiet, and therefore easy to order around. I was crushed that something positive had just been revealed as yet another flaw.

In hindsight, I'm sure the majority of my behaviour that was picked apart was mostly mundane when compared to that of the other girls in my year group, but of course nobody realised I was a girl. Instead, more and more, I was branded as a weird and broken boy. This is one of the biggest issues when it comes to trans children as a whole – very rarely does anybody consider that we could be trans, unless we blatantly spell it out, or our parents are armed with foreknowledge of the trans community. I was notably emotional and sensitive but never enough for anyone to realise the truth. Instead, I internalised a lot of those failures and assumed that the problem had to be with me. Throughout my entire primary school life I longed to shake off that label of 'too quiet' so I could be seen as the person other people expected me to be. If you don't know that being trans is even a concept, you're unlikely to realise there's a valid reason why you don't fit in – you just assume the problem is you. All you know is there's a standard and you're failing to hit it.

Even if someone had come to me and explained that I could be a girl if I wanted, that it was quite possible I was in fact a girl, it would have taken enormous willpower to tell them I agreed. Society as a whole does a really good job of convincing you that showing gender variance is a terrible idea. Boys are taught that anything pink is practically radioactive, while girls are teased if they pick racing cars and wrestling figures over dolls and dresses. Although the tomboy label does give girls some leeway, there's no equivalent term for boys that's not intended to be derogatory. When you realise what we're essentially doing as a society is placing lifelong loaded expectations on children based on nothing but genitals, it seems quite ridiculous. Gendering children based on their bodies seems even more grievous when you remember that kids are not oblivious to this. They're very aware of these expectations as they start to mingle and enter school. Children know they're at risk of being scrutinised and mocked for shaking up their gender presentation in any way. This devastates those who want to express themselves outside of these rules and it encourages other children to enforce these expectations themselves.

One particular occasion that demonstrates this perfectly was when a boy in the year below me brought in three glimmering trophies. The school often encouraged children to show off any awards or accolades they'd earned in the community and would make a special mention of them during the weekly assembly. Trophies were nothing new, but what made this occasion different is that these weren't the usual football or rugby trophies. These were for horse riding. The fact that a boy had brought in awards for this was deemed absolutely hysterical. That morning I was yanked into a band of boys who, between fits of giggles, explained that they'd spotted a boy showing pride at taking part in a girl's hobby. I didn't really appreciate what was so hilarious about it myself. Laughing at other people always felt wrong and needlessly mean, but I definitely got the message behind it: In so-called feminine hobbies lies ostracisation. Hindsight makes me wonder if those boys even found it that funny to begin with, or they were simply just playing the parts that had been thrust onto them. By publicly rejecting the boy who had broken the rules on acceptably boyish pastimes, they were differentiating themselves from him, establishing themselves as being on the right side of the gender divide. These children – some not even old enough to have reached double digits – were convinced that deviating from gendered expectations was deeply wrong.

Embarrassingly, I wasn't beyond performative disgust either. When visiting a friend from school, his big sister was babysitting and asked what movie we'd like to watch. In front of my friend and his gruff older brother, she suggested we could watch *Beauty and the Beast*. 'Eww no! That's a girl's film!' I recoiled from the VHS tape as if looking at something so feminine was blinding. In actuality I adored Disney movies, but there was no doubt in my mind that I had to reject princesses in public. I had to look tough and disinterested while other boys were around because that was the unspoken rule.

In the same year, not long after I'd registered disgust at 'girl films', I sat mesmerised watching *A Little Princess*, the 1995 remake of the 1939 original. The film was about a girl who's sent to a strict boarding school while her father is dispatched to war. With only my own dad in the house, as he sat in the bedroom in front of our pioneering new 'Windows 95' computer, I had the living room to myself and was free to watch it without judgement. During the film, the young protagonist gave a passionate speech to her teacher about how every girl deserves to be a princess 'even if they're not pretty or smart'. Inexplicably I felt a lump growing in my throat as my eyes filled with tears. I felt inspired and full of admiration for this brave character. Something about what she said deeply resonated with me. I quickly pulled a blanket over myself and stretched out on the sofa as if I were asleep. I was terrified I was about to be caught crying over a princess film but was too enchanted to stop watching. Through a gap in the blanket I watched the rest of the film and desperately tried to keep any tears from leaking out. As the film started to come to a close, I heard my dad walking down the stairs. In a panic I buried my head in a cushion and stayed as still as I could. With eyes closed I heard him sit down and flick over the TV channel, cutting off the final moments of the film. I stretched and rolled the blanket off me, pretending to yawn as I did. 'Oh I fell asleep!' I lied, trying to avoid any suspicion that I was enjoying a film so clearly aimed at girls.

Although I loved violent TV shows like *Power Rangers* and *X-Men*, I had a huge soft spot for endearingly cute media when it wasn't characterised as being exclusively for girls. I worshipped *Winnie the Pooh*, finding the quaint and ambiguously gendered character endlessly lovable. *The Tale of Peter Rabbit* was one of my favourite books, along with Beatrix Potter's other adorable animal stories. And while I loved my superhero action figures, I also kept a consortium of soft cuddly animals dotted around my bedroom. My favourite fluffy companion was a tiny round bear who I unimaginatively called 'Little Bear'. To label my interests and possessions purely 'boyish' or 'girlish' would be a gross simplification. There was a varied amalgamation of themes in my hobbies, just like the ones of most children of any gender.

Looking at my own childhood, I find it ridiculous that there remains a myth today that parents can pressure their children into being transgender against their will. Such claims are seen in common trashy stories of 'boys' who suddenly claim they're girls after their parent has allegedly brainwashed them with the idea. In truth, as a child I didn't know I was trans because I didn't know being trans was possible. Had there been television shows that illustrated what being trans meant, I could have used that to understand myself. But without anything like that to open my mind, I solidly believed that I was a boy and that expressing anything deemed feminine would leave me punished and humiliated.

I feel it important to point out here that no child is ever given surgery related to being transgender. Despite what the newspapers will scream, it just does not happen. At most, trans teens are sometimes given puberty blockers, safe and reversible drugs which will delay puberty. This gives them time to decide what they want and figure out who they are. For anyone younger, nothing is given or done for them medically. Trans healthcare for children simply comes down to gently providing mental and emotional support to both the child and the parents, the result being that the child then gets to wear what clothes they want and use the pronouns and name they prefer.

There have been a number of surveys on trans youth and they often paint the same grim picture. A survey undertaken by PACE over four years found that 56 per cent of young trans people had considered suicide, while 48 per cent had made at least one suicide attempt.[1] Contributing factors to suicidal feelings were found to include rejection at school and at home. Meanwhile, supportive actions

---

1   Nodin, N., Peel, A., Tyler, A. and Rivers, A. (2015) *The RaRe Research Report: LGB&T Mental Health – Risk and Resilience Explored*, PACE, available at www.queerfutures.co.uk/wp-content/uploads/2015/04/RARE_Research_Report_PACE_2015.pdf, accessed on 23 February, 2018.

from their social circle were said to directly counter these feelings and build self-worth. Considering that supporting trans children is harmless and has no irreversible long-term effects whatsoever, it's tragic that many are still left without support even when they know exactly what the cause of their distress is.

Often trans kids grow up with an upbringing loosely like mine. They might feel out of place at key moments, but otherwise they're as much in the dark as everyone else around them. The problem with expecting trans children to have to exhibit overwhelming evidence of distress in order to be noticed and treated is that kids like me will never be recognised as in need of help. Although there were noticeable flashes of the truth and windows into my feminine personality and discomfort around boys, these were sufficiently counteracted by the times when I seemed mundane and content. Outside of school I bashed action figures together in dramatic recreations of my favourite cartoons, I ran around the garden pretending to have dynamic adventures, and I raced my skateboard up and down the neighbourhood's quiet streets. The truth is that it's possible for unaware trans kids to be okay, to survive, and to find happiness, while still not being quite as comfortable or as at ease as their peers. Usually, it's when we start to creep into puberty that things can really start to get noticeable. For me that was when the volume of my discomfort was abruptly cranked up to maximum.

Chapter 2

PUBERTY, PART ONE

When I was 11, I went to secondary school, which I consider the most miserably difficult period of my entire life. At my primary school, we were told there were really only three options of where to go next: a Catholic all-girls school (tragically unavailable to me for obvious reasons), a Catholic all-boys school, or a Catholic mixed-gender school. The idea of attending a school only populated by boys was about as enticing as attending one entirely made up of starving panthers, so of course I selected the mixed-gender school. This meant I was arriving with only five other people from my school – all boys. Everyone else was going to the single-gender schools. Every single girl I had grown up with was moving on to a school I was barred from attending. As it turned out, the school I ended up at made me feel more like an outcast than primary school ever had.

Over the years, I've grown to think of my primary school as a kind of isolated and cushioned bubble. The school was strict in the sense that if anyone even remotely broke one of the rules – like nudging another child too hard or uttering a forbidden word – the school would enter a state of emergency. Multiple teachers would confer and interrogate the child as a team, impressing upon them the deathly severity of their actions. Afterwards all children would be informed of what had happened, and a warning would be given that repeating such an offence would see them face cataclysmic justice. When coupled with its religious teachings, which instilled a rather unhealthy fear of hell and damnation in all its young pupils, this meant that the school was about as genuine a reflection of the real world as Mario Kart's simulation is a reflection of driving to the supermarket. For kids like me, who simply got on with their work, it was a place where no other pupils could ever harm you. Upon arriving at a new school, for the first time I was encountering kids who had grown up outside of my safe bubble. At times it felt like these other students hadn't even grown up on the same planet; instead they seemed honed by some harsh post-apocalyptic wasteland, where only the brutal and ruthless were wild enough to survive. While I nervously stepped through the front door into a terrifying new world, they barrelled in cursing and brawling their way down the corridor without consequence. To say I was stunned by the change in tone is an understatement; I would have had less of a culture shock if I'd moved to Saturn.

I had grown up attending a school within walking distance, surrounded by spacious retirement bungalows and kindly old couples. My new one was several miles away, encircled by a dense housing estate, opposite a rundown graveyard, and next to a bustling retail park. It was also gigantic. My new year group had five times the students that had populated my former one. Due to the distance between the school and my home, I had to catch one of the many dedicated school buses every morning. As our school couldn't be trusted with a precious, clean, modern bus, the local bus company used what were presumably the oldest and most expendable vehicles they had. Every morning

I stepped aboard a decrepit old bus painted in 70s mud brown and sat on stiff, uncomfortable seats, hoping that I could be ignored until we arrived.

Even at the time, I described riding the school bus as like travelling with a group of hyperactive chimps. There were many instances of misconduct on that bus over the years: windows were shattered with hammers, seats were torn open with knives, small fires were lit, and outright brawls took place on a regular basis. The culprits were, of course, almost always boys. But there was also no shortage of girls to cheer on the behaviour, usually from within a thick smog of cigarette smoke. Early into the year, one girl stepped onto the bus one morning, burst into tears, and ran back into her mother's car. I watched through the window, feeling nothing but sympathy and a vague desire to hop in and join her. Another time I remember one girl was riding the bus for the first time. She turned to her friend and said, 'I really don't like this bus.' There was a look of fear in her eyes which perfectly encapsulated the horror that partaking in this journey impressed upon anybody who was unprepared. I simply nodded in mutual understanding. 'Welcome to my life,' I thought, as the juvenile carnage continued around us. Riding the school bus was the lowest point of my day.

The worst thing about being a teenage transgender girl, when you're not yet aware you are one, is that none of the boys your age got that memo either. Being treated like a seven-year-old boy when I was actually a seven-year-old girl was gruelling, but at least I never felt like I was in actual danger. At my new school, I learnt through painful and terrifying experiences that teenage boys asserted dominance over others through intimidation, humiliation, and violence. The fact I wanted nothing to do with them, and found their reckless desires for attention and kudos completely alien, wasn't something they cared about. One lunchtime at the start of the school year, a boy whose name I hadn't even learnt yet punched me in the stomach and screamed that he wanted to fight somebody. I hadn't even gotten my breath back by the time he'd marched away. I felt completely unequipped to deal with this behaviour and couldn't comprehend why so many people here were staggeringly cruel.

Another instance that demonstrates what school life was like for me took place on the school bus home. That afternoon I was doing my usual activity of looking blankly out the window and hoping everybody would ignore me. While counting the minutes until it was my turn to escape, I glanced across the aisle back inside the bus to see one boy my age staring at me. He was glaring with such intensity I half expected to burst into flames. Although I'd never spoken to him before, he seemingly despised the look of me. Later he walked over and decided to punch me in the face. For no reason. Being the savvy and prepared kid that I was, my response was to immediately spring to my feet and adopt a combat-ready pose, plotting my retaliation. Unfortunately, that last sentence is a complete lie. In actuality, upon being punched I burst into tears in shock and despair over why this was taking place. My new bully was so put off by this bizarre reaction that he simply walked off, clearly not about to get the fight he was hoping for. I was so embarrassed by this event that I returned to school the next day and just pretended it hadn't happened. For some blessed reason, nobody talked about it – at least not to my face – allowing me to continue as normal. I never actually told any teachers or even my parents, finding the whole event another instance of how abysmal I was at making the shift from child to teenager.

With this new school I felt like I had entered the real world for the first time, a place that I was completely unable to acclimatise to. It was as if my entire personality and instincts were wired wrong. I just didn't match any of the boys around me and I couldn't fathom why. Why was I so different? In reality I was a frightened and sensitive girl who'd been dropped into a school full of angry boys who saw me as one of them. Being perceived as a boy, I was fair game for their brand of violence and humiliation.

As the revelation around my gender was still just out of reach, I continued to blame myself for being so bad at fitting in. One morning I was being driven to the bus stop by my dad – something he occasionally did when our schedules aligned – when he chuckled his way through a retelling of some of the escapades that he got up to in his time at upper school. He said that he realised I must now be up to similar boyish hijinks with my friends, such as pranking each other and humiliating teachers together. I smiled, feeling I had no choice but to play along and not disappoint him, despite knowing that my time here was nothing like his. I'd managed to find a tiny handful of friends who I could talk to about video games or books, but connecting with them on any level beyond that was a task I wasn't able to master. It was a very tenuous friendship – even among them I still felt very much like the odd one out. But sitting beside them in lessons and pretending I was at ease around them was far preferable to being alone. Across the school the other kids my age seemed to be enjoying themselves on at least some level, forming meaningful connections and growing into new people. Meanwhile, I just wanted to be at home, away from everyone and the weight of their expectations.

During our one-hour lunch breaks, I often retreated to empty corridors and quiet corners. The school was a messy amalgamation of old and modern architecture, with the oldest parts of it dating back over 40 years, so there were plenty of odd little spaces. Very few areas of the school were off-limits during this time, and most of the pupils wandered freely through the building in packs. The teachers understandably left the kids to take over while they sequestered themselves in the spacious staff room. Just like the school bus, this was another chaotic time of day when vandalism, bullying, and smoking were popular pastimes. The teachers either didn't notice or didn't care as teenage mob rule became the status quo. I chose to bring my own lunch rather than eat the lukewarm chips or cardboard-textured pizza that was on offer in the cafeteria, and this gave me some flexibility to mostly stay out of the way. Still, there was no shortage of incidents over the years as I was punched, spat on, tripped up, playfully electrocuted, attached to a door handle, relentlessly pummelled with snowballs, and even slapped in the eye with a mouldy banana.

Although a lot of what happened to me sounds absurd and akin to the usual abuse that teenage boys inflict on others, there was no limit to what was considered acceptable. Once, when trying to pass a friend a plastic bag of his things, my finger got twisted in the handle as he yanked it away. My hand ignited in the worst pain I had ever felt. Being visibly upset, I inadvertently attracted a small crowd. One boy stepped forward and asked to see my finger. After I explained I literally couldn't move it, he grabbed it between both hands and squeezed. I didn't even know who this boy was, but seeing an opportunity to publicly hurt someone, he had giddily embraced it. His face contorted in concentration as he exerted himself to inflict maximum pain. Despite the agony it caused, I wasn't even surprised. This was exactly the sort of behaviour I saw every day. I later went to the hospital and found out the finger was broken, but I didn't tell anybody about the boy earlier that day. I simply didn't think there was any point – students regularly got away with far worse.

Several times in my adult life, my dad has joyfully recounted a story from back in my first year of upper school. Although I don't remember it taking place, I think it's worth retelling here. Apparently one morning I awoke, ate breakfast, put on my uniform, got my bag ready, and then refused to leave the house. Despite the demands of my parents, I insisted I was staying home and wouldn't leave for the bus. As my dad tells it, he had already left for work but returned from his commute at the request of my mother. He then came in and physically dragged me out of the house while I tried to fight him off. Allegedly, I even clung onto the door frame. After getting me outside, he tossed me into his car and drove me to school himself. Whenever he repeats this story, I explain that I have no recollection of it, to which he laughs and insists that it happened. I believe him, not just because of how many times I've heard him tell this story to somebody, but because it perfectly fits. I hated going to school. Every morning I awoke queasy with dread, wishing that I was still blissfully asleep. It's very easy to accept that, being as timid as I was, there would have been days when the thought of who and what awaited me at school was enough to ignite a refusal to leave the house.

Over dinner I once tried to articulate to my parents what the atmosphere was like at school, explaining that I couldn't walk from one classroom to the other without seeing students being violent or loudly cursing at each other every ten seconds. I felt like I was in a prison and that attending was some form of punishment. But they waved away my examples as exaggeration, refusing to believe that things could really be that bad. With this growing stack of evidence, it confirmed something I had long suspected: the problem was indeed me. The feeling that I was different, in a very undesirable and irreparable way, had been planted back in primary school but blossomed into full-blown self-loathing in those early teenage years. I accepted that there was no point in trying to change schools, because every school would presumably be as intolerant and oppressive as my own. Why would they be any different? All the boys around me were entering puberty and adjusting nicely to this loud and horrific environment. They were thriving. It seemed to be just me who was struggling.

Looking back, it seems blatantly obvious that I was a trans girl. It's why I felt so perpetually different from every boy and so uncomfortable with every attempt to push me to be more like them. It also explains why puberty was giving me such profound feelings of regret, as my body began to change in ways that felt entirely unnatural. But how can you diagnose yourself with a problem you don't know exists? Instead, I did what everyone does when they realise there's no escape from a new scary situation: fake it. I pretended everything was fine – with friends, parents, and teachers. Inwardly I still desperately willed myself to become stronger, more like the people around me. On the rare occasion when someone asked if I was doing okay, I dismissed their concerns and said I was simply tired and feeling a bit groggy. I knew that showing weakness was to invite further ridicule and attention, so I figured all I had to do was cover up my flaws and in time maybe I'd finally grow up and fit in. Spoiler alert: it didn't work.

Video games remained an escape for me during this period. I fled into fantasy worlds to retreat from the misery that was my day-to-day life at school. One game I greatly enjoyed was *Baldur's Gate*, a high-fantasy role-playing game in the Dungeons & Dragons setting. A rarity then, the game allowed you to customise and name your own protagonist. Being the lazy kid that I was, I simply created an avatar of myself, using my own name. A big focus in the game was killing monsters to find better equipment and to make your character stronger. One afternoon my hero felled an ogre who dropped a belt. I opened the inventory screen and popped the belt on the young masculine mirror of myself, who then promptly turned into a woman. Cue a moment of surprise as I digested what had just occurred. Inadvertently, I had equipped myself with a 'cursed' belt which changed the gender of whoever wore it. Furthermore, the belt couldn't simply be replaced, it had to be magically removed, which I didn't have the ability to do right then. For some inexplicable reason, I found this idea bizarrely appealing. I decided to continue adventuring with the belt, even declining a later opportunity to have it removed and transform my character back into a man. What was intended to be a curse reinvigorated my interest in the game. Happily, I kept playing with my hero as a young woman, enjoying the fact that, within the context of the game's storyline, she had originally been seen as a boy but now continued her life as a girl. I of course neglected to tell anyone how I was playing the game, avoiding this detail if I ever spoke about it to friends. I knew enough to realise that what I had found so enticing was not normal and not the intended way to play the game. Just like when I wanted to be grouped with the girls back in primary school, I knew what I was doing was taboo and must be kept a secret.

Another escape was Japanese anime and manga, which were enjoying a boom in popularity in the early 2000s.

My favourite was a comedic series titled *Ranma ½*, about a boy who turns into a girl when splashed with cold water. I'm sure from that detail alone you can see why it appealed to me. Amusingly I've noticed that a lot of trans women my age found a quiet solace in *Ranma ½* as teenagers, thanks to this alluring detail about the protagonist. What was refreshing about it was that the titular character willingly used the ability to become a girl as an aid in various schemes and adventures; it wasn't always depicted as a damnable curse. Meanwhile, the cover art of each volume routinely showed Ranma as a pretty girl, wearing feminine outfits and smiling happily. This was an inspiring juxtaposition when compared to how other media handled gender-changing characters, who were often insulted in ugly punchlines.

Perhaps the most significant interest I developed with the onset of my teens was rock music. Previously I'd had no interest in music whatsoever, with no collection or favourite artists to speak of. This changed when one afternoon I was watching television and saw an advert for an Aerosmith documentary. The energetic backing music of frantic drum beats and screaming guitar riffs was intoxicating. I had to learn more. With the help of the Internet I looked up other classic rock artists and came across a sea of results. The entire aesthetic of hair metal was enchanting. I saw men with long, feminine locks, colourful outfits, and sparkling, extravagant makeup, yet they still somehow were seen as masculine and powerful. They were millionaires with legions of fans despite being openly flamboyant and playfully twisting gender norms. Even better, I found the music exhilarating and rapidly became a fan of everything about the genre. As my fandom became known in the family, I was given old CDs which relatives had dug out of forgotten collections. Gleefully I then took them to school in a portable CD player. The school bus became a little more bearable as I now spent it with loud thumping music exploding in my ears, listening to albums by KISS, Boston, Mötley Crüe, Whitesnake, Guns N' Roses and many others. Most of my new favourite tracks had been recorded before I was even born, but listening to them made me feel at home.

Music also allowed me to begin an outward reinvention of myself, one that took years to fully bloom, but which would eventually help supplant my reputation as the overly sensitive and shy kid with that of being a rocker and music lover. The best part was that it provided the perfect cover for growing out my hair. I desperately wanted to look more feminine, and the most obvious way to do that was to grow out my short, spiky hairstyle until I could part and style it like the other girls in my class. Until now I'd never had an excuse for why I wanted long hair, so I lied. I pointed to my music fandom and blamed my idolisation of shaggy-haired rockers as the reason for my decision to stop visiting the local barbers.

When I was 13, I finally found an answer. I would love to say that I discovered the concept of being transgender in some heartfelt and touching journey of self-discovery. But I didn't. It was because of video games. While trading stories about *Phantasy Star* on an online international message board, the girl I was chatting to casually mentioned that she was transgender. When I took a trip to Yahoo!'s search engine, I was presented with a handful of personal websites and the definition of what it meant to be transgender. I had found God. Something within me erupted with exuberant celebration. This was the key to my identity, the puzzle piece I'd been denied. It was the answer to a question I didn't even know I was asking. I couldn't even articulate why this felt so utterly and completely right for me; it simply did. It was like my brain had been anxiously waiting for me to reach this conclusion for years, and now that I had, it couldn't contain its excitement. My entire outlook on who I was and what my future would be turned inside-out in an afternoon. Thanks to a bunch of websites built in the late 90s, with lots of pink text and sparkly low-res GIFs, I realised why I'd felt so out of place my entire life. I wasn't a boy, I was a girl. I was transgender.

Through autobiographical websites, I read stories of women who had transitioned earlier in their lives and were now recounting their stories to help the next generation. I gobbled up information about how they'd thought they were men for years, completely unaware of who they were, just like me. After their revelation, they'd started hormone replacement therapy (HRT), which caused their bodies to essentially undergo a second puberty and come out the other end more feminine. Photos of glum-looking 'men' were juxtaposed beside smiling women, a before-and-after demonstration of how they'd changed. It astounded me to learn this was something you could actually do. There were pills that would make me look like a girl! I was utterly amazed and filled with a desire to follow in these footsteps. I wanted what they had more than I wanted oxygen.

Nervously, I reached out via an e-mail to the owner of one of the larger websites. Her online home was full of transition advice and data on the medical practicalities – a kind of amateur 'how-to' guide for transition. I figured she was a good bet in terms of someone who might know what to do in my situation. Typing up my letter, admitting to someone for the first time how I felt, I explained who I was and what I had just discovered, as well as asking for advice. I felt like I had just confessed to murder or given someone nuclear launch codes. At the time, I imagined myself writing a significant but eloquent introduction and request for information, but really it was more of a typo-ridden panicked confession and plea for reassurance.

A week of obsessively refreshing my inbox later, while I was still reeling from this revelation and trying to pretend that my world hadn't just exploded, I received a response. I still remember my heart jumping as I opened the message and scanned down its contents, frantically trying to take everything in. This was privileged information, the secrets to my universe. Although she was from the USA and considerably older than me, she kindly explained to me how transition worked with gentle patience. She elaborated that the effects of HRT took years to finish, just like any puberty. Although I was longing for a quick fix, one didn't exist; the only answer was to begin a slow process. The younger I would start, the better the effects would be as the 'wrong puberty' would cause some changes that could never be undone; for example, my voice would soon permanently deepen, while my frame and face would become more traditionally masculine. 'If you transition now, you'll be indistinguishable from other girls.' Those words burnt into my soul. They became a haunting prophecy that shaped my entire worldview. As well as this hope, she also warned me that transitioning wasn't all curves and pretty clothes – I'd encounter vicious abuse from society and likely from my own family. According to my new idol, I would have to end my transition by moving to another part of the country, going undercover and formulating believable fables of how I'd grown up as a mundane girl like everyone else. Being trans was much more scandalous than being gay, which back in 2002 was still fairly controversial. I was going to have to be careful and guard this secret with my life.

The encouraging but bleak tone of the e-mail was emblematic of trans-related discourse at the time. The help sites back then discussed transition as if it was deeply dangerous black magic. It wasn't something that took place in the public eye. Transition needed to be swift, silent, and secretive. We were outlaw witches, intruding on nature and buckling it to our will, fixing the injustices of our birth to the horror of respectable society. The idea of an open and pleasant transition did not exist, at least according to all the 'how-to' websites I scrambled through. The stories I found were full of violence, terrifying intimidation, and endless shattered friendships. Transition was often talked about as a new beginning because your old life would be burnt to the ground, whether you wanted to strike that match or not. Recommendations often included a note on how to integrate yourself into a new job and social circle. To stay still and live as visibly transgender was to invite endless controversy and expect all job security to evaporate. It was unthinkable. These grim warnings, often pulled from accounts of transitioning in the 80s, established my entire understanding of transgender issues for years to come.

There was nothing special or unique about my teenage situation that allowed me to find all that information on being transgender, when many in my situation don't until they're older. It was luck. If I hadn't decided to talk about that particular video game, on that particular website, on that particular day, I would have missed that chance and never known. It might otherwise have been a handful of years or even a decade or more before I had a chance to make that discovery.

The depictions of transgender people I'd seen on television at the time consisted almost entirely of exaggerated talk-show participants – the ones where the trans person was presented as a laughable concept, a nonsensical clownish figure for everyone else to gawk at. If we were glimpsed beyond reality TV, then we were corpses or killers in gritty crime dramas. The overwhelming message was always the same: Trans people are strange, perverse, and disconnected individuals. They exist on another plane of society altogether. There was nobody who resembled any sort of visible role model, fictional or otherwise, outside of these websites I had found. Incidentally, this reinforced the narrative that being transgender was inherently secretive, an entire concept kept hidden from normal society for our own protection. But more than anything they demonstrated with their stories that with enough time and effort it was possible to be seen as a girl despite how you were born. That gave me hope.

The side-effect of having no visible representation of anyone my age was crushing isolation. When you do realise you're trans, it's easy to feel you're the only person for a thousand miles who feels that way. I had never knowingly met another trans person in my entire life, and all I saw online were middle-aged women with jobs and partners. However, that was soon to change as a new band of friends was about to enter my life.

During my early teens, I hung around on Gaia Online a lot. Depending on your age, you may have heard of it before, or you may have no idea what it is. Back in the days when MySpace was the only social media platform around, Gaia was a giant mega-forum that attracted a huge teenage audience. With cutesy anime avatars, which you could dress up in colourful outfits, Gaia had a sprawling message board with topics covering just about everything. The website was so vast you could hang around in the same small category every day and never bump into the same people. One morning, while skulking around a section of the forum intended for serious and thoughtful debate, I came across a thread for discussing trans people. Clicking inside I expected to find a cold and detached discussion between cisgender youths, discussing their thoughts on gender-affirming surgeries. Instead I found an intimate clubhouse of trans teens talking about their day and laughing together as friends.

As there was so little interest from the rest of the Gaia community in talking about trans people, it had allowed this safe space to sit in plain sight with virtually no disruption from anyone else. It was populated by a small handful of regulars, who were all trans, using the space to socialise and connect with people like them. Once I realised this, I joined in and excitedly introduced myself. Over the following weeks I became a regular member myself and soon spent all my free time in there. I would visit the thread on a daily basis, checking in every single evening after school to see what posts I had missed during the day. I became firm friends with the others and soon felt right at home. As the thread didn't update in real time, everyone had to refresh the page to see any new messages that were posted. Essentially, it was like taking part in an agonisingly slow chat room, with minutes passing between messages at busy times, and hours between updates at other times of the day.

Collectively, we were a very young group, but there was also the occasional 'older' member in their 20s who would pop in. We talked about what any group of teens would chat about: how school was going, how annoying our parents could be, and what we liked watching on TV. The fact that we were all trans gave us a common foundation to build from, but it was our personalities and interests that really helped us bond. With these new queer teens for comparison, I realised that my friends back at school were always being kept at arm's length. I called them friends, but they didn't know who I truly was – I never felt comfortable enough to show them. Instead, I would sit with them and force myself to chuckle along to repulsive jokes, while pretending that I was at ease. It was survival, not friendship. Meanwhile, my new online companions were seeing the real me: the good and the bad. It was incredibly liberating to let go of that pressure to conform and it was something that I desperately needed.

With my friends on Gaia, I got to experience what it was like to be referred to with the right name and pronouns. After a few months of talking within the group, I'd picked a new name for myself: Rebecca. Evidently, it's not a name that stuck long term, but at the time it made me giddy to see it pop onto the screen. It was a small gesture, but after years of wearing an ill-fitting name, being called one that finally felt like my own was like being *seen* for the first time. I was profoundly comforted to see female pronouns used so effortlessly for me too. They were a pleasant surprise every single time.

That little forum thread on Gaia had opened up a whole new world for me. Thankfully, these days vital spaces for trans youth are much more common. There are now countless Facebook groups and virtual communities openly dotted around the Internet for questioning teens to stumble across. Physical support groups also seem to be cropping up more readily too, I know of many supervised groups for under-25s that exist around the country entirely for trans folk to meet and be themselves. Companionship is absolutely vital at that vulnerable age. When you're a trans teenager, you really do feel like an outcast from your peers and society at large. It's very difficult to know who's safe to come out to and who will spread your secret through your whole social circle like salacious gossip. Unfortunately, I didn't feel like I could trust any of my school friends, so I spent all my evenings typing away online.

The number of hours that I lost on the computer did concern my parents. What I couldn't articulate was that online I felt like myself, and everywhere else I didn't. My body was continuing to change in ways I wasn't particularly fond of, and school remained a nightmare. Online I had friends who actually liked me for me, and even cared about my wellbeing. It was mind-blowing for someone whose day-to-day life felt like a forced act. I tried to appease my parents by spending as much time away from my paradise as I could manage, but this didn't amount to much beyond a few token hours sat on the couch waiting for time to pass. At night I'd sit illuminated by the computer monitor's glow, feeling protected and linked to the invisible friends I had dotted around the world. More than once I was caught defying my parents by sneakily staying up late to chat, which resulted in them temporarily banning me from the computer altogether. My dad even started to take our modem to work with him, so I couldn't access the Internet during the day until he had reinstated it. Once I figured out this was his go-to plan, I started to pre-emptively hide the modem the night before, removing it before he could do so himself. That didn't go down very well, but it did mean I had an extra day online before he returned from work that night and confronted me.

As this was before the era of smartphones and tablets, my bulky computer was my only way to get online and keep in touch with my friends. Back during school hours, I had no way whatsoever to reach out to them. It left me silently secluded, trapped among a crowd who I feared would never understand how I felt and who I really was.

During my time in school, a lot of varied topics were touched on outside of the traditional syllabus, such as ghosts, class A drugs, polar bears, the origins of reggae, and how to play 'Twinkle, Twinkle Little Star' on a keyboard. However, despite this diverse range of topics, we were never taught about trans people in any capacity. There was even more time spent discussing heterosexual sex than there was on the existence of anyone in the LGBTQIA+[1] community. Keep in mind this was a Catholic school, so even our sex education consisted of little more than a blurry video tape from the 80s and a blushing teacher hurrying through the material. Trans people weren't just ignored, it was as if nobody knew we even existed. However, I do recall gay men were mentioned once, in a sort of sniggering manner including an 'Aren't queer people weird?' tone. (This took place during a single religious education lesson.) There were no queer pupils out at the school – all of us knew it was a death sentence to own up to being one. Across my entire five years at the school, which had over 1,000 kids and more than 200 new children arriving every year, nobody ever came out. Any reference to queer identities was only slung from pupil to pupil as the ultimate derogatory insult.

I couldn't perceive any outcome where coming out as trans at school would go remotely in my favour. In a school where even the teachers openly mocked my long hair, it was unthinkable that I would find any support there. One teacher was an ex-nun and once exclaimed in utter horror that one of the pupils in our class had not been baptised. Had I told her I was transgender, I'd have expected to be burnt at the stake. My loose plan was to do as those women I'd read

---

1 An umbrella term for the queer community, specifically referring to those who use one or more labels from lesbian, gay, bisexual, transgender, queer, intersex, and asexual, while the plus symbolises the other marginalised identities related to gender and sexuality such as pansexual.

about online had done: begin to transition discreetly, then once enough changes had occurred, escape to somewhere fresh with a new identity. I dreamily pictured moving to a new school located out of the city, where I'd arrive as a girl and nobody would know who I was. That way I could enjoy a speedy and comfortable transition and never have to talk to anybody outside of my family about being transgender. Of course, none of these naive ideas came to pass even remotely, as my little optimistic fantasy was about to be slashed to shreds.

Chapter 3

DISBELIEF

One of my online friends who was a little older than me, the ancient and wise age of 16, had recently come out to her mother. The reaction she'd gotten was not very positive, but it wasn't overly negative either. Her mother was mostly confused, but as my friend hadn't been booted out of her house like we feared, it was generally considered a win amongst our little digital family. Encouraged, I decided it was my turn to come out, time to put the wheels in motion and get my transition started. I sat and wrote a lengthy letter explaining how I felt, being careful to include the basics: I had been struggling with feeling out of place for a long time and now I knew why; I was transgender and needed to transition so that I could live as a girl. I even said that I wanted to start hormones, that a doctor would be able to provide them, and that they'd help change my body into what I wanted it to be. I printed the letter out and planned the exact evening that I would present it. I chose a night where my dad would be working late, as I didn't yet want him to know – for now I only wanted to tell my mother.

My relationship with my dad had always been strained, but had recently gotten even worse. He was incredibly stressed with his job and struggling to keep our patchwork

Victorian house from collapsing. After recently moving in, it seemed that every weekend there was a plumber, electrician, or carpenter working on another aspect of the house which had fallen into disrepair. Coming from a traditional upbringing, my dad saw it as his sole responsibility to keep the family afloat, and to do so he was sacrificing his physical and mental health to remain in a well-paying but punishing job. I understood what he was doing, but I didn't think it was worth it. I rarely saw him at all. He began to return home late at night only to immediately crumple into bed. On weekends he zipped around the city stressed and on edge, either visiting family or picking up more supplies for the house. Whenever we did interact, he was frosty and tense. Gradually, I resented that I felt more like his unwanted employee than his child. I dreaded how he'd react to the news I was trans. At best, I knew he'd be displeased but I was scared of how bad the outcome could really be.

With my mother chosen as the recipient of my letter, I still couldn't bear the idea of her reading my revelation while I stood there beside her, waiting for a reaction. So I came up with an alternative plan to deliver it. Ridiculously, my idea on how to present this important and extremely personal news was to put the letter down in front of her, yelp that she had to read it, and then literally run away. So that's what I did. After fleeing the kitchen, I went and sat in the bathroom and locked the door behind me. My heart was drumming so fast I could hear it pounding in my ears. I felt like I was going to have a heart attack but I was also dizzy with relief at knowing I had just made some practical progress towards my transition.

Later that night my mother took me aside to talk about what I'd just told her. All my confidence evaporated. 'This must be someone else's writing,' she said, waving my letter in her hand as I felt a sickening sense of foreboding. 'It's mine,' I confirmed, with my mouth suddenly dry. I went to say, 'I wrote it. I'm transgender. It's the truth.' However, my voice failed to make a sound. Instead I feebly gestured back to the letter and reiterated that I had written it. I had always pictured this going so differently, eloquently laying out the truth to a patient and understanding parent. But now the words wouldn't come. Overwhelmingly, I felt that I was doing something wrong, as if by having this conversation I was breaking a sacred rule and should be ashamed of myself. 'It says you always felt like a girl. But I raised you… I know that's not true. I remember you running around shops as a toddler – you were a terror, pulling clothes off of hangers and making noise.' I didn't remember what she was referring to. As my mother she had access to memories of me that I didn't. She continued to describe childhood behaviours that retold a typical boyhood in my formative years, truths that stomped over my own memories. I'd felt certain, but suddenly being questioned like this caused my belief to fracture. The conversation swirled in circles, but with my dad soon to arrive home, it ended with no resolution. She didn't want him to find out yet any more than I did.

That night I went to my online friends for help and shared how anxious I was. As always, they were supportive and reassuring. I didn't admit it to them, but I was starting to wonder if my mother was right. I had read other stories of transgender teens who talked of childhoods coated in pinks and surrounded by dolls, which didn't sound anything like my history of Batman and video games. Surely I hadn't made a mistake?

The next day was a Saturday. With my dad back home, neither I nor my mother had mentioned the letter again. As we all ate our evening meal as a family, my dad absent-mindedly mentioned that my mother hadn't seemed to sleep well. 'You were tossing all night,' he revealed between mouthfuls of food. I knew why, so did my mother. I looked down at my plate, not wanting my face to betray my sudden anxiety. I was terrified that she was about to reveal my secret. I wasn't ready to have this conversation with my dad, I had barely gotten through it with my mother. I couldn't do it again, not yet. 'I don't remember,' she said. Her voice was hollow. It was an obvious lie. But my dad had no reason to suspect anything, so he accepted it and the moment passed. She was protecting him from the truth, but I knew that couldn't last forever. Soon this tension would break and he'd know. In that moment I wished I'd never told her. I wanted to be back in the closet, safe in my fantasies of transition, the ones propped up on hope and optimism where anything was possible. Coming out had brought with it a crushing sense of guilt for saddling somebody else with my truth, as well as establishing the grim reality of how far away transition really was.

At the end of the following week, my mother came back to me to talk again. She closed the bedroom door and asked me to shut off the video game I was playing. This time I had even less confidence than the first time we'd spoken. My doubts had festered and grown as I'd failed to find enough justification in my past. It then turned out that my mother's understanding of transition was far messier than I'd hoped. 'So you want to speak to a doctor to make this go away?' she ventured. Despite what I'd said in the letter, she mistakenly thought I expected a 'cure'. She assumed that I wanted to attend an appointment not to transition but to eradicate my desire to. Meanwhile, she reiterated that she still couldn't believe I was trans: 'I just can't see it. And I'm not new to this. I know what I'm talking about.' She referenced sensational and borderline offensive television appearances of transgender people, pointing out that they didn't resemble me in the slightest, so how could I be transgender when that was the definition? I tried to counter her arguments but I couldn't convince her otherwise.

My mother's belief that she had a clearer idea of transgender identities than me, despite the fact I was openly explaining that I was trans, is telling of a larger problem. As we see the same narratives over and over, it underlines in people's minds that there is only one way to be transgender. It causes people to believe, like my mother did, that they have a solid grasp of what a trans person looks and acts like. Yet I'm confident in saying that nobody can really know what it's like to be trans unless they themselves are trans. There are no universal signs or nullifying cues; our experiences are simply too diverse and personal. But back then even I didn't know that, and it was working against me.

My mother stated that I must have been led astray by dizzying internet babble and hypnotically clever strangers; that surely I had gone looking for a quick fix answer and stumbled onto this obscure and bizarre label. I wanted to repeat myself and scream that she was utterly wrong, that I was a girl and transition was vital to me, but my confidence was destroyed. I gave up.

In the days that followed I went to school as normal and pretended nothing was amiss. But behind my facade there had been an apocalyptic shift in my identity. I now felt like an intruder amongst my online friends, a fraud who had rudely infiltrated their digital clubhouse. I now believed I wasn't trans and never had been. This thought spread like rot, poisoning my sense of peace and belonging until I became convinced that my mother was right. I had clutched so tightly and readily to the idea that I was a trans girl, I hadn't stopped to see how much of an obnoxiously simplistic excuse it was. I had only questioned my gender once before last year, in a fleeting thought. Trans people didn't do that. They always knew.

The idea of saying goodbye to my online friends was impossibly painful to comprehend, especially as I'd have to admit that I didn't belong with them and had inadvertently lied. So I didn't say anything. Instead I chose the selfish option and deleted my accounts. Even today I still regret that I never told them what was going on. I shut them out when I needed them the most. I simultaneously hurt us all. I'm grimly aware that these poor teenagers would have feared the worst. I desperately wanted to talk to them again, to go back to who I'd been, but in a twisted way I didn't feel worthy of their friendship. I had accidentally tricked them into letting me into their private and personal world by believing I was one of them when I wasn't. I couldn't bear to tell them that, so I ran away.

I wish that suddenly hitting dead-end progress at that age is unusual, that I could say I'm an aberration amongst a sea of success stories. But I've since learnt that I'm not the only person with this past; it's not even rare. Coming out at any age can be a horror show, and all it takes is a lapse in confidence or a cruel response from a family member to send you running right back inside the closet. A friend once grimly joked with me that we trans people often have multiple coming out stories, because it's so hard to make the first attempt stick.

More than anything, I think what happened shows the overwhelming resilience needed by transgender children and their families. There's still so little support and understanding on offer that to continue to maintain your truth with so little affirmation is nothing short of heroic. Yet increasingly often these days, kids are equipped with the knowledge to understand their feelings. I have enormous respect for those trans kids and teenagers who are able to tell the world they're transgender and stand tall through all the backlash and doubt. Back then I wasn't able to do it.

At 14, it was the first time I consciously thought that I wasn't trans enough to be transgender. If I had more diverse role models or a better understanding of what it meant to be trans, I might have been able to cling onto my identity. Instead, I rejected all personal reflection and instead dived into escapism, using it to grit my teeth and get through the rest of my adolescence. This was made even easier by the fact that my mother never brought up my letter again. I hadn't even told her I didn't identify as transgender anymore, she just never came back to talk about it. This helped me slip right into denial.

Just because I no longer saw myself as transgender, it of course didn't mean I had an easier time at school. For instance, P.E. was possibly the only school activity that rivalled my utter distaste of the school bus. Part of it was a natural aversion to the changing room environment. Surrounded by rowdy boys, who were either preparing for or returning from a competitive game of sports. Pranks, roughhousing, and even theft were common in that changing room, and I of course wanted nothing to do with any of that behaviour. Without the balancing presence of the girls, or even a teacher, the testosterone ran rampant. Having to spend two hours a week jogging around a wet, muddy field with a group of boys was as unnerving as it was exhaustingly dull. My interest in sports had not increased at all since primary school, ensuring that P.E. was as uninviting as possible.

Luckily, my complete ineptitude in physical activity often meant that in P.E. I had an easier time than some. When you're known for being terrible at sports, nobody really expects anything of you once you're on their team. I mastered the art of doing as little as possible, knowing what positions to take in football or hockey that involved the least amount of work. I also figured out exactly how many times I could 'forget' to bring my P.E. kit before it became obvious I wasn't actually that forgetful, just eager to avoid joining in. As the years went by, my increasing laziness led to bolder actions to escape from P.E., the most significant being when I stopped attending altogether. Whether I was so forgettable the teachers couldn't recall who I was, or whether I was so notably terrible at sport that hunting me down was clearly a waste of everyone's time, nobody ever confronted me about my non-attendance. Instead, I took refuge at the back of one of the art workshops. One particular art teacher was famously understanding when it came to finding students bending rules, so he was my first bet for someone who might let me hide out in their class. The agreement became that if I was ever caught, he had never approved my staying in his classroom, but otherwise I was unofficially free to do whatever I liked. This meant I spent my P.E. lessons sketching characters from whatever video game or TV series had currently captured my attention.

Luckily for me, that same art teacher later became my form teacher after my original one retired. This meant that I would see him twice a day – for morning and afternoon registration – and he was also in charge of rallying my class together for events such as weekly assemblies. Although he never said it to my face, I suspect he knew that I was being bullied and having a difficult time. He was particularly lenient with me and would let me skip school events under the same agreement, where I had his unofficial permission but nothing that would protect me if I was caught. Notably, he also never confronted me about my increasingly ghastly attendance record, which virtually every other teacher did. I never felt comfortable enough to confide in him about how fragile I really felt, but he remained my favourite teacher for the rest of my time at school. Compared to the other teachers, who were arrogant and aloof, he was kind and talked to the students with a respect and a quiet sense of humour. Sadly, three years after I left school I was told that he had recently died. Apparently an army of past and present students attended his funeral, which wasn't a surprise to learn. I've no doubt I wasn't the only one who he made special exceptions for over the course of his career. At the very least he's left behind a legacy of people who still remember him fondly, myself included.

I always had a poor reputation for turning up to school, but it became even worse in later years. If my nose was the slightest bit runny or the faintest of tickles formed in my throat, I would declare myself stricken with the plague and retreat to bed. Even if I felt in prime condition by mid-week, I wouldn't go in, taking any excuse to not have to return to that awful place. The school responded with warning letters and demands that I stop taking time off, which I ignored. Often teachers would take me aside and threaten consequences for my tardiness. When this happened, I would plead ignorance and tell them that my immune system was weak and useless, that I contracted horrible illnesses on a regular basis. Whether they bought my excuses or not, the result was the same: I continued to spend weeks at home and minimise my time in that suffocatingly uncomfortable environment.

The apathy I had towards P.E. and my lack of attendance had begun to bleed into my other subjects with each year that ticked by. Where once I was presented as a shining example of a hardworking student, teachers openly expressed bafflement at how I had returned for my final two years stunningly apathetic and outright lazy. When I had given up my identity of being a trans girl, I likewise lost my motivation for everything else in my life. There was no longer any fear of failing, because success brought me no joy either. Even attempting to play along at school for my own good felt pointless.

That same year I found a new group of friends, one as clownishly averse to work as I was. I quickly learnt I could channel my disinterest and self-loathing into grim humour, which went down well with my new friendship circle of idle misfits. After a lifetime of feeling like an outcast and a complete weirdo, and having carried around a hell of a secret about my gender, I developed a dark, pessimistic sense of humour. As a survival mechanism, I embraced my new reputation as a slacker and clown. I cast myself as someone who would rather sit listening to heavy metal at the back of the room than bother to pay attention to what was going on at the front with the teacher. My headphones were only removed to crack a joke to a friend about how terrible my grades were, or how pathetically inept our school and teachers were.

The first time I snapped back at a member of staff was when a teacher zeroed in on my passive refusal to partake in her lesson. With the rest of the class in total silence, she rhetorically asked if I was prepared for her to write a letter home about my behaviour. Surprising her and defying my former well-behaved reputation, I flippantly responded that she should feel free and I really didn't care what she did. On another occasion, an assistant at the school tried to humiliate me by mocking my mop of long hair, so I quipped back that I'd consider cutting it off when he found a real job and didn't spend his day cleaning up after children. I used sarcastic retorts like these as shields, covering up my underlying vulnerability. They were opportunities to project a cocky confidence that I didn't have. Outwardly, I had gone from an uptight, nervous, and quietly emotional student, to a relaxed and confident layabout. But behind the flippant exterior I was as miserable as ever. I'd just become a better actor.

Although I was still attending a Catholic school, it was at this point that I lost the last of my faith. My first school had taught the Bible as hard fact. We learnt about Noah's Ark and creationism in exactly the same way we were taught about the Tudors and multiplication. Although mass was reserved for special occasions at my new secondary school, it had been a weekly event back at my primary school. Mandatory prayers had felt as mundane as every other part of the day. For the first 13 years of my life I believed that God had my back, as long as I didn't step out of line and tick him off. Once I became a teenager, that sense of somebody watching over me dissipated to nothing. I saw so much casual cruelty at school, I simply could no longer imagine the existence of a benevolent and kind man keeping an eye on me. Thanks to my digital excursions, I'd also been talking to people from other cultures and religions. This really opened my eyes to how diverse the world was and how much my school had selectively shielded me from everything outside of Catholicism. I felt duped, used by the school as a performative prop for the community audience in our church services, with no thought to our own agency or freedom to choose. This new perspective on my childhood became another contribution to my growing outlook of dispassion and cynicism.

Although it never vanished altogether, the bullying at this age finally faded and became quite rare. This was partly because of my new demeanour, but also in part due to me befriending a boy who terrified people. Gavin was the prototypical rebellious teenager, with a reputation for breaking rules and punching anyone who dared to insult him. Looking like a cross between James Dean and Jack Sparrow, with the personality of The Breakfast Club's John Bender, other students avoided him as wild and volatile. Even the older teens in the Sixth Form groups knew he'd promptly push back if they tested him. Thanks to an identical taste in music, we became unlikely friends in my final year of school. When stood with Gavin, I had nothing to fear from bullies due to his invincible, self-assured nature. While I saw others look at his arrival with trepidation, I would playfully tease him for his smoking habit or openly argue with him about who was the greatest lead guitarist in the world. Better yet, I managed to convince Gavin to start taking the school bus with me, which changed the dynamic of that hellish time of day altogether. Suddenly it was like having a bodyguard. In a way, Gavin was a sort of flawed role model for me. He had long hair like me and all the same geeky tastes in pop culture, but there was a fierce confidence to him that I could never emulate.

The only part of Gavin I didn't like was his intermittent mean streak. I knew he sometimes exercised pointless cruelty by mocking other students that he disliked, although he rarely did so if I was with him. More than once I saw him throw out sharp insults that were completely unprovoked, just because he was in a bad mood. He knew I was uncomfortable with it, and that was why he curbed it in my presence, but it was an innate part of his impulsive personality. I guiltily realised I was reaping the benefits of being on his good side and not one of his targets. I did my best to chastise him for anything I saw as unprovoked but I never broke off the friendship. Despite my attempts to soften his attitude, his reputation as a dangerous kid remained, and by association it kept me safe for my final months in school. To onlookers I probably looked like a sidekick or even a groupie, but Gavin was genuinely a good friend to me at times and looked out for me when I really needed help. He would also remind me implicitly that I was a person worthy of friendship and attention, something I really needed back then.

As the end of school approached, teachers reminded me that I had made absurdly little progress on my coursework. It was a warning I ignored as I was feeling unconcerned and uninterested in my future. Most of the projects I ended up handing in I'd begun writing earlier that week. My media project in particular I completed in four days: a pop culture magazine that I'd been expected to have worked on all year. Likewise, when school ended for my final exam season, I treated it like the start of an early summer holiday. When queuing for an exam later that month, an acquaintance asked how many hours of revision I'd done. I shrugged, 'None. I've been playing the new Transformers PS2 game for the last two weeks. It's a lot a more fun.' He found my answer less amusing than I did. Although I'd found a bizarre satisfaction in no longer letting schoolwork stress me out, I honestly felt little for anything else. I wasn't happy, sad, annoyed, or even worried at the poor choices I'd made – the same ones that had ruined my chance to leave school with useful GCSEs. I just felt empty.

I remember, years later, thinking back to that time and realising how heavily I leant on humour in almost every interaction. I'd been talking with a friend who had explained that from experience the funniest people were often the most depressed. I had to agree. Making people laugh is a good way to get people to like you when you know they'd recoil from the disturbing things you really want to say about yourself. Trans people are often impeccable actors. When we're closeted, we learn how we're supposed to move and talk, the difference between the expectation of us and the reality. We then force ourselves to adopt an expected persona like a snug costume. Being the funny person is an easy part to play when you hate yourself, because it feels like your whole life is a joke written by somebody else. Some of the best laughs I got came from deadpan deliveries of the truth. Absurd self-deprecating punchlines are sometimes just a way to hide the fact you don't know how to ask for help.

I would be lying if I said I've never felt so low that I started to experience suicidal thoughts. But I've been lucky in that they've never developed beyond simply being thoughts. Suicide is an epidemic issue in the trans community and, as mentioned previously, attempts among trans youth are tragically common. Beyond the obvious issues of family rejection and so much of society working against you, trans teens have to witness their bodies morphing into something alien and sometimes even repulsive. It really causes a special kind of panic and dread when you realise that the source of your sadness is that you're going through the wrong puberty but you have no way to halt it or even slow it down. Puberty begins when it wants and its pace is relentless. This is why I believe puberty blockers are vital and should be made more widely available. They're entirely reversible and have been recommended by medical practitioners who have studied or worked with transgender children.[1] They're reassurance that your body is no longer going through the wrong changes against your will. In an ideal world, any teenager who suspects they're transgender should be allowed ready access to blockers. It's one thing that the trans community is fighting for that I passionately believe in. However, when it comes to the topic of puberty in general, it does sometimes divide us.

The idea of the trans community as a group that encompasses all trans people and furthers trans rights is an attractive one. However, in reality, the community is often splintered into countless sub-groups and divisive opinions are common. To reiterate, the views in this book are mine in that they are the views of one transgender person in the trans community. These views are not the unanimous opinion of the community as a whole, because no such view exists. One thing that I disagree with in some trans circles is the belief that puberty is the only ideal time for us to transition. I enthusiastically agree that all transgender teens should be supported and given blockers if they wish to transition before or during puberty, but I don't agree that they've somehow doomed themselves if they miss this window, or that it's ultimately the best time to transition in their life.

---

1 Kuper, L. E. (2014) *Puberty Blocking Medications: Clinical Research Review*, IMPACT LGBT Health and Development Program, available at http://impactprogram.org/wp-content/uploads/2014/12/Kuper-2014-Puberty-Blockers-Clinical-Research-Review.pdf, accessed on 23 February, 2018; Olson, J., Forbes, C. and Belzer, M. (2011) 'Management of the transgender adolescent', *Archives of Pediatrics & Adolescent Medicine, 165*(2), 171–6.

It's true that there are many benefits to transitioning earlier. Avoiding puberty for a trans boy means not developing breasts, which can be a significant source of distress, and a trans girl can skip developing facial hair and a broken voice. However, there's a myth peddled on some trans-focused websites – less so now, but miserably popular back when I was a teenager – that if you don't transition before puberty you've lost your chance to be happy. Instead, you have to exist as a visible trans person, a damned and hollow consolation prize. I entirely reject this idea, but at the time I sadly took it to heart. Even at the laughably young age of 14 I was convinced that I had already missed my chance to look like a girl. I felt doomed and constantly felt like giving up. As my confidence over my trans identity was wavering, what encouraged my surrender was believing I'd already missed my prime transition opportunity. I know now that I was wrong...completely. Not only will HRT work at any age, but looking like you're cis is certainly not the root of happiness and not the reason to transition. The reason to transition is to be yourself, to find happiness in the freedom to be open and honest. That can happen at any age, and it's never too late.

Transitioning post-puberty or well into adulthood does have its advantages. It's easier to form a support network with the resources of adulthood, and of course you're likely to not be as limited by an unsupportive family. The opportunity to go to university is also worth mentioning, as student loans and housing can be a vital resource and backup plan during transition. When I hear adults say they wish they'd known they were trans as a child or young teen, I can't help but feel conflicted. If you're a trans teen who is tragically unlucky enough to be surrounded by an unsupportive family, it can be impossible to transition.

Coming out in that situation could even destroy the safety net they have, which is how trans youth end up homeless and living in poverty. There's stability in transitioning later, which I think is often overlooked in favour of assuming the best-case scenario has already flown by unutilised.

At 16 I wouldn't learn for years that transition was still entirely viable for me. Before I could get into that headspace, I first had a whole lot of distractions and denial to get through. The biggest distraction of all? A girlfriend.

Chapter 4

DENIAL

Having finally left school for good, I did little that summer other than sit on the computer playing video games and aimlessly browsing the Internet. I was in denial, actively suppressing the memory that I had once identified as a girl. If it ever came to mind, I would frantically focus on anything else until it was pushed to the back of my thoughts. As September approached and it was clear I had no plans whatsoever, my parents rightly confronted me and demanded that I do something productive with my life. Finding it the easiest way out, I decided I would go to the local college. It turned out that being an apathetic slacker at school meant you didn't end up with much to show for your time once you left. As expected, I had little in terms of useful grades and thus few options of what courses or jobs would take me. Since tinkering with computers was the only useful skill I had, I picked a computer course from the glossy college prospectus and decided that was how I'd spend my year.

The first time I ever saw the college was when I arrived for my induction day. A colossal set of towering buildings right in the heart of the city, it made my former school look tiny. Once the course began, I found college refreshingly mature compared to the school I had just left, with a classroom full of adults, and teachers who no longer patronised, insulted, or talked down to me. The only downside was that there were literally no women on the course whatsoever, and as the vast majority of my peers had come from the foundation course a year earlier, they had all already established themselves as friends. I really felt like the odd one out on that first day. I was quite a bit younger than everyone else there and dressed in a baggy heavy metal t-shirt, while the rest of the class wore sporty tracksuits and snazzy shirts while happily talking amongst themselves. I remember running through an exercise on Microsoft Word when I noticed two other students whispering about me from the corner of my eye. 'He looks like a little girl,' one murmured to sharp laughter in agreement. Although intended as an insult, it really didn't bother me. I had long, silky brown hair running down past my shoulders. I liked that I looked small and pretty, compared to the tall and boisterous young men who made up the rest of the course. If ever confronted about my appearance, I explained away my preference for androgyny as a desire to look different and express my love of rock music. When my tutor once proclaimed confidently that I'd certainly one day grow sick of my hair and cut it all off, I strenuously denied that would ever happen. I knew going back to short hair would make me look like a boy, which sounded abhorrent. I felt awkwardly different from boys my age, and cultivating a radically different aesthetic was my way of owning that difference as something to be proud of, or that's what I told myself anyway. I wasn't quite ready to confront the fact that I still just wanted to look like a girl.

The comments I got about my unconventional appearance were the closest I got to being bullied at college, which is to say not very close at all. I still found the environment there uncomfortably masculine, but juvenile behaviour and violence had thankfully been left back at school. Due to the location of the campus, there were plenty of places to go and things to do at lunchtime. I was no longer penned into a dense school ground for 60 minutes every day, hiding out from bullies. Now I could go window shopping on the high street, grab lunch in a cafe, or simply listen to music undisturbed on my trusty MP3 player (which held a staggering 1GB of music).

Although I was unsuccessful in making any new friends at college, I did reconnect with one from school: a fellow geeky teen named Ruben. He was never harassed as much as me – probably due to the fact that by age 14 he was the tallest person in the school – but he was another person who was seen as an outsider back then. We'd become friends early on and although we didn't always see eye-to-eye, and the amount of time we spent together did fluctuate, he was the closest thing I had to a friend I could actually confide in. When I went to college, Ruben had decided to take the year off, living with his mother in a tiny flat and spending all his time playing video games. Since they lived near the college, I often visited and ate my lunch in Ruben's room. More than once I'd walk in at lunchtime to find him in pyjamas, only having just woken up to groggily answer the door. Most of the time he'd be in the middle of an online video game and would sprint back to his computer after letting me in. Usually we'd then just chat about our geeky interests or watch anime together, very rarely bothering to eat outside or head somewhere else.

One of the more serious things I talked about with Ruben was how we had no idea what we were doing with our lives, and each of us possessed a disturbing disappointment in ourselves. We'd lost contact with everyone else since we left school – very much intentionally on my part – and we were becoming isolated and directionless. We had the same sense of self-loathing, sharing a similar belief that we were useless and broken people, without any ambition or pride. Worst of all, we had no optimism that things were ever going to improve. Although we often smothered these feelings by gorging on pop culture, they would always return and inevitably we'd again find ourselves sat solemnly questioning our apathetic attitude and academic failings. These talks were the closest I ever got to spilling the details of my recent past. I realised that Ruben at least somewhat understood how I was feeling, even though the source of his brand of negative feelings seemed rooted elsewhere. The conversation always ended the same way, with a grim acknowledgment that we were likely never going to be able to shake these feelings. Each of us had experienced depressing teen years, and with adulthood looming we knew we weren't ready or willing to take on any new responsibilities. We still felt like two childish screw-ups.

As Ruben was the only friend I had left, in my spare time I had returned to Gaia Online in search of new people to talk to. This time I was using a fresh account. My former pink-haired and smiley female avatar had been replaced by a grumpy-looking boy with a shaggy bob of red hair and a tiny pinprick mouth. I stayed well away from the transgender discussion thread, still nursing guilt and conflicted shame over how I had considered myself part of that community just a few years ago. I now used the website exclusively to talk about pop culture with strangers. One afternoon I ended up striking up a conversation with a girl, who also lived in England, while chatting about a new TV show we were both enjoying. Nicole was a lot like me – another geeky teenager with a huge video game collection and a love of sci-fi – and we very quickly became friends over our shared fandom. After talking for a few days on the forum, we then upgraded our correspondence to instant messaging and blurry circa-2005 webcams. We found that beyond having a lot in common we also had a similar sense of humour and would spend hours making each other laugh with silly jokes. Within a month we had awkwardly admitted how attracted we'd become to each other, and with that clear go-ahead I asked if she wanted to become my girlfriend. She accepted and thus began my first relationship.

Nicole was kept a secret from my family for the first few months, simply because I was too nervous to tell them that I had a girlfriend. By this point I was barely speaking to my parents at all. My dad now worked away every weekday, only returning for weekends, and my mother had gone back to work herself. My difficulty in connecting with my immediate family extended to my other relatives. Although I didn't see them very often, any conversation with grandparents or aunts and uncles felt clumsy and forced. Although I'd once been close to my cousin Lydia, we now only saw each other at family weddings or Christmas dinners. During these family events I'd spend most of the time on the outskirts of the room, before excusing myself early.

It was only when I became frustrated with having still not met Nicole that I sat down and told my parents about her. My dad seemed especially delighted to learn about Nicole's existence, which at the time I was certain was his way of being relieved that I wasn't gay. Neither of my parents were openly homophobic, but I had picked up enough to know it wasn't something they wanted to hear from me.

It was one winter weekend that I took a four-hour train down the country to see Nicole. Intensely nervous at going to see my first real girlfriend, I wondered if I would dissolve into a jittery puddle upon meeting her. After rendezvous-ing in the train station, I found Nicole was just as I'd expected, with a bob of jet black hair and a funky fashion sense outlined by her lacy gothic jacket and purple waistcoat. I found her clothing style intoxicating and longed to be wearing something as outlandish and loud instead of my black jeans and gory Iron Maiden shirt. Holding hands, she led me to the town centre as we excitedly chatted about how strange it was to finally be together. As the day drew on we found ourselves snuggling on a bench by the river, cuddling up to keep warm and gushing about how happy we were. In our delusionary romantic teenage love bubble we felt inseparable and indestructible. Convinced that we'd be together for the rest of our lives and overcome any obstacle, we promised to meet again soon. At the end of the day, I kissed her goodbye and returned home with a renewed sense of self-worth.

Suddenly, all I wanted from life was to be left to talk to Nicole, either in person or typing away on the Internet. As my computer course was coming to an end, I was told that the college was soon launching a two-year computer game design course and that I might be a good fit for it. As computer games were still my favourite source of escapism after Nicole's company, I signed up, thinking that it would buy me more time. To my delight, Ruben enrolled too, meaning this time I'd actually have a friend in the classroom and not just be surrounded by older strangers. Embarrassingly, I was looking for an easy ride, not a career in the video game industry. That course felt like an easy way to lose two years. I had no interest in my future because I had no sense that I really had one. Even if I'd never admit it back then, I was depressed. My relationship with Nicole was like a drug, something that numbed the pain and helped me forget how empty I felt. Otherwise, when left alone I felt like my life was pointless and I struggled to feel anything other than a quiet sense of unease and disappointment. As usual I blamed myself for feeling this way, but I now know what all those feelings really were and had been the whole time: gender dysphoria.

Gender dysphoria is usually understood in very simple terms. It's most often described as the disconnect that transgender people feel, the juxtaposition between what the mind says the body should look like and the reality of its actual shape and appearance. While that's often true, dysphoria isn't always that simple. Dysphoria can also lurk in the background of your life, draining all colour out of your world and dulling your emotions. It comes from having to live a life of suppression and compromise. I've talked to a lot of trans people in recent years who've shared stories of suffering from dysphoria without realising that it was the cause until later in life. Dysphoria can become your status quo so effortlessly, it's difficult to discern when you're having a normal reaction to something or if your entire outlook has become warped. One way to understand the deeply draining effects of dysphoria is as an emotional and mental saboteur, a quiet passenger ensuring you feel as miserable as possible.

A recognised medical diagnosis, dysphoria is steadily replacing gender identity disorder as an understood condition. This is obviously a fitting change since being trans is not a disorder or a mental illness, but it does require treatment. Personally, I support the move to de-medicalise being transgender as I believe otherwise it encourages the myth that trans people are cisgender people who develop a need or desire to 'change gender'. The truth is that we're making changes to match who we already are. However, even de-medicalisation has attracted critics who cry that it shows that trans people should not benefit from medical care on the NHS, or via health insurance. But to that I argue that being pregnant isn't an illness either, but you wouldn't expect people to be left to deal with it on their own. Surely the goal of healthcare is to assist people who are otherwise in danger or deeply distressed, and with dysphoria unchecked that perfectly describes trans people.

There have been debates in the medical community about whether the extent of gender dysphoria is actually caused by being transgender, or if it's an effect of the stigmatisation faced as a result of being trans. As someone who lives with dysphoria and has experienced it evolve and change with my transition, I disagree with the assessment that it's rooted in outside sources. That belief simply doesn't explain its extreme effects and its presence without the knowledge of even being transgender. A common effect of dysphoria is that it places a cap on your emotions and tricks you into confusing contentedness for happiness. It tells you that being numb and dissatisfied with everything is the normal way to be. It was only years later that I realised my own understanding of being happy was a piteous substitute, a small victory amongst buzzing and exhausting dysphoric feelings.

Dysphoria also twists what you hear and perceive from other people, seeing slights and prickly condescension where no ill-intent exists. When you're dysphoric, the world feels like a grim and dreadful place, full of pettiness and callous strangers. Plenty of trans people, me included, have spent years with a reputation for being short-tempered and irritable, only to completely shred that status once they transition.

It's important for me to mention that dysphoria isn't a requirement to being trans. Although it's very common for trans people to suffer from dysphoria, not all of us do. Also, the physical effects of dysphoria can manifest very differently for different people. Stereotypically trans people are said to find their own bodies repulsive and cry that they're 'trapped' in the wrong one. In reality, lots of trans people seek to alter their bodies in small and subtle ways to improve comfort and thwart dysphoria, but they're not overcome with grief at the sight of themselves. It is true that some of us do require surgery to counteract substantial negative feelings stemming from particular features, but like many things involved in being trans, dysphoria is something that's personal. It's impossible to properly distil a universal description of dysphoria, because we all experience it in individual ways.

One source of dysphoria for me was knowing that my teenage years were coming to an end. I didn't feel like a man, nor did I want to become one. The idea repulsed me. All the men I knew were either stoic, cruel, or crass – adjectives that didn't describe who I was or who I wanted to be. Men were large and ugly. I wanted to protect my androgynously youthful appearance and stay an ambiguous teenager. The only thing in my life that cut through the dysphoria and distracted me from its clutch was Nicole. Or to be more specific, it was the idea of her. By being somebody's partner, I felt wanted, loved, and worthwhile by default, regardless of how she was actually treating me. The relationship's existence was evidence of my worth and progress. It became a fragile substitute for every emotion I was missing, everything that dysphoria had swallowed up.

As an infatuated teenager, I didn't really see the problem in arranging my life and sense of worth entirely around a single person. Of course, I can now see how disastrous and detrimental such a plan is, but at the time it was the perfect distraction. Every time I had a set of days off at college, I would jump on a train and visit Nicole, staying over in the small house she shared with her mother. When we were together it was easier to forget how lonely and lost I otherwise felt. We spent all that time simply doing the typical things that geeky teenage couples do together: playing video games, trading comic book theories, going to the cinema, and binge-watching TV shows. We seemed like a normal and happy couple from the outside. Yet there was one little secret in this dreamy and wholesome vision of young love: I consistently wanted to wear her clothes. It wasn't just one outfit or particular style that had spellbound me; I wanted to wear makeup, I wanted to buy my own feminine fashion, I wanted to style my now considerably long hair into a more girlish style. Altogether, I desperately wanted to shake up my outward presentation to get away from my drab and masculine look. I also entirely hated the fact that I wanted to do these things.

My desire to wear dresses, skirts, and other feminine attire didn't blossom out of nowhere. It had been there throughout my teenage years and was a supporting piece of evidence when I'd been identifying as transgender, but it became difficult to ignore when I was with Nicole. I saw her don corset tops over fancy blouses, and draw on dramatic eyeliner as I sat and wished that I felt comfortable enough to ask her to share her wardrobe with me. Did I want to transition? No. That would be going too far, but I did want to look like a girl. I lived in baggy jeans and dark t-shirts, the boring uninspired wardrobe of someone who's given up. I wanted to go wild, dress extravagantly, and incorporate colours and cosmetics. I wanted swishy skirts and funky jewellery, all the things that girls my age were sporting, things I'd never been able to experience. But I knew giving in to that temptation was taboo. More importantly, I knew my partner would sooner see me drop dead in the street than walk beside her in heels. Although Nicole liked my hair, she saw me as a rebellious rocker and certainly not a girl like her.

In silent privacy, I despised the entire part of myself that craved to explore my femininity. I saw it as a dangerous void, one that would swallow me and crush my relationship if I came too close to inspect it. I knew Nicole would be upset and angry if she learnt the truth, so telling her wasn't an option. Likewise, I couldn't think of anybody who wouldn't be baffled by my confession.

I became completely convinced that I'd be violently condemned if I dared to tell a single person about what I wanted, but I didn't trust myself to not be one day drawn into the allure of experimentation. Therefore, I vowed to stay well away from even the idea of indulging in makeup or dressing up. In my intense paranoia to not jeopardise the relationship, I even went as far as to research self-control exercises, so scared was I that I would weaken and give in. I started to treat my desire to express myself as a dangerous addiction, a habit to be kicked.

At this point, some of my old friendship circle from school started to re-enter my life, albeit at arm's length. At Nicole's insistence, I joined Facebook, the trendy new social media platform that everyone our age was signing up for. I found that people like Gavin and my old slacker-inclined friends were already members and welcomed a chance to use me to increase their friend count. While I'd last seen them as a nervous and awkward 16-year-old, burdened by the baggage of recently being the bullied outcast, now

I was 19 and holding down a multi-year relationship. Unhealthily, being able to talk to them about Nicole boosted my sense of worth amongst them. Having a girlfriend, while my former school friends struggled to keep a partner for more than a handful of weeks, felt like evidence that I wasn't a loser after all. There must be something of worth to me, I thought, because evidently I had achieved that tested heteronormative masculine demonstration of maturity: the long-term girlfriend. In the same way that Nicole would parade me into her school grounds to impress her Sixth Form friends, I used her existence to wipe away my former reputation and try to cement a new one. In hindsight, the fact I cared what they even thought, and the way I used my relationship like a status symbol, was a giant red flag that I was struggling with deep feelings of inadequacy, not to mention how pitifully immature I was being.

What I was doing with my relationship at the time is something I'd learn in future isn't uncommon for trans women deep in denial. Sometimes it's a girlfriend, but other times it's the military, bodybuilding, marriage, a sports team, or even priesthood. By suddenly defining your life around something easily sold as a traditionally masculine pursuit, there's the futile expectation that perhaps it will purge away these unwanted thoughts. Maybe if you suddenly act like a macho image of virile masculinity, or a mature paternal figure, then you won't long to wear dresses and wonder what it'd be like to be a cute girl anymore. Chasing a masculine stereotype also allows you to redefine your life with something to live for. It's food for that insatiable dysphoric abyss. But of course, it's never satisfied with these pursuits. That abyss is a side-effect of what's missing from your life. Until you replace it with exactly what it wants, it's not going anywhere. It'll sit back and let you chase your new idea of who you are, but it won't stop reminding you that something's wrong. It knows what gender you are, even if you don't.

Remembering that I once defined myself in my younger years as a 'boyfriend' is now bizarre and quite cringeworthy, but it's also quite sad. I was hurting, but lacked the self-respect and emotional intelligence to understand what I needed to get out of that ditch. So instead I just kept digging. As my social life expanded, in the background my acute desires to unconventionally express myself remained unchanged. No matter how much willpower I extended in trying to shoo those feelings away, they never budged. When I was distracted or busy, they could be quiet but they would always creep back. Countless times I shuffled through the town centre and wondered what it would be like to wear the dresses I saw in shop windows or to dye my long hair a bright, attention-grabbing colour. If I ever sat with Nicole's all-female group of friends, I'd inevitably wish that I was one of them and not the odd one out. Altogether, these desires left me perpetually uncomfortable and trapped, feeling that I was saddled with a chunk of troublesome personality that I wanted to chip off.

I didn't know why I had these feelings. I simply knew that something in my gut was telling me I'd be happy if I gave in. In response, I repeatedly told myself that I wasn't a girl and that everything I was feeling was just a silly personality quirk. I couldn't be a girl because I simply wasn't trans enough. In my mind, only stereotypically feminine trans girls chose to transition, ones who grew up with dolls and wept at the sight of their own body. I believed my ambivalence and numb disinterest in myself was proof I didn't have gender dysphoria. I even retconned my own history. I used my desire to don dresses as an explanation for why I'd previously come out as transgender. Despite the fact that clothes and makeup had rarely factored into how I felt as a child or a young teenager, I persuaded myself that they must have been the sole driving force behind wanting to transition at 14. Therefore I wasn't trans, I just wanted to dress up and admired feminine fashion. It was a shoddy answer full of holes, yet less frightening than the possibility that these feelings were actually symptoms and coping mechanisms of pushing myself into denial. If being trans was true instead, then it meant my whole life was a delicate sham – something I simply couldn't accept.

Despite my refusal to identify as a girl, I still didn't feel like I could compare myself to other men either. This was a thought that emerged from time to time, such as when reluctantly reconnecting with people from school. It was most perfectly and confusingly highlighted by a particular occasion towards the end of the year when I went to get a haircut. As it had been years since I'd decided to grow out my hair, I now had an overwhelming amount of it. When I stood upright, it fell all the way down my back. If I ever went swimming, my hair made me feel like a mermaid, swirling and fanning out around me. I loved how it looked, but it was with a mass of damaged and split ends. Despite how impractical it had become, I had resisted visiting a hairdresser the whole time it was growing, almost entirely because I was terrified it would be lopped off without my permission. My hair was intensely important to my identity. I saw it as something that marked me as different from young men my age and allowed me some comfortable distance from the expectations of my perceived gender.

Finally, with some heavy urging from Nicole, I relented and found myself walking into my childhood barber's, the only one I'd ever visited. Although most places nearby were explicitly gendered, this place catered to men and women, with a men's barber's in the front room and a women's salon in the back. There was no waiting area or lobby – the front door simply led right into the men's part. It was a room that reeked of hair gel and was decorated with generic photos of beached boats, dusty roads, and other completely miscellaneous scenes, with seemingly no theme tying all of the art together. That day, I remember passing by men of all ages who sat slumped shoulder-to-shoulder, making no conversation or eye contact. The only woman in the room was stood in the corner, talking to one of the barbers as he carefully shaved a client's hair so short it was practically a fine fuzz. Awkwardly, I approached the counter and explained that as I was here visiting my hometown, I was wondering if I could have my hair trimmed. The woman glanced over and casually explained that she could do it as she had no appointments for the rest of the day. Inwardly, I was relieved by the prospect of having my hair cut by a woman as I'd stereotypically assumed that she might understand how important my long hair was to me.

Sweet smells and soft aromas tickled my nose as I walked through a short corridor and was led into the spacious back room. Despite being through a tight doorway, the women's salon was much larger than the men's barber's in the front. Comfy sofas made an incomplete circle in the centre of the room as the spacious perimeter was peppered with mirrors and sinks. While the shelves had been sparse in the front, here there was a colourful selection of bottles and sprays everywhere. The hairdresser who'd offered to trim my hair introduced herself as Stephanie and nodded towards an empty chair in the corner. As I sat down and spun towards the mirror, I looked at the inverted salon reflected back at me and digested how different it was. The stifling atmosphere of the barber's had been replaced with the comfortable and patient air of a friend's living room. It was the first time I'd ever been anywhere that felt so exclusively intended for women.

Stephanie then surprised me by plunging her fingers into my thick drape of hair. She tweaked and fluffed it while I stared blankly at her via the mirror. She asked what specifically I wanted done with my hair, while I hastily explained I wanted to keep it long but that I needed it tidied up. She eyed the length of my hair thoughtfully, scrunched up her face, and then suggested she take off about seven inches. When I paused, she added that trimming it would make it lighter and take out the split ends. I agreed, trusting that she knew what she was doing but reluctant to agree to losing any of it.

As she snipped away locks of my hair, I started chatting with her. I talked about Nicole and of how I was always bouncing between my hometown and her southern city several hours away. Stephanie meanwhile regaled the dramatic story of her leaving the salon across the street to come here, having clashed with her boss over accusations of underpayment and theft. A platinum-haired hairdresser was walking by during a lull in the conversation but stopped upon seeing me. 'You have lovely hair,' she remarked, stepping closer. Stephanie agreed and paused to nod at me. 'Much better than mine,' she said. I smiled but wasn't sure how to reply. It was rare for me to receive any compliments at all, especially like this. I felt comfortable and at ease with the realisation I was being treated like any other woman here. Tipping her head, she pointed at her bright, unnatural hair colour. 'It's all the dye. I'm always doing stuff with it,' she added. I nodded and said, 'I've never dyed mine, so I guess it's still quite healthy.' The truth was that I of course wanted to dye it. I wanted to experiment and try difficult colours and styles, maybe even blonde like her. 'You lucky bitch,' she quipped with a wicked grin, before walking away. I laughed off the comment as I was hit by a swirl of mixed emotions. It had been a very quick, flippant comment, a derogatory insult for a woman, but clearly delivered as a joke poised on the premise that I didn't really belong here. Depressingly, it had revealed the truth: I was different – a guest and an outsider in this feminine space – and everybody knew it.

Once my hair had been trimmed and layered, I was shown the result with a handheld mirror. I nodded appreciatively, feeling I really had no other choice but to chirp happily. Truthfully, my hair did look much neater and healthier than it had in a while, but a considerable amount of its length was missing. I was reminded that she'd been cutting a man's hair and thus had seemingly been more careless with the length than she might have been otherwise. When I stood up, I fully realised how much had changed. My head felt oddly light and cool, the ends of my hair now tickled my shoulders and no longer trailed down my back. The floor was covered in thick clumps of my hair, the original strands from back when I'd vowed to grow it out to become more feminine. Getting another look at my reflection, I saw I looked undoubtedly more masculine now, less of a mermaid and more a metal-head.

When I'd finished judging my own reflection, I paid Stephanie and walked back into the men's barber's to reach the exit. It was like passing into another dimension. The gruff, silent men had been replaced by other equally disinterested patrons. Some in the exclusively male room cast a curious eye at me as I reached the door. This felt like the real joke: how I was supposed to belong here and not in the back with the colours and the friendly laughter. The whole experience had a strangely memorable effect on me.

That night, because I knew deep down that this experience had special significance, I recorded the whole event in my diary, which is how I've been able to describe it here with such clarity. But, as with every moment of lucidity back then, I soon put it to the back of my mind and returned to being wilfully distracted. I didn't acknowledge that the experience had significance or consequences for me at that time because I still didn't want it to.

Chapter 5

BARGAINING

The uncomfortable status quo of ignoring my own instincts continued for the entire two years of my new college course. For that time my life remained essentially the same, as I split my weeks between college and Nicole. When my computer game course came to an end, it also took away my excuse to continue ignoring my future. I'd finished with the highest grade in the class, mostly due to all the time I spent quietly getting on with my work, but I had no interest in pursuing things to the next level. Unlike me, Ruben had fitted in exceptionally well with our peers and had become particularly popular. He seemed to have shaken off his former slump, while I was still trapped within mine. He decided to leave the region altogether, to head to university with a handful of other boys. Incidentally, that would leave me with no friends in my hometown and no reason left to stay. I'd later come to wish I had joined him, but rolling right into even more education sounded exhaustingly dull. I was still only interested in my relationship and anything else I could do to distract myself from my fractured mental health. My solution of what to do next turned out to be completely moving in with Nicole.

With heavy boots, mirrored sunglasses, tank tops, and a no-nonsense attitude, Nicole's mother reminded me of Terminator 2's Sarah Connor. She was not exactly a very cuddly woman and I was certain she didn't like me. But generously she did offer to let me stay with the two of them if I would help look after her horses. I agreed. Every day I would travel to the small stable where the four horses lived. Once there, I'd spend a few hours running down the checklist of everything that needed to be done to take care of them. Although working in stables and taking care of horses may sound glamorous in a romantic and wholesome way, in reality it involved pushing around endless wheelbarrows of horse poop in a giant swampy field drowning with thick mud. When not carting around poop, I carried huge bales of dusty hay or led disobedient horses up a steep slope and back into the stable. It was monotonous but it meant every night I got to fall asleep next to my girlfriend. At the time that was the only thing I cared about, and for all the wrong reasons.

After years of being a couple, I still longed to express myself away from the gendered box I'd been dumped in at birth. But now my resolve was finally starting to erode. I wanted a compromise. It didn't have to be flashy or obvious, but I needed some sort of concession for how drab and uncomfortable I felt presenting myself as male. One evening, while browsing the Internet on Nicole's computer, I noticed that amongst the Doctor Who action figures on Nicole's desk there was a bottle of jet-black nail polish. Well, Ozzy Osbourne sported black nails and passed it off as part of his masculine rocker persona, so why couldn't I? While she was on the other side of the room, engrossed in another romantic vampire novel, I painted my nails. My shaky hands produced a blotchy mess on each finger, but

I figured it was forgivable for a first attempt. Now I had to find out what Nicole thought of them.

Whether this was going to ignite a supportive or an outraged reaction, I wanted to get it over with quickly. I hopped onto the bed and wiggled my fingers at Nicole. 'Oh for God's sake,' she said, looking at me like a disappointed parent. After chastising me she went back to her book. I should probably remove the colour, I thought, maybe even apologise. I waved away that instinct. It was the fear talking, not me. This was something I'd wanted to do for years. I would downplay what it meant to me, but I wasn't going to stop.

I was the first to wake up the next morning. While still laid in bed, I stretched my arms into the air and danced my dainty fingers across the morning sunbeams. My nails were still highlighted, shiny and black. I felt peaceful. The familiar pressure that had been stalking me for years wasn't as distracting as usual. Although I didn't realise it, this was my taste of what it was like to beat back dysphoria. In trans circles this feeling is sometimes called gender euphoria.

Unlike dysphoria, gender euphoria is a fairly loose term. It's not medically defined and even in the community it's not often used, but I've found it a helpful concept. The exact definition can differ quite significantly, depending on who you talk to. However, the meaning that I've come across the most, and the one I subscribe to, is the sense of happiness that descends when your presentation matches how you feel. When you've been dysphoric for years, even a tiny gesture like painting your nails or binding your chest can make you feel comfortable and safe. Sometimes gender euphoria is the silence and peace of being granted a break from dysphoria, other times it's an astonishingly energetic giddiness from feeling at home in your body at last.

A week later, I bought a handful of my own nail polish, including my own bottle of black. I silently decreed that I would keep my nails permanently coloured from then on. When I returned to visit my parents, I nervously pointed out that I had glossy black nails, playing it off as something playful and flippant. I was met with bewildered disappointment. Both parents acted as if I had done something utterly ludicrous. At first I was determined to persist in my new form of self-expression, but when I swapped to purple nails and my mother called them out as especially ridiculous, I started to falter. So far nobody had supported me and I didn't expect my friends to be any different. Was this really worth it? If simply painting my nails was causing such a backlash, how could I ever expand to what I really wanted to do? Striding into the room with a dress on would probably end with me being run out of town. Defeated, I stopped. I went back to doing what was expected of me. But even in sulking failure I didn't throw out the nail polish. I knew one day I might feel defiant enough to use it again. So instead I tossed the bottles in a dusty drawer, somewhere I knew others wouldn't check, but where they could lie in wait if I ever changed my mind.

Again, what happened to me here isn't unusual amongst trans people. Often the reactions of those around us carry immense importance, especially if we're already riddled with guilt for shaking up our presentation or pronouns. It's very easy to think that we don't deserve this happiness, that maintaining current relationships is more important. As trans people it's common to feel like a burden on those around us early on. We shouldn't. I maintain that transition is not selfish but is in fact a beautiful process of self-love and exploration. But that's a message which is presented virtually nowhere. Even before we tell anybody what we're planning, we know that society demonises transition. It's presented as pathetic and silly. It's there in the jokes, in newspaper headlines, and in the underlying narrative of exploitative documentaries. That stuff sinks deeply into our psyches; it fosters feelings of doubt, guilt, and shame. It can stop progress dead in its tracks, all in the name of protecting the status quo.

Even though I was determined to not explicitly act on my 'gender identity issues' (as I came to label them awkwardly and secretly), they found ways to slip out anyway. One comical example took place once again via video games. *Fable 3*, a story-driven role-playing game that was similar but much more advanced than the older *Baldur's Gate* series, was released while my girlfriend and I were 150 miles apart. However, the game did have an online mode where we could meet up and adventure as a swashbuckling, spell-slinging duo. Designing our characters separately, in the single player introduction, we planned to virtually meet up a few hours into the game's storyline. Upon first laying eyes upon each other, I couldn't contain how hilarious I found our choices. Awkwardly, our two characters had arrived wearing exactly the same outfit: a crimson highwayman-esque jacket and a matching gold-rimmed skirt, with styled auburn locks to match and trendy buckled boots. Nicole grumpily accused me of inappropriately wearing virtual women's clothes, while I explained that in the fantastical setting of *Fable*, such an outfit was obviously gender neutral on my handsome male hero. That was, of course, a lie. I had chosen the outfit specifically because I appreciated the chance to wear more feminine clothing without outrightly playing a female character, something that few video games allowed. It was an example of a recurring trend. I was now bargaining with myself, trying to appease my desire to feminise my appearance through loopholes and facsimiles. If I began to indulge my feminine tastes virtually, then maybe I'd stop wanting to in real life.

A similar example took place privately in *World of Warcraft*, a huge online video game with a persistent shared world to explore. Over the years, I had often played monstrous and sinister-looking characters when playing with friends, but as I was looking for a new way to experience the game, I chose something very different. One of the two new races added that year was a sapphire-skinned alien species with hooves and decorative horns. While the men were brutish hulks, the women were slender and cute. For the first time, I selected a female character, giving her a traditionally feminine name to match. My justification for doing so was that she would look more fitting in the intricate robes that this particular character class had to wear. A male character would appear comically clumsy, so I had to play as a woman. It was a weak excuse, but as always I took the easy answer rather than confront what my desires really meant.

When I logged into the game as my new character, I loved how fresh the familiar experience felt. A few hours in, I received a private message from another player, who asked if I wanted a couple of useful items he'd found – specifically, potions that would restore my character's health in a pinch. I responded that it was kind of him to offer and, if he didn't mind, I'd happily take them off his hands. Moments later, his avatar came bounding across to mine and traded the items over to me for nothing. I expressed my thanks to which he replied, 'No problem, hon.' I had never been called 'hon' before. I realised that he had assumed because my character was a girl, so was I.

Awkwardly, I felt a jumble of gratitude and guilt. My pretty-looking avatar, in her ornate blue and gold dress, was left stood statically in the road as I contemplated how I felt. Inarguably, I liked the assumption, but I also felt deceitful, like I had done something wrong and inadvertently tricked him. Over the next few days, I intermittently logged back into that character, one I kept a secret from Nicole, and had a number of similar encounters. Every time, I dreaded being asked what gender I was, because I knew I couldn't bring myself to say that I was a girl, but I also found being presumed to be one uniquely pleasant.

Playing that character came with a noticeable absence of the usual chafing irritation of being perceived as a man. I was comfortable and at ease wearing that persona, more so than with any of my other characters. One night, it became too much. I abandoned the character in a fit of guilt, consciously choosing to never play her again. My sense of duplicity and wrongdoing won. Ironically, I had a male friend who often played female characters openly, and with no thought to how it affected who he was being seen as behind the keyboard. Yet for me, I knew I couldn't duplicate that flippant attitude – it felt like something I didn't have permission to do.

As another winter approached, I found myself feeling restless and gloomy. Experiencing glimpses of gender euphoria that year had inadvertently highlighted how unfulfilling my life was when that sensation wore off. My relationship's ability to supplant my self-worth had begun to weaken. Eternally shovelling horse faeces into a wheelbarrow no longer seemed like a rewarding career path either. I suggested to Nicole that we draw up a plan to save money and move onto the next phase of our life together, to finally find our own place to live and do something new.

She disagreed. Nicole was content with our status quo of being financially wasteful and saw no reason to change anything. We were unable to come to any sort of consensus about our future, or even an agreement on which city we should live in, and we began to bicker regularly.

In a rushed panic, I phoned my old college and asked if they had anything I could do as a step up from the BTEC I'd finished the previous year. They broke into a marketing pitch of a new video game degree course they had just launched. It was part of their 'university centre' – that is, the course was taught in careful co-operation with a nearby university. They continued to boast of talented tutors and a meticulously constructed set of modules, tantalisingly explaining that as a former student I could slide right onto the course despite the fact it was about to begin. Scared that I wasn't going to be able to secure anything better, I accepted. In the months to come I'd think of this moment often, usually with expletives on my lips and plenty of regret.

To attend the course, I moved back in with my parents, something I had already second-guessed on the day I left Nicole behind. For now, she was going to stay with her horses. When the course actually began, I had a bad feeling from that very first day. The teaching was stunningly lax, while the first few weeks consisted of recapping what I had already learnt back at college but at a fraction of the speed. Save for a couple of other students, the rest of the small class loved the plodding pace and heaps of free time. One glance around the computer lab during a workshop session and you'd find the majority of the class watching mischievous cats on YouTube, or playing on portable game consoles. If the lecturer bothered to show up that week, he usually stumbled in stinking of booze and having done no preparation for what he was going to talk about. I started to wonder if, instead of industry professionals, the academic staff were just a band of local drunks who'd been ushered in from the pub across the street. Ironically, I'd have probably gotten along with the other students and relished the slapdash organisation if it had been two years earlier, but now I actually wanted to learn something new and earn a respectable qualification. Since my relationship was fraying, I swapped my aspirational identity from 'long-term boyfriend' to 'erudite student'. I needed this new identity to fill the empty abyss. But with the shoddy state of this course, I felt more like a slacker than a scholar.

I raised my concerns with the head of the computing department, comparing our deadlocked progress to competing courses that were zooming through a challenging syllabus. My persistence escalated my complaints so high that I ended up speaking with the institution's dean. Sat inside his spacious office one afternoon, he nodded along to my list of concerns and promised me that everything would be fixed. He assured me that new supportive staff were in the process of being hired and a much more formidable learning plan had been developed for the second semester. On his word, I hung on and didn't drop out, but his promises turned out to be hollow. Things got worse. The only vaguely competent tutor on the course suddenly vanished, with concerning rumours that he had fled the country. No new staff materialised, replacements or otherwise. I felt conned. The smiling dean kept promising that, any day, everything would be reversed. I was suckered into hanging on, praying that my investment of time and money would soon pay off.

Meanwhile, my relationship with Nicole continued to decline. I ignored them at the time, but friends began to warn me about her. After we all travelled to Manchester and attended a lively comic book convention together, one friend took me aside and said that she was concerned by how Nicole spoke to me. She gently pointed out that she was often manipulative and would guilt-trip me into doing things that I didn't want to do. If I ever dared to say no to Nicole, she would sulk until I showered her with apologies. I dismissed my friend's worries, explaining that she was only seeing a certain side of Nicole. I claimed that, inside the personal confines of the relationship, things were much different. I knew there were problems with our relationship, but as usual I blamed myself for not living up to other people's standards. Yet manipulative behaviour wasn't even the worst of it, when in private Nicole could be violent too. She would often hit me as a 'joke', punching my arm or pushing me. When I complained and reminded her that I didn't like her being aggressive, as it reminded me of being bullied, she'd shy away as if deeply hurt. She always defended her actions by claiming that she simply showed affection by roughhousing. If I ever tried to hug Nicole, she'd dive out of the way as if dodging a hail of gunfire. According to her, I needed to stop being so picky and start seeing her violence as a compliment instead. I took my inability to play along as another failing of my masculinity, an example of me being too sensitive for a boyfriend. Looking back, I know that her behaviour was unacceptable and arguably abusive. But as a primary source of my self-worth, I was incredibly reluctant to even consider ending the relationship. Without it, what did I have left?

Meanwhile, I was back to bouncing between two parts of the country, staying with Nicole in my spare time and then spending the remaining time at my parents' house. As it always did when it lacked a distraction, my gender dysphoria stomped back into my life and demanded attention. Since I now had some space from Nicole, I guiltily considered buying some makeup in addition to my forgotten nail polish, or perhaps even some feminine clothes. I had no plan for what I'd actually do once I owned them but I wasn't thinking that far ahead. Once I'd toyed with the idea, I found it returning with regularity. It could be fun. Nobody had to know. All I needed was an opportunity to buy something without getting caught. One presented itself when my parents left for a week-long holiday and asked me to house-sit in their absence.

If I was ever going to expand my wardrobe, I knew now was the time do it. It was a rare chance. No Nicole, no parents, no friends. Nobody would be around to judge or scrutinise me. Unsure what I was going to buy, or even why I was doing it, I caught the local bus to the town centre, with the very loose plan in mind of buying a dress or a skirt of my own. There was a nervous energy to having made this decision. I felt like I was on my way to partake in an elaborate jewel heist. I knew that what I was doing was wrong on some level, but also it was too irresistible to back out of. Once the idea had occurred to me, I was powerless. I had to try to pull it off.

Apprehensively, I wandered into the largest clothing shop in town. First, I dallied around the men's section, pretending that I had an interest in the stacks of identical jeans or the racks of shirts in various shades of beige. I was warming up and collecting my courage. Slowly, I edged closer to the women's clothing department, the forbidden zone, readying myself to charge through its imaginary force field. In preparation, I ridiculously concocted a story that I was there shopping for Nicole. Mentally, I mocked up a dialogue tree of potential questions and answers that I might encounter. I was shopping for her birthday, seeking to surprise her – that was my carefully crafted lie. If asked what size she was, I would say that she was about my size but slightly smaller. I considered myself a genius for coming up with that last part. By introducing a clear difference between us, and not just saying we were the same size, I would surely demolish any suspicions that I was actually just shopping for myself. Reassuringly, I also reminded myself that I had photos of the two of us on my phone. If for some unfathomable reason I was pressured to prove she existed, I could whip out photographic evidence.

As I circled the same rack of skirts, too apprehensive to actually pick one up, I saw two familiar faces nearby. I barely knew their names but I recognised them on sight – two boys from my college course. They were chatting to each other and slowly stumbling in my general direction, but thankfully they hadn't seen me yet due to predictably browsing in the men's section. Panicking, I made a beeline for the exit as stealthily as I could. Once back outside, I retreated into the sheltered entranceway of an abandoned shop, and cursed. That was close. If they had seen me, they might have come over to talk to me, right at the moment when I was eyeing dresses and skirts! I considered quitting. This was just too risky. But I was already so close. It could be months before I felt brave enough to do this again. After a few minutes of waiting, I saw the two boys emerge and wander away, far too immersed in talking to spot me.

I lingered in that entranceway just long enough to confirm they weren't coming back. Determined to ride out my momentum, I then marched back into the shop and grabbed a black, smart-looking skirt from the rail and triumphantly hooked its hanger over my finger. As I turned towards the checkout, my grandmother walked in. I almost cried from the sheer terrible luck I was having. It was the middle of the week and the chances that two sets of people I knew would walk into the exact same shop just as I was trying to stay anonymous were ludicrously slim. Yet it had happened, and now I had to decide what to do about it. With delight, I watched as she ascended the escalator to the second floor, while I hid at the back of the shop and remained unnoticed. This was the window I needed to escape.

As I joined the queue to pay, I pulled out my mobile phone and became utterly engrossed in typing an imaginary text message. Entering gibberish into my phone was a good distraction. Once it was my turn, I stepped over to the cashier and handed her the skirt. As the black fabric moved across the scanner, she met my gaze and smiled warmly. '*She knows*,' I thought, with melodramatic certainty. '*She's picked up on my body language and knows what I'm doing. I'm buying a skirt and she thinks I'm a hilarious weirdo. She's going to tell everyone she knows. She'll remember this day for the rest of her life.*' Fighting the urge to flee, I paid and silently left the store at a stumbling pace that was only somewhat awkward. Knowing I would feel the need to stash the clothes out of sight, I had brought a backpack with me, and I hid the skirt inside. Finally my adrenaline subsided. Now it was time to go home and actually wear it.

Locking the front door with both the key and the bolt – just in case my family made a surprise return from outside of the country with no warning – I went up to my bedroom to try on the skirt. Slipping into it, there was no miraculous wave of euphoria, no explosion of celebratory fireworks, and I wasn't struck by any stunning revelations. Likewise, no wormholes to hell were torn open, the apocalypse didn't begin, and nobody was summoned forth to tell me how gross and wrong it was to wear this. Despite how much I had built up this moment, it was quiet and personal. I was wearing a skirt. It was nice.

Cheerful to be indulging such a long-held desire, I booted up my computer and started to browse for similar clothes. After an hour or so, I'd put together a colossal virtual shopping list of outfits and jewellery – all the things I had eyed up and never let myself wear. I wanted them all. Then I looked at their price. I could not have them all. In fact, I could barely afford half. I hastily whittled down the list to a few favourite items and then hit purchase. I stretched for the fastest shipping option, not wanting to risk it arriving later in the week and have it potentially intercepted. Guilt and excitement mingled together in a confusing mess as I waited for the package to arrive. Two days later, a courier hand-delivered a box of clothes and thankfully didn't ask what was within. I retreated to my bedroom, once again double-locking the front door, and tried on my new outfits in privacy. I felt great. Like the skirt earlier in the week, wearing these clothes made me feel calm and comfortable. Looking at my reflection especially gave me a sense of profound joy. The clothes changed my silhouette to something not quite as boxy. I couldn't put my finger on why that felt so nice; it simply did. Unfortunately, I didn't look like a girl but I did look different. Better. My gender dysphoria had just been thrown something substantial, enough to temporarily stop its relentless draining assault on my mental health.

When you've been longing to buy more colourful and bold outfits and finally let yourself do so, it's like unleashing your starving feral fashion sense. Free for the first time, mine charged towards the loudest and most noticeable things in sight. I can guarantee that none of the outfits I bought during this experimental phase have survived into my wardrobe today. They were all ghastly creations with clashing colours and nonsensical designs. Those old garish dresses were all eventually donated to charity shops. I like to think that they went on to help the next style-starved trans woman looking to experiment. Perhaps that wasn't the last time they were purchased in tense secrecy.

Dressing up in feminine clothes went from a one-off indulgence to a private pattern. Crushing guilt and self-loathing quickly became a recurring part of the routine. The more I did it, the worse I progressively felt. It wasn't unusual for me to spend some time in a new dress early in the day, and then spend the night interrogating myself over why I had wasted my money on something I was wearing only in secret. I didn't have much to spend, yet instead of buying things for myself and Nicole to share, or saving for our future, I was drip-feeding this pointless hobby.

I was terrified that soon I'd be found out, that Nicole would see the clothes I'd bought and leave me in disgusted fury. But I struggled to stop. The soothing effect on my mental health was too potent to resist, even with its nasty aftershocks. But the guilt became so intense that in my darkest moments I started to self-harm. I was convinced by my stress and shame that the pain would act as punishment, a deserved deterrent for continuing this extravagance. I didn't see this as the warning sign that it was, I believed I was still acting logically. I differentiated 'real' self-harming from what I was doing, as if my motive justified the means. Unbeknownst to me, I had just begun to lose control.

Self-harming is another risk that plagues the trans community. It goes hand in hand with the widespread levels of poor mental health. A Stonewall report on Scottish trans students in 2017 reportedly found that well over 90 per cent of trans teens had deliberately hurt themselves at least once.[1] This is a staggeringly high statistic compared to the NHS's prediction for all young people, which sits at just 1 in 10.[2] It's another fact that highlights how incredibly important it is to support trans people and ensure they don't feel isolated.

One of the most alienating things about my situation was that I had no name for what was going on or what I was. I had tentatively browsed self-described crossdressing websites but found them distastefully unappealing. Most had a sexual element to them and were populated by self-identified men in outlandishly absurd outfits. There was a spectacle and performance aspect to the examples I came across that I couldn't remotely relate to. Their community seemed accepting and harmless enough, but even at a glance I knew it wasn't for me. On the other end of the spectrum, I maintained that it was still impossible that I was transgender. I thought I was somewhere in the middle, with nobody. Alone.

Realistically, I needed queer friends but I had none and knew of nobody remotely like me. I'm confident now that I did have at least one or two friends who were safe to confide in, but I never became comfortable with dropping them even a single hint. I was ruled by paranoia and pessimism. Privately, I never stopped imagining how nightmarishly sickened I suspected Nicole and my family would be if they knew what I was doing. I was already convinced that both my parents didn't like the person I had grown into. I felt that whenever I stepped outside of the tightly defined idea

1 Bradlow, J., Bartram, F., Guasp, A. and Jadva, V. (2017) *School Report: The Experiences of Lesbian, Gay, Bi and Trans Young People in Britain's Schools in 2017*, Stonewall and Centre for Family Research, University of Cambridge, available at www.stonewall.org.uk/sites/default/files/the_school_report_2017.pdf, accessed on 23 February, 2018.

2 Ibid.

they had of who I was supposed to be, by doing anything from voicing a political opinion they disagreed with to once again refusing to lop off my long hair, it would inevitably end with an argument and me getting upset. If they learnt I was wearing dresses, it would cause the biggest clash yet. By staying silent I believed I was protecting myself from them, and them from me. I was preserving the status quo as best I could so that nobody had to be disappointed by the truth.

As I was growing overwhelmed with the guilt, my mental health continued to plummet. Likely as a result, I then developed anxiety. Sleeping became impossible as I would suffer panic attacks in the dead of night, where my mind became a machine-gun of fearful thoughts and nonsensical worries. It wasn't unusual for me to still be awake with adrenaline when dawn arrived. Exhaustion would eventually push me over the edge and I'd lose consciousness; then I'd spend daytimes catching up on sleep. I regularly skipped my morning lectures as I slept right through them. Elsewhere, I would be travelling on public transport and suddenly feel like I was suffocating. I'd sit staring out of the window while I fought the urge to panic and charge out of the emergency door. I was perplexed where these symptoms had come from, with panic attacks occurring with frightening regularity and no conceivable explanation or pattern. Ridiculously, I convinced myself that the anxiety must be self-inflicted, a placebo effect of thinking about the last panic attack too much. It was another straightforward and sloppy answer to a scary problem, an easy way out that meant I didn't have to ask anybody for help. With all the stress that I was under, I was now falling apart.

If I ever wanted time to myself when Nicole wasn't working, she'd demand an explanation and a precise estimation of how long I'd be away from her. When I raised the point that this scrutiny was unreasonable and stressful, she dismissed my objection. She explained that she had no interest in doing anything alone and expected me to feel the same way. But I didn't. As the problems in our relationship became worse, Nicole began threatening to end things altogether. We simply couldn't communicate. Any conversation between us was a difficult slog and neither of us seemed to be getting anything out of the relationship anymore. All stability and security was gone. She would wildly brandish the idea of a breakup around like a knife, as if warning me about the power she held, but she never followed through. For a month, I consciously tried to fix the relationship, doing my best to appease her and return things to how they used to be. It exhausted me. By the end, I had begun to question why we were even still together. One night, after another lengthy and tense discussion over the phone about how miserable we both were, I surprised her by agreeing that the relationship was dead. I was sick of all the stress that it was putting me through and I wanted to break up, even knowing that this was the last thing in my life that felt worthwhile. Nicole insisted that I had to be the one to do it, that she would never end things between us herself, despite how many times she'd signalled she was about to. So I did it.

I cried that night, as I went to bed newly single. I feared I'd lost the only thing of worth in my life, that without it I had nothing. I was still keeping a diary at the time and melodramatically wrote that I had made a horrible mistake. It would probably make a better story to say that I was pushed to end things as I finally realised my own self-worth, but there was nothing that triumphant about the decision. We had simply each evolved into two very dissimilar people. The gap between our personalities and politics had widened too far. Although a large part of me genuinely believed I'd never find anyone who'd love me the way that Nicole had, I could tell that we'd been bringing out the worst in each other.

I was now at rock-bottom. My life was in shambles and my mental health was a quivering ruin. I needed time alone to sit amongst the mess I'd made and decide what the hell I was going to do. With each passing day, I felt a little lighter and a little more certain that I had made the right choice. After a week of silence, Nicole sent me a message to say that she wanted me to come over and talk, to collect my things and neatly tie the relationship off. I refused, telling her that she could keep or throw out whatever few video games and comic books I'd left behind. Despite everything, I didn't trust myself not to give in and call off the breakup if we reunited. Tempting as it was, I knew any reconciliation would be a mistake. There had been no passion left, no love, no security, and even no happiness. We were finished. We'd stayed together so long simply because it was all we'd known. I wanted to stay away from her for both our sakes. Our relationship had started as something endearing and sweet, two teenagers lost in puppy love, but it had undeniably grown into something toxic and destructive. I didn't want to see her again, and I never did.

I've wondered since, did Nicole suspect I was trans? I left so many hints during our time together, both accidental and deliberate, I was sometimes waiting for her to bring it up. But if she knew anything, she never said it. Although it is vaguely tempting to track her down and catch up, I don't think it's a good idea. It's been years since we separated and I'm sure she's become a new person too, though maybe not quite as dramatically as I have. When we were together, Nicole did occasionally say things which made me wonder if she knew more than she was letting on, or that she was worried there was something queer bubbling below the surface. More than once she exclaimed in exasperation that I was clearly a gay man in denial and would one day leave her. Her frosty reactions to my gender flexibility might have been driven by the same thing that was behind my earlier determination to hide it: a desire to not lose the relationship. Being young and unaware of what was going on in my head, I don't think I can really blame her. She seemed to value the relationship in the same harmful way that I did – that is, as the primary evidence of her worthiness.

Despite the forgiveness I would retroactively extend to my ex, I do think the partners of trans people have an obligation to support their loved one's transition. A lovesick teenager burying their head in the sand isn't very kind but at least this is vaguely to be expected. An adult should certainly know better than to ignore the signs that their partner is unhappy. Trans is something you are, not something you become. There's no trans-vampire that nibbles on an unsuspecting cis person's neck, causing them to undergo a sudden transformation. Likewise, you can't be brainwashed into becoming trans. If someone is trans, they are trans, and it will come out eventually. Partners can make that process easier by expressing support and encouraging exploration, or they can make it much harder. The one thing a partner cannot do is make someone cis. I personally know of trans people who are not transitioning because their partners do not approve. They know they are trans, they know precisely how transition works, but they withhold their desire so as not to upend their relationship. I find that absolutely tragic. Transition is the act of freeing oneself from a lifelong prison. It's ultimately a selfish practice to try to keep a trans person in place for your own comfort and stability.

When it comes to the topic of couples staying together through transition, I've found that most cis people assume that transition must mean separation. Yet more often than not, I've seen couples stay together through it. A lot of that depends on how comfortable the non-transitioning partner is with their relationship changing from a perceived heterosexual one to a homosexual one, or vice-versa. Despite how it may seem from an outside perspective, transition doesn't drastically change people. Generally we become more of ourselves, more open, more honest, happier and calmer. The idea of a radical personality change, one that turns a partner into a complete stranger, is essentially hyperbole. When we transition, we're still the same person underneath; we just might shed or pick up some quirks on the way. Therefore, if you love your partner for who they are, chances are you'll still love them when they transition.

Now single and entering my early 20s, I was still not thinking about transition at all. But I did understand enough to know that my former partner had, willingly or not, left me feeling unable to express myself the entire time we were together. With the relationship over, I decided I wasn't going to let that happen again. Something had to change.

Chapter 6

ACCEPTANCE (KIND OF)

That summer, I did two very significant things that each changed the direction of my life. The first thing I did was to start attending a real university. I abandoned my old degree course, leading a handful of other dissatisfied students to an alternative institution. I was able to negotiate our way onto the second year of the course by demonstrating the software skills we'd taught ourselves over the last two years. Thanks to YouTube videos and a stack of academic books we'd shared, we'd substituted our missing lectures and picked up enough to show that we could hit the ground running. We arrived on our new course amazed by the extensive resources on offer and excited to experience teaching that would presumably be delivered sober. With this, I felt like I was making some real progress in my professional life, aligning myself with the path I should have been on before and regaining lost time.

The second significant thing that I did was attempt to accept that there wasn't anything wrong with me. I owned a stash of dresses and longed to be more feminine. That was considered bizarre by wider society, but did I really have to buy into that belief and condemn myself too? I realised I was dragging around a lot of baggage and that this cycle of guilt and shame wasn't working. I was always beating myself up, but it was making absolutely no difference to what I wanted to do. I had physically hurt myself and spewed venomous warnings at my reflection, all to remind myself that these feelings were too repulsively selfish to indulge in. But no matter what I did, that demonised part of me would shrug as if to say, 'Well I'm not going anywhere, dummy. I'm you.' So I decided to stop expecting these feelings to magically go away. Instead, I decided to negotiate.

What sparked this newfound acceptance was the fact that I had started to read self-help blogs after one of my favourite authors had shared an empowering article about acceptance that had profoundly resonated with me. These weren't the harsh, masculine, judgemental websites that I had also read in my attempt to suppress and eliminate my gender variance; they were much fluffier, positive ones. They were full of warm advice preaching self-acceptance. On one of these excursions, I came across a method that I knew I had to try. It sold itself as a self-help trick, something you can do in minutes. Dubious, but in need of some sort of relief, I read on. It explained that the first step was to look in a mirror and think about the part of yourself you disliked, and to do so until you felt that familiar shame. The second step was to look yourself in the eyes and explain that it's perfectly okay to have this feeling and that there is nothing wrong with you for having it. Even if you passionately despised your supposed flaws, this method could allegedly help you make peace with them by consciously confronting them. I figured there were absolutely no drawbacks to trying, other than privately feeling ridiculous, so I gave it a go.

I remember vividly the night that I tried it, staring at my reflection in a brightly lit bathroom mirror and ignoring my prickling self-conscious feelings. It was so rare that I really looked at myself, I almost didn't recognise the shaggy face looking back. Thankfully, I still looked young for my age but I had changed a lot since my time at college, which did spark hints of regret. Slowly, I spoke aloud to myself. 'This feeling is never going to go away,' I began, shakily admitting the obvious as I homed in on that warm feeling of panic, dread, and guilt. 'But there is nothing wrong with feeling like this. You like wearing feminine clothes and makeup. You wear dresses and skirts. You want to look more feminine. That's perfectly okay. It's really not a big deal that you want to express yourself like this, even if other people don't understand it.' I finished with a shrug and continued to stare silently into my own eyes for several minutes, as my mind reeled. Then I started to laugh. Ridiculously, it had worked. I hadn't believed what I was saying when I'd begun, but each new word had triggered more relief. I had finally granted myself the permission to stop punishing myself. Thinking about what I wanted to do and who I wanted to be no longer summoned shameful embarrassment. I actually felt almost silly that I had dedicated so much time and energy to feeling bad about a harmless hobby for so long.

Although that day the effect felt immediate, there had been a lot of legwork leading up to that moment – it wasn't the magical transformation that it appeared to be. The biggest step in getting to that point was admitting that this feeling was permanent. After years of hiding and burying how I felt, I was bored of the farcical nature of expecting it to vanish. At times over the years, it felt like I was beating myself up for being born with blue eyes or for enjoying the taste of chocolate. It was a mundane part of my personality that I had persuaded myself was akin to a drug addiction, something dangerous and unhealthy. When I broke up with Nicole, I realised that my most judgemental critic had never been her, or my parents, it had always been me.

The affirmation that I wasn't doing anything wrong slapped me out of a daze. I'd been living in fear of other people's potential reactions, letting it twist my own self-worth into nothing. I stopped short of announcing my newly discovered self-love to anyone else – that was still a little too frightening – but that night I did finally accept who I was, or at least who I thought I was: just a guy who happened to appreciate clothing from the other side of the shop. With that in mind, I vowed that it was time to live for me, to have fun on my terms. The first step was to buy some more clothes and makeup, without the sense of wrongdoing. I had learnt my lesson last time, when I almost bumped into familiar people, so I travelled one city away and went somewhere new. Unlike before, when I had been a jittery mess of paranoia, I was much more confident this time, feeling comfortable with the fact that these were my clothes I was buying.

The next few months were the fun break I needed. University began and gave me an excuse to follow my passion. I spent my days drawing, writing essays, and tinkering with animation programs. The work was much more intense than it had been at the university centre and I never lacked for something challenging to do. Meanwhile, in private I bought more feminine clothes and freely allowed myself to dress up. To save money while attending the fairly local university, I decided to stay at my parents' home instead of going into student housing. This felt like a savvy idea to reduce debt and my food bill. What it meant in practice was also sacrificing my privacy. When I wanted to try out my new outfits and express myself, I had to do so when nobody was around, which thankfully was often. I would wait until the house emptied, get changed, then generally sit around watching TV, chomping on snacks or playing video games, enjoying how comfortable I felt with my gender dysphoria appeased. If I heard someone return, I would change clothes faster than Clark Kent in a telephone box. I never dared leave the house, though I did debate going for a walk or enjoying a book in the garden. The fear of being spotted by neighbours, and how the scandalous news could spread back to my family, slapped away any thoughts of going outside.

Even dressing at home wasn't without its unexpected problems, however. One night, my family was away, meaning I had a rare opportunity to take my time and not worry about having to get changed before anyone came back. I'd also bought some new makeup earlier in the day and I was looking forward to trying it out. When I figured it was late enough in the evening that nobody was likely to come knocking at the door, I sat down in front of my mirror and started playing with my cosmetics. The result was predictably clownish for someone who had never been taught how to use makeup and still had very little experience. But being photogenic wasn't exactly my concern, so I was happy enough with how I looked.

I decided to pop into the bathroom after finishing my makeup, so I could marvel at the final result in better lighting. However, upon walking in, I was greeted by the most terrifying spider I had ever encountered in my entire life. With a string of creative expletives, I ran back to my bedroom in panic. I'd never been good at dealing with insects, but spiders especially sent me into shrieking hysterics. I knew I couldn't ignore it; I'd never sleep knowing it was lurking in the house somewhere. I imagined it crawling onto my face as I slept, a creeping behemoth scuttling across my skin, and shuddered at the very idea. In the past whenever I'd encountered a spider, I'd grab the nearest person and recruit them to take it outside for me. Being alone, that wasn't an option. The next thought was my neighbour, yet I had to either run there in my dress and full made-up face, or get changed and risk the spider escaping while I did. I was far too squeamish to capture it myself, so begrudgingly I realised I would have to squash it. First, I filled a nearby cardboard box with my old hand weights, relics from the time I had comically planned to build muscle. Carrying the box as far as I dared into the bathroom, I leaned over and dropped it onto the horrifically huge spider. Satisfied I had done all I could, I returned to my bedroom with a pounding heart and went back to admiring my sloppily applied makeup. Unbeknownst to me, the spider lived, having scrambled away at the last moment. Thankfully, it didn't reveal itself until my family had returned. By then it was blessedly no longer my problem – it was my mother's job as the house's designated spider slayer to help rehabilitate it into the garden.

Ideally, I'd love to recount more amusing stories, but the truth is it wasn't all silly fun. Regret did return, albeit never with the ferocity of before and no longer aimed at myself. Whereas before I had blamed my own hobbies and personality for being outside of the norm, now it was our cisnormative society that disappointed me. I longed to live somewhere, or some*when*, that didn't demonise gender variance. I wanted to go outside and feel safe wearing whatever I liked, instead of fearing the very idea of doing so. Depictions of trans people had evolved little since my teens, with disgustingly disrespectful gags everywhere.

Meanwhile, I still didn't even know what I was. All I knew is that it was exceedingly rare to see a sincere depiction of anybody like me.

I began to have a common daydream, one that would come to me when I felt my most dejected. It was always exactly the same. I saw myself at the end of my life, laid in a bed with little time left to live. I was reminiscing on my wasted life, thinking back to how I'd never pushed through the fear, never shared what I wanted to do or openly explored who I wanted to be. I knew this future wasn't just likely, it was a certainty. This was prophecy, not fantasy. I was doomed to become that miserable man unless I did something. But I felt trapped, completely caged in by the expectations of others. That daydream recurred regularly and never failed to completely depress me. At night my dreams regularly revolved around the same topic, usually materialising as wish-fulfilment. I often awoke disappointed from scenarios where I'd freely dressed and acted how I pleased in a busy public place, with no concern for backlash or judgement. Ultimately, I still believed I wasn't trans enough to go all the way and transition, but I knew I was enough of something to require some sort of change. I was just too scared to actually do anything.

When I broke up with Nicole, I declared that to simplify my life I would remain single until I graduated. Yet with graduation still well over a year away, I spectacularly broke this promise. It began when I struck up a fast friendship with a woman named Loretta. She was also a student in the region, attending a different university to my own, but she had just suspended her studies due to a slew of serious health issues over the past few months. We originally met only in passing, when in groups of mutual friends, but we began to get to know each other more online. After a short time, she invited me to start hanging out as a pair. We got along spectacularly. Thanks to an identical sense of humour and similar interests, our personalities clicked with ease. There was a playful excitement to her which made spending time with her a joy. She found everything either fascinating or hilariously charming. Despite coming from a difficult family and living in a tiny bedroom barely big enough to cram her bed inside, her approach to life was enthusiastically optimistic. Undeniably, I was attracted to her, but in practical terms we still barely knew each other. I was afraid of coming across as a creep and ruining our growing friendship by telling her. When one afternoon she leaned in and lightly kissed my nose, pulling back to reveal a gleeful grin, my fears were quashed. Evidently, she felt the same spark. I kissed her back and later that night we both agreed to become a couple.

I knew that from the outside our relationship surely looked like a sham. We had gone from strangers to partners in under three weeks and still had a lot to learn about each other. But we were having too much fun to care what anyone else thought. Unlike Nicole, Loretta made me feel at ease and never guilty or nervous. I realised that this was what relationships were supposed to feel like, that I had settled for an imitation last time. However, I was grimly aware that by falling into a new relationship I was at risk of stepping back into that old cage, of burying who I was and trying to appease the security of the relationship at all costs. Although Loretta seemed to be much more accepting of my openly sensitive personality and feminine appearance, she was of course unaware that there were dresses and makeup stuffed under my bed. As a first step, I started painting my nails again, nervously showing Loretta that I'd done so. After asking for a closer look, she exclaimed that the colour suited me. To my delight, she even opened up her nail varnish collection to me, letting me pick from a treasure trove of diverse colours instead of my puny handful. I didn't feel safe enough to tell her everything plainly just yet, but I had a growing sense of hope that she would be okay with my secret.

A few months after we'd gotten together, Loretta had a dress delivered to my parents' house, as it was easier than sending it to her student housing. It was knee-length with a red polka-dot pattern and a 50s-style cut. It looked like the type of fun retro outfit you'd wear to a party. I was on the phone to Loretta when I took delivery of the dress. She was at her new flat, while I was staying with my parents again. She asked if I'd open it up and see how it looked. It was gorgeous, I couldn't deny it. I booted up my computer and showed Loretta through my webcam as I laid the dress out on my bed. 'You should try it on,' she said, mischievously. I almost fainted with shock. This was what I'd always wanted: for someone to give me the go ahead to wear an outfit like this. 'Are you sure?' I asked, wanting to be certain this wasn't a joke or that I was about to make her uncomfortable. Loretta just shrugged, 'Go for it. Why not?' From her expression I could see her amusement, but seemingly this was a wholesome and good-natured reaction, without mockery or judgement. I slipped on the dress and positioned the camera so she could see me clearly. This felt like staggeringly unexpected territory, the first time I'd ever shown somebody what I looked like in an outfit like this. I could barely believe it was happening. Loretta just gave me a kind smile. 'You look nice,' she said. I knew then that things were definitely going to be different.

It was approximately a week later when, with extreme care, I broke the news to Loretta that I owned more dresses. I explained that nobody else knew and that it was an entirely private pastime. As far as she was concerned, it was an unlikely hobby but not an undesirable one. This was a ridiculously huge relief for me, having kept this secret tightly held for years. With Loretta aboard, I continued to dress up in my spare time, except this time I had company. I no longer had to sneak to the shops as Loretta would come with me and we'd shop for outfits together. She showed me the best shops to go to for inexpensive and age-appropriate outfits. As I'd been living in bulk-bought jeans and black t-shirts, I was woefully uneducated about the most suitable shops to head to and what a reasonable price for makeup was. It's a common problem trans people can encounter if we've stayed in a safe and simple shopping pattern prior to coming out. We can lack context for where to go and how not to get ripped off as we build a replacement wardrobe. Though that said, it would be a lazy generalisation to say it's the norm. I've met plenty of trans people who were stylish and savvy when it came to clothes long before they came out to anybody. But I was most certainly too inexperienced back then to even have known the difference between different high-street shops.

With new outfits to play with, I started to stay at Loretta's flat and spend entire days in makeup and feminine clothes, before swapping back and going to university. When my course started to wind down at the start of summer, I had no reason to go back, and the frequency of dressing up dramatically increased. There was one night in particular where Loretta had said she wanted to see how I looked in her old business suit, a formal outfit she'd bought for university events. I agreed, always happy for an excuse to wear something new. Unusually, I actually put care into assembling the full outfit. I even wore one of her bras, which of course didn't exactly fit properly seeing as my chest was completely flat. Altogether, I was in a white blouse, black tights, a smart pencil skirt, and an accompanying blazer. Loretta even did my makeup, carefully applying everything from foundation to colour-matched eyeshadow and lipstick. Excitedly, she dragged me over to the bathroom's full-length mirror so I could see the final result. I certainly looked better than I ever had doing my own makeup. This was the most stereotypically feminine I'd ever looked. After grabbing my phone, I started to snap photos of myself, posing in a mixture of silly and serious expressions. Afterwards, Loretta even took a few of me as I sat back down in the bedroom and began to daydream. When I looked back at the photos later that evening, it was one from that moment that stuck out for me: a picture of me still in the outfit but looking away, as if distracted and forlorn. Despite the radically different presentation from my everyday look, it had just become my favourite photo of myself. There was something to it that looked genuine and pretty, though tenderly poignant, compared to how dead-eyed and distant I normally looked in photos. Yet I couldn't show it to anyone else without inadvertently revealing my secret.

The lengths we'd just gone to – preparing me in a full feminine outfit simply in order to sit in the bedroom together – made me uneasy because of its implications. As I wiped away makeup and slipped into my pyjamas at the end of the day, I stressed to Loretta that this was still just for fun – it didn't mean anything more, it was an innocuous game. I worried that she'd see this escalation as a sign that I wanted more and therefore was endangering the relationship. To her credit, Loretta didn't seem fazed by what I'd just worn. If she was concerned, she didn't show it. Twinges of guilt had caused me to make such an assertion just in case, but

I wondered who I was truly trying to reassure. Was I really just worrying about what I'd find out about myself if we didn't stop?

As trans people, there are countless coping mechanisms that we can flit through before we learn who we are. Some of us don't have an interest in clothes at all and never enter a phase like the one I was tangled in. But nor is it uncommon to regularly dress up in a wildly different presentation and pass it off as a hobby or a lovable quirk. For those of us who find solace in shaking up our outfits, that desire to dress up can work as a useful gateway to understanding dysphoria, even if we still lack the vocabulary for it (like I did). For us, changing our presentation to one that matches our gender can unveil temporary peace of mind, or outright gender euphoria. In the process, this reveals the potential for sustainable happiness. It highlights dysphoria as something solvable, not an immovable aspect of everyday life. That way, dysphoria goes from a draining and painful shroud that you've learnt to live with, to something you endure on a short-term basis. You just have to hold out to shed your presentation and slip back into the one that feels right. I have friends who came to the realisation they were trans through comic book cosplay, drag acts, and crossdressing clubs. Some people spend years in that phase because they're too nervous to go further or they still need more time to understand themselves. For example, people like me.

When autumn came and my university course resumed, I spent more time at my parents' house again, as it was much faster to commute to university from there. While Loretta restarted her degree on a more fitting path, moving from hospitality to business management, I was heading into the fabled final year of my degree. Allegedly, this would be the most intense and difficult set of semesters by far. In the first week, I was offered the chance to write a dissertation, an extended piece of research on a relevant topic of my choice. The offer came with a warning. Being on a creative course, I had a collection of practical projects to juggle. A dissertation would be an entirely different challenge, an extra set of spinning plates to tend to at the same time. Arrogantly, I assumed I could handle the pressure and accepted, seeking the excuse to practise my writing in an academic challenge. Weeks later, I was drowning in PowerPoint presentations, 3D models, animation graphs, and a stack of books to speed-read. As a side-effect, I stopped wearing makeup and dresses altogether, as I simply had no time. Whenever I wasn't at university, I was hunched over my laptop, working. I only crawled away at night to catch up on food and sleep.

One night when returning from the computer lab, I spotted a colourful poster advertising the university's LGBT+ society. Absentmindedly, I took a photo of it with my phone, telling myself I would decide later what to do about it. Despite the intersectional language of the poster, I dreaded turning up and being dismissed as not trans enough or queer enough to be allowed to take part. After all, was I even queer at all? I was in a relationship with a woman and never thought about my sexuality. Although I was growing consciously uncomfortable with being gendered as male, I still did see myself as a guy and therefore also cisgender. I worried that trying to find friends in the society would come across as co-opting experiences that weren't mine, even if I arrived and admitted that my identity was fuzzy. Because of these fears, I didn't get in touch and I never discovered if I'd have found a place there or not.

This poster wasn't the only time I'd noticed trans people being mentioned at university, but the next time was particularly memorable. As part of my degree I had to take a mandatory module on creative industries and ethics. Although it's admittedly an interesting and important topic, I found the lectures dull and a waste of precious research time. Each week I was packed into a giant lecture hall with students from various other creative courses such as film, television, visual effects, and animation. We were then given generic lectures that unreliably changed in quality, depending on that week's speaker and topic. This particular week, the lecture was set to be delivered by my course tutor, a socially conscious and witty woman who I greatly respected. Therefore, I expected to enjoy her talk, but I failed to predict how familiar her subject would be.

The topic my tutor had chosen to cover was diversity in the video game industry. In the middle of the lecture she started to tell a story of a transgender colleague who had transitioned in a studio she'd once worked at. I glanced around the room and saw a few smirks and confused faces. As this predated the media's modern obsession with trans people, a lot of the students seemed to be learning about their existence for the first time. Of course, I knew exactly what she was talking about. I awkwardly sat in feigned ignorance as she talked about what hormonal transition was, how trans people adopted new names and pronouns, and how scared trans people can be to come out. Steadily, I felt the familiar tightness of anxiety growing in my chest. I didn't want to be in the room anymore at all. I wanted to be outside where I could breathe and think. With my traditionally poor judgement, I had sat towards the back of the room, while the door was at the very front. To leave I'd have to get up, walk down the stairs, and exit in front of everybody, including my course leader. Given how weak my legs had gone, I didn't trust myself not to tumble down the steps if I tried to flee. Instead, as I broke into a cold sweat, I fumbled for my phone and discreetly scrolled to my small selection of video games. My favourite one at the time was a simple colour-matching game that relied on repetitive actions but also required you to think and plan ahead to maximise your high score. When I had been struggling with panic attacks in prior years, I'd found that simple games like this were good for distracting me until I was free of whatever situation was sparking my anxiety. Trying to tune out the lecture, which was still inexplicably sending my brain into a flustering mess, I started to tap away at my phone until the session was finished. I knew that to any onlookers I probably looked lazy and disinterested, but that was a preferable assumption to the truth. When it was over, I shakily stepped outside with my friends and tried to cover up how frail and exhausted I now felt. One friend mentioned that he'd enjoyed the lecture and learnt some interesting things. I smeared on a smile and said that I agreed, not daring to even hint at how much I had already known, thanks to my confidential teenage years.

When the academic year came to an end, I hobbled into university on my final day, burnt out and empty. The last nine months had driven me to the precipice of oblivion. I'd wrestled with endless technical problems, seen countless sunrises during late-night research sessions, and led a group project where everything had gone spectacularly wrong at every single intersection. But I had done it. Everything had been cobbled together in time and slipped in just under the deadline. Now it was time for a break.

Once again, I moved back into Loretta's flat, and with no distractions and the return of my free time, I started to dress up again. As with the previous summer, I kept things private, only going outside in feminine presentation on a single occasion when a fire alarm suddenly sounded one evening. I briefly considered diving out of the window and into the overgrown bushes down below us on the ground floor so that I couldn't be spotted in a dress. Eventually I relented and awkwardly shuffled down the stairs and into the yard, wrapped in a loose coat. I then hung silently behind a cluster of chatting and smoking tenants, who were busy complaining that their end-of-semester party had been interrupted. With a baggy hood over my head, I turtled myself into the collar and hoped nobody would recognise me. To my relief nobody did, or at least nobody cared enough to say anything, and I headed back inside with no incident or embarrassment to speak of.

During my final year at university I had become disillusioned with the video game industry. Guest speakers repeatedly told of the passion required to endure the industry's relentless schedule, and the complete lack of job security. I wasn't exactly jumping at the chance to join in. Truthfully, there was little I did have a passion for, but I had found myself surprisingly comfortable when writing my dissertation. At the time, I'd asked my supervisor what options I had if I wanted to keep going down the academic research route, to which he'd told me that a Master's degree in whatever interested me the most would be the best way to keep going. He'd also explained there was no rush to apply, as those types of postgraduate courses were often still accepting students as late as their starting weeks. I talked this idea over with Loretta, who was due to continue attending her undergraduate course in September, and she agreed it sounded like a good idea. Since she was lukewarm about her current campus, we started to throw around the idea of going somewhere new. The answer to where we'd go if we had a choice was the same for both of us: the south coast. We both loved the beach, craved warmer weather, and adored the idea of being significantly far away from where we'd grown up. However, after looking at practicalities, especially the cost of getting down there and settled without any friends to meet us, it seemed a little too tricky to pull off. Therefore we concluded we'd stay put, with Loretta continuing her course as normal and me applying for a Master's at a local university instead.

My new MA Media Studies course turned out to be a combination of fascinating and excruciatingly demanding. Once again, I found myself with no free time. I buried myself in my work and became distracted from any self-reflection and any more trips back to clothing shops. The first two semesters were similar in structure and involved absorbing an onslaught of new information, then delivering several seminars on topics that I had researched, before expanding those into full essays. Having to give so many seminars had the unintended consequence of turning me into a much more confident speaker. I became completely comfortable addressing a crowd, simply because I had to do it so often. Strangely, I even found the attention enjoyable.

My third and final semester was entirely involved with writing another dissertation, but this time a much bigger one. It was set to last the whole summer. Although having just a single project to work on sounded like it would give me a fortunate break, the sheer amount of research needed meant I was chained to my computer for the entire season. When the end of September came, Loretta had just begun her final year, while I had finally finished higher education altogether. As a short-term replacement, I became self-employed and began to design websites. It was something I fell backwards into, simply because I had the skills while the demand was already there, with friends of friends and old acquaintances wanting personal websites to advertise their own skills and businesses. I didn't want to do it forever. I still had my sights on academia but I also needed the break. With the freedom to work whatever hours suited me, for the first time in a year I had free time again. I inevitably felt drawn back to wearing my dresses and makeup more often, having rarely done so that year. It was at this point that I curiously realised I had developed a pattern. For three years running, I consistently sprung right back into enjoying my feminine wardrobe every time I had nothing left to distract myself with. It was like a default state of mind, something I always went to when I had time to think and space to explore my identity.

During the previous 12 months, I'd occasionally talked directly with Loretta about my dressing up, treating it as something sensitive and important but also privileged and private. When sat watching an informative documentary which followed two people transitioning, Loretta turned to me and said that she was surprised I had never suspected I was a trans woman. She mentioned that she wasn't just alluding to the clothes I liked but my personality and demeanour too. I looked away, knowing I couldn't say it if I saw her face. 'I used to,' I whispered, cringing as I confessed. Loretta waited for me to elaborate as I instinctively wanted to flee and snatch back what I'd just let slip. For a decade I'd vowed to never share what happened in my teens to anyone. It was a painfully personal story, locked away where I never looked. I felt like I'd be exposing the most vulnerable part of myself to the possibility of a lethal strike. Rejection would destroy me. 'I thought I was a girl for a year,' I blurted out quickly, spilling the words before I could regret them. 'I even told my mother. But she didn't think I was transgender. We talked about it twice and it didn't go how I wanted. We've never even talked about it since. Afterwards I changed my mind.' I dropped my head onto Loretta's shoulder, bracing myself for her reply and praying she'd show the kindness I'd come to expect. 'You deserved better,' she said. Her voice carried concern but also something protective and regretful. 'Maybe,' I uttered, not daring to think what might have happened if things had gone differently back then.

As graduation approached, I was feeling strangely reflective. A lot had changed in the last few years. I was no longer unhealthily drawing my self-worth from my relationship status or planning on coasting my way through life. I'd grown to feel that I had a future and had collected measurable, worthwhile skills. My dissertation supervisor had heaped praise upon my work and assured me that I was ready to become a PhD candidate, which was a big boost to my confidence. Yet despite it all, I was struggling to feel any sense of accomplishment or fulfilment. I even declined my graduation ticket, electing to collect my degree certificate quietly at a later date. The thought of attending a grandiose ceremony and having my picture taken all day felt undeserved and tedious. What I'd achieved recently felt useful on a practical level, but personally I was oddly detached, vaguely unhappy and bored. It felt like it wasn't enough, that nothing would be. Something inside me was still glaringly empty.

I stared at my reflection one evening and was disheartened to see that I could barely recognise myself. The stress of the last two years had worn away my soft and androgynous features. I could no longer joke about my youthful appearance or pass for a teenager with clueless cashiers. I was clearly an adult. Despite my soft, long hair, I looked like a man. I hated it. A twist of anxiety tightened as I realised my feminine-looking face was gone forever. I'd surely look more and more masculine now as time progressed. The face looking back at me was the start of more changes to come. I had found it bearable being a young male with amorphously gendered features, but was I prepared to live and grow into a blatantly masculine man? I didn't sleep well that night, with too many new questions tumbling around my head.

Days later, on a chilly autumn evening, I laid back on the bed while wearing another newly purchased dress. Hanging around the flat in my feminine outfits was fun but it wasn't enough, it had never felt like enough. I knew that now. While staring blankly at the ceiling, I thought aloud something that I hadn't dared to consider since I was a teenager: 'What if I'm transgender?'

Chapter 7

ACCEPTANCE (BUT FOR REAL THIS TIME)

In the spare time I had while at university I had become a blogger, often writing about pop culture such as comic books, movies, and video games online. In doing so, I'd started using Twitter, originally to build up an audience for my blog, but eventually just to socialise and connect with people worldwide. My social media feed was a cacophony of varied voices that I had handpicked along the way, including a number of vocal transgender activists. Coupled with my own recent realisations, the catalyst for beginning to question my gender again was the fact that I repeatedly kept seeing trans women who were remarkably like me. In the back of my mind, I was still carrying around the assumption that all transitioning trans people were in constant dysphoric anguish. The fact that I wasn't perpetually excluded me from transition…except here there were women casually explaining that dysphoria came in many shapes and sizes, and that sometimes people didn't even have dysphoria to any notable degree, but of course they were still trans. So if they were trans, maybe I could be too? I knew that wasn't a question I could answer without help, so for the first time in my life, I admitted I needed to go to counselling.

Loretta agreed that counselling sounded like an excellent idea. I had kept her updated on my evolving feelings and she readily agreed that it could be just what I needed. She'd seen my comfort level change over the years and had always gently nudged me to ignore the fear and follow what my gut was telling me. I didn't know what this road would mean for our relationship, but both of us agreed that I had to keep going and expose the root of these feelings.

I knew that the easiest, and cheapest, way to go to counselling was to see what my university offered. Considering that the graduation ceremony for my course was weeks away, I realised I had picked the worst possible time to decide that their support services were worth checking out. Regardless, I sent an e-mail to the counselling services and asked if I could have an appointment anyway, being open about the fact that I was soon to no longer be classed as a student. Thankfully, I was told that they weren't overly strict with a student's status and I was welcome to come in for an introductory session that week. I also saw that they had assigned me an appointment with one of their male counsellors, which made me hesitate. My mind automatically imagined a burly lumberjack with bulky arms, a no-nonsense man raising an apprehensive eyebrow at my confession that I liked to put on dresses and thought I might be a girl. Although aware of the ridiculous nature of my speculation, I decided there was some validity in that fear and I wanted to talk to a woman. I wrote back and explained that I had 'gender identity issues' and therefore would feel more at ease speaking to a woman. With a sincere reply, they explained that was fine and rearranged my appointment with somebody else.

When the appointment day came, I sat on a faded sofa in the student union and nervously wondered what was about to happen. As it was almost Christmas, the lobby was covered with sparkling decorations and a tree three times my height, but there was nobody around to appreciate the festive atmosphere. The semester was over, most people had already headed home, and soon the university would shut down entirely for the holiday period. I looked at Loretta, who had come to keep me company and was sat on another sofa opposite me. 'What if I freeze up?' All my life I had fiercely instructed myself to never reveal these details, never admit how I felt about my gender or the fact I once suspected I was trans. I pictured myself arriving at the appointment and evading the question, chatting about the weather or showing off some cute animal pictures I had on my phone. Maybe I'd even run out of the door screaming.

With ten minutes left until the appointment, I reluctantly got up and squeezed through a tiny side-door that apparently led to the counselling department. In my three years at university, I'd never been down this corridor; in fact, I had always thought that the door led to a storeroom. Instead, I found a cosy, windowless waiting room inside, a hidden haven of houseplants and plush chairs. With the reception desk empty and nobody around whatsoever, I slouched into one of the chairs and waited. Before long, a kindly, middle-aged woman with a gentle voice came and led me away to a private room. Her office was a small and softly lit space with drawn curtains and two oversized chairs that looked ready to swallow anyone who went near them. I felt like I'd just walked into a miniature spa. This room felt safe, calm, and completely cut off from the world. Patiently, the counsellor introduced herself as Holly and explained how the counselling service worked. She listed off disclaimers and instructions in a manner that spoke to the countless times she had surely done this before. She stressed that everything we talked about would be confidential, unless she was legally obligated to reveal anything for someone's protection. With that out of the way, Holly looked across to me and asked what I wanted to talk about.

I paused. Feeling my mouth go dry as the spotlight shifted to me. I readjusted myself in the intimidatingly squishy chair to buy myself a few precious seconds through hesitation. 'Well,' I began, once again pausing, 'It's about my gender.' I then told her everything. The whole story you've read so far up to this point came gushing out in a rapid stream of abridged information. I even told Holly about coming out to my mother as a teenager, an event I'd tried my hardest to erase from my own memory. I finished by explaining that I was now craving some sort of conclusion to all of it. I described the last month like finally turning around to look at the complicated baggage I was dragging around. Seeing it properly for the first time, I was now admitting I needed help to work out what to do with it all and what it meant for my identity.

The act of talking about myself to a third party was overwhelmingly liberating. At the end of the session Holly thanked me for giving such a detailed summary of the last few years, explaining that it would be a helpful head start if I wanted to move forward into a proper set of sessions. She asked if I'd like to arrange a follow-up now or if I wanted to go away and consider my options. I eagerly arranged another appointment on the spot and walked out feeling better than I had in weeks. I was excited and eager to get back into that room and continue.

The following few counselling sessions were similar, as I returned and reiterated stories and ongoing thoughts about my gender in further detail. Delicately, Holly guided me with simple questions, such as asking how specific interactions had made me feel in the moment, or what I'd been trying to achieve when things hadn't gone the way I wanted them to. After explaining the effort that I'd put into hiding parts of my personality from my friends and family while at university, Holly looked at me in a way that made me feel exposed but still secure and respected. 'That must have been very difficult for you,' she stated sympathetically. Hearing those words was intensely validating. 'It was actually,' I replied, almost phrasing it like a question and really considering it myself for the first time. It had been difficult, but I'd never stopped to realise that it had been. Hearing it from someone outside of the situation made the whole experience feel legitimised. Altogether, my sessions with Holly were turning out to be enormously worthwhile. With her help, I was steadily seeing that there was something tangible and real behind my lifelong discomfort. The possibility that I was transgender was becoming palpable.

The first result of attending counselling was that I stopped identifying as male. Though I kept the decision private, it felt good to separate myself from that gender. Considering myself male always felt like trying to wear shoes that were far too tight. Finally kicking off that label felt well overdue. Although I suppose it was a significant step to do so, it didn't feel like a big change at the time but a natural evolution of how I understood myself. However, I didn't identify as female either. If anything, I was refusing to play by gendered rules altogether. I was abandoning all perceived ownership and belonging within masculinity, and stepping away with nothing to replace it. In practical terms, all it meant was that I stopped using gendered language to refer to myself. I now tenuously saw myself as agender, a term often used by those who consider themselves genderless.

With my new identity, I realised that it meant I was potentially non-binary. I had only come across the term over the last year but was encouraged by the fact I saw countless people on social media happily using it to describe themselves. Seeing it used made it feel valid and real, like there was a legitimate chance it could be for me after all. At this stage I didn't reach out to anyone else, or make any public declarations of my new understanding of my gender, as it still felt too fragile to share. There was comfort in the term, but I was too steeped with imposter syndrome to feel like I had a right to it.

Pinning down a definitive description of non-binary gender identities is tricky as they're incredibly personal. Some non-binary people consider themselves transgender, coming under the umbrella of everybody who isn't cisgender, but others see themselves as separate from the trans community. The most basic explanation of the term could be considered to be someone whose gender is outside of the traditional binary of male or female. Although it can be tempting to think of gender as a linear spectrum, with male on one side and female on the other, that understanding doesn't gel for all non-binary people. They can be somewhere between male and female, or they can be somewhere entirely removed from the gender binary altogether.

My next few counselling sessions continued to take place weekly, and across them I started to realise something: I was looking for validation. Even when talking with Holly about my growing pile of evidence, I would never call myself transgender. I would cautiously say, 'I believe I may be transgender' or 'It's possible I'm transgender.' When I started to explore these feelings, I realised that I didn't just crave validation, I craved permission. I didn't believe I was worthy of calling myself transgender, even though I wanted to. I felt like I had to be told I was trans for it to be true, to ensure I wasn't snatching up a term that I wasn't allowed to touch. I believed I was the very definition of 'not trans enough', someone just outside of eligibility. However, I reserved that label for myself alone. I knew I would never doubt or question anybody else who announced themselves as transgender but I was measuring myself against severely firm standards and criteria.

I realised that one of the reasons I'd been able to come back to this conclusion and seriously inspect my own gender was that I now had people implying that I was allowed to toy with these suspicions. Previously, nobody had told me it was okay to be transgender, ever. Not in explicit terms or even implicit ones, nobody in my family, nobody at school, and not my previous partner. All of my behaviour that had pointed to the possibility of being trans had been demonised and criticised as flawed, weak, or embarrassing. I'd internalised these feelings, treating parts of myself as shameful or silly, when they were in fact valid coping mechanisms and glimpses into who I really was. Only with Loretta and Holly was I receiving the signal that all of this was okay.

Unfortunately, I know a lot of people who have struggled with the same feelings. Even when faced with overwhelming evidence that they are trans, it's that sense of intrusion that can hold people back. As the recognition of being trans is presented as such a significant step, the identity takes on an almost sacred level of reverence, something reserved only for those who've proved they belong to that community and need it. Meanwhile, if everybody else in that person's life is implying that it's wrong to come out as transgender, it leaves them feeling trapped in place. With the prospect of not being welcome in either group if they dare to come out, the safest thing to do is nothing.

At the end of one counselling session, I found myself talking about my parents. I explained that if I was honest with them and told them how I was feeling, I'd expect them to dismiss my distress as temporary and something that would eventually pass. Holly asked if I believed the questions and feelings I had about my gender were temporary. I laughed. I'd had these issues for such a long time, they felt like an intrinsic part of me, inseparable and permanent. Using my childhood as an example, I talked about being at school and feeling out of place for the entire time I was there. I explained that if you factored in my early discomfort with my gender role and expectations in that setting, then I had known something was amiss for almost as long as I could remember. I then paused as something occurred to me: My feelings had never changed. From being a child through to being a teenager and now being an adult, how it felt was identical. All that had changed was my understanding of it and the labels that I used, but I was still that same person with the same consistent feeling. With that, Holly leant forward and asked me an important question: 'In that case, what do you know is the truth about yourself?' I began a grin that broke into nervous laughter. 'Know is an interesting word. That's one I always avoid using,' I replied. Holly didn't accept my dismissal. She didn't even crack a smile. She was waiting for my real answer. I swallowed a lump in my throat and began, 'Well, I think–' Before I could even finish, Holly had cut me off. 'No, no. I'm not asking what you think, I'm asking what you know. What do you know is the truth?' she said. I hesitated before the words slipped out on their own: 'I am transgender.'

As soon as I'd said the words, there was a rush of relief. It was obvious that I was not only transgender but a trans woman too, but until I had been gently led through my own thoughts and experiences by Holly, I wasn't able to accept it. Once I'd unlocked that realisation, it illuminated what I'd been doing this whole time: protecting other people. I had stayed closeted and quiet, not because I was afraid of what they'd say to me but because of how it would make them feel. I detested the idea of making people uncomfortable. I was still trying to be the nice kid, to not rock the boat or upset anybody. My family and friends were comfortable with their perception of me as a man. If I came out as a trans woman, they'd have to deal with the consequences, they'd be upset. It was the same reason I'd never told Nicole – I didn't want to hurt her. I knew I couldn't go on like this, protecting people's comfort at the cost of my own. It wasn't healthy and it wasn't worth it to anyone.

Perfectly, that revelation came at the end of our session. As always, I thanked Holly for her help and scheduled another for a week later. Stepping outside, I was still in awe that I could now say 'I'm transgender' without the sense of doubt or the dread that I was invading someone else's space. Holly had also helped me reach this conclusion by changing how I viewed my hidden gender identity issues. I'd always pictured them as an isolated shard of my personality, something I kept buried and worked around in my daily life. But in reality, it was an integral part of who I was. Even when I hadn't known the truth, throughout my childhood and my teenage years in denial, I had been a girl. The 'issues' that I had struggled with were the conflicting feelings of not being able to articulate, comprehend, and demonstrate the truth about my gender. I'd worked to hide the most obvious and telling indicators that I was carrying around desires and distress, but suppressing my gender altogether had been impossible. I'd never been longing to become a girl, I'd been struggling with pretending to be a boy.

Now that I realised I was transgender and had a much firmer grasp of my identity, I started thinking about how I would get onto the waiting list for trans healthcare. Here in England, it meant talking to a doctor and asking for a referral to a Gender Identity Clinic (GIC). There are a few GICs around the country, all run as part of the NHS. They offer various services, but in practical terms they diagnose people with gender dysphoria, refer people for surgeries relating to transition, and arrange a prescription of HRT. Due to their incredibly long waiting lists, which can stretch anywhere from 6 months to over 36 months, it's important that trans people join the queues as early as possible. There was one problem, however: just because I knew I was transgender, it didn't mean I thought I should transition.

Transition looked terrifying. I knew the statistics. Trans women especially were at a higher risk of harassment and discrimination, even violence and murder. I was a white graduate in my mid-20s, definitely not the most vulnerable type of trans woman by a long shot, but not exactly safe either. The fact I blatantly lacked job experience worried me the most. The thought of working in a customer-facing role while transitioning was terrifying. And then there was the fact that there were no guarantees when it came to results. I wondered what would happen if I did transition but I was still unhappy and ended up being treated like a man anyway. I could end up desperately poor and miserable. My life felt bland and unfulfilling at present, but at least there was safety and security in that. Transition was a gamble, one I couldn't be sure would pay off.

I was no longer asking myself 'Am I trans enough to be transgender?' but now 'Am I trans enough to transition?' I would ask myself this question over and over, playing out endless scenarios and drawing imaginary conclusions about how my theoretical transition might go. It haunted me for weeks on end. I perpetually pictured worst-case scenarios, such as being screamed at in the street every day, beaten to a pulp by drunks, or slowly dying of starvation in poverty. Every time I would interrogate myself on whether I was prepared to accept these far-fetched possibilities in return for being myself, and consistently I couldn't reach an answer.

While I was busy wrestling with the decision, I decided that the sensible thing was to get myself on a GIC waiting list anyway. If I decided I wasn't going to transition, I could simply cancel and leave the queue. Meanwhile, if I finally decided I was going to transition, then I'd have a head start. Coming to that conclusion was easy. The hard part was actually finding the courage to stand in front of a doctor and tell them all of this.

As I was still registered with the same GP surgery I'd been with my entire life, I knew which ones were the easy-going doctors and which were the stern-faced and deadly serious ones. As with counselling, I wanted to talk to a female doctor as I suspected I'd find it easier to come out to them. This time I knew precisely who I wanted to talk to: a young, kind doctor who had helped me with my last eczema flare-up. After hyping myself up for ten minutes, I grabbed my phone and punched in the number for my GP, wanting to dial before I lost my nerve. Once the cheery receptionist answered, I requested an appointment with my chosen doctor. No luck, she didn't have a single available appointment. Perhaps sensing that I specifically wanted to talk to a woman, the receptionist did say they had one slot free with a different female doctor, but otherwise all the women were booked up. At the mention of her name, I remembered my last encounter with the alternative doctor, a grim woman who liked to blaze through appointments with ruthless efficiency. I responded with 'No thank you! I'll try again later.' I put the phone down, wanting to hold out for a doctor I'd be more comfortable with. I was disappointed but secretly relieved I had found a way out – it was an excuse to avoid that scary conversation. But I did promise myself I would try again the following week. I knew I was only fooling myself by escaping the inevitable.

A week rolled around and after another positive and affirming counselling session, I decided to capitalise on my post-counselling buzz and call my GP again. Once again, there were no appointments with the doctor I wanted to see. Predicting this might happen, I reluctantly fell to my backup plan. 'I'll take any other appointment,' I forced myself to say, dreading who I might end up with. As it turned out, there was a free appointment slot with another calm and kind doctor, but a male one. I pushed myself to accept the one on offer, knowing that I would eternally delay otherwise in search of the perfect opportunity. Now I just had to mentally prepare to come out to a third person.

At this stage, my family still had no idea what was going and I was in no rush to tell them. I had admitted I was seeing a counsellor earlier that month, which itself felt like a huge thing to reveal, but I was nowhere near ready to declare anything else. My mother took the news in her stride, as if I'd just mentioned I'd been going to the gym every week. Meanwhile, my dad had offered to lend me money for private therapy instead, explaining that it felt like the right thing for him to do under the circumstances. It was a generous suggestion, but I was glumly aware that such a gift would likely be rescinded if he knew what I was actually talking about in there. It didn't feel right to accept. Besides, I was getting along so well with Holly I wanted to remain in her care. I was already where I needed to be.

My relationship with my parents at the time could still be generously described as lukewarm. I had tried so hard for years to pass myself off as an easy-going slacker, someone who skipped through life with blasé boredom, I couldn't remember the last time I'd had anything resembling a serious conversation with either of them. As we always seemed to be disagreeing on everything anyway, I'd been trying to avoid talking to them about anything more nuanced than the weather. Telling them I was dealing with this stressful identity crisis was something I inevitably had to do, but I really didn't feel like blurting it out just yet. The night before my GP appointment, I stayed over at my parents' house as they lived much nearer the surgery. When my mother saw me leaving the next morning, I lied and claimed I was going for another reason entirely.

I grew more and more nervous as I sat in the GP's waiting room, painstakingly counting down the minutes until my appointment. I had already rehearsed exactly what I was going to say. I knew that I would struggle to bring the topic up, so I had to either get it all out in one go or ease into it with a pre-prepared introduction. Although I did debate just screaming 'I'm a woman!' to get it over with, I instead decided that I would present it in a breezy and light-hearted manner. When the time came, I was called into a small office as I prepared my mental script. 'So, what can I do for you today?' the doctor said expectantly, after I had taken my seat. Chuckling to myself, half sincerely and half out of pure panic, I said, 'I realise this is going to be very left-field all things considered. I'd like a referral to a gender identity clinic, please. Because I've been struggling with my gender identity for many, many years and, thanks to attending counselling, I've realised that this is the next step that I'd like to pursue.' I wasn't sure what to expect as a result but I was relieved to have gotten the full explanation out succinctly. In that brief moment I felt like I'd just tossed a grenade onto the desk and was waiting to see if it would explode or not. Thankfully, the doctor nodded and began tapping away at his computer. 'That's fine, we can do that,' he explained happily. I nodded and smiled, acting like this was a routine and casual appointment and ignoring the pounding of my heartbeat in my ears. The appointment lasted a few more minutes as he took some simple details from me and then explained that they'd be in touch if anything else was required. I thanked him and walked out of the room feeling indestructible. I laughed hysterically to myself as soon as I got outside, amused at how absurdly nervous I had been for such a straightforward request.

Although I assumed my part in joining the GIC queue was now done, it turned out there was still one more step. Before I could be accepted onto the waiting list, a local doctor had to fill out a questionnaire with me. This list of questions had been sent by the GIC itself. My answers would apparently speed up the process of assessing me once I arrived. I learnt all of this in a phone call, in which I was told by a receptionist that an appointment had been made for me to fill out the form with one of the most direct and stony doctors at the GP surgery. When I walked into the appointment room that day, his expression betrayed that he was as thrilled to be having this conversation as I was, which is to say he looked like he'd rather be getting trampled by elephants. Once I'd sat down, he explained that there were about ten questions he had been instructed to ask me; once I answered one he was going to write the answer down and move on to the next. The first questions were simple, with the doctor just asking me to reiterate my name, my address, and why I wanted a referral to the GIC. But then things got weird. 'Are you a homosexual?' he asked, with disturbingly little emotion in his voice. I wasn't even sure how to answer that question. Was he asking if I was a gay man, or a gay woman? And what was with the bi-erasure? I supposed in a way I was gay, if I was actually a woman, then by virtue of being in a relationship with Loretta I certainly wasn't heterosexual. But I hadn't thought about my sexuality in years. 'I don't know!' I unhelpfully blurted out with a dramatic shrug. When the doctor continued to stare at me with his robotic stillness, I fell into a nervous babble about being in a long-term relationship with a woman but not knowing what I was. After a long pause, he wrote something down and moved onto the next question. I didn't think it worth asking what he chose to write.

Now it was the doctor's turn to shift uncomfortably. The questionnaire now requested a written account of my 'sexual characteristics', based on a physical examination. Neither of us moved or spoke as we blankly looked at each other. I mentally prepared for the possibility that I might be about to get naked, when he cut in with 'We'll skip that' and scribbled something down as I let out a breath that I hadn't realised I was holding. The rest of the form was about my mental and physical health, with more strangely personal enquiries. With the appointment finished, a large part of me was insulted and irritated that such a questionnaire had been necessary. My sexuality had absolutely no bearing on my potential transition. What possible reason was there for asking me that? And I didn't even know where to start with that sexual characteristics question. What did that even mean? Grimly it aligned with what I'd heard of GICs so far: that they were antiquated and required an outlandish library of personal information on each patient to judge if we were worthy of help. But regardless of what I thought of the questions, I couldn't deny that it felt good to have continued making progress. Both appointments had felt far more terrifying in theory than they turned out to be. And now they were over. The sheer relief of having them behind me was wonderful. It was only later that this euphoria wore off, when I remembered that I still had to decide if I even wanted to transition or not.

Knowing that you're transgender is not the same as knowing you want to transition. For starters, many of us don't want to transition because it's not even right for us. Transition is presented as the ultimate goal for trans people, but many who don't identify on a binary spectrum don't want to publicly change their name and pronouns, or make any changes to their body. They may simply shift their appearance through fashion and hairstyle, or even make no new changes at all. Meanwhile, there's the group of us who need the effects that only a medically assisted transition will enable, but we still might not want to transition because of outside elements. This can be social pressure, apprehension over job prospects and financial stability, or just a fear of harassment and violence from the general public. I was struggling with every single one of those factors.

I knew my family wasn't going to take the news well. They were hilariously heteronormative, with no queer friends or family to speak of. Trans people just didn't really exist in their worldview. To them, we were strange and odd people who you sometimes heard about on TV but never actually saw in the real world. The revelation that they'd have encountered many trans people in their lives and never noticed would have been met with an assured denial. This knowledge dug a pit of dread in my stomach. I wondered how much time would need to be spent on helping them come to terms with what was happening and on defending my decision to transition. Probably a lot. Meanwhile, my biggest worry was still harassment. I was afraid that if I transitioned I could end up being leered at every time I dared step out of the door. Was the risk worth it? I just didn't know.

One week in counselling, Holly phrased a hypothetical question to help me solve this conundrum: 'What if transition didn't exist? Imagine there is no way to transition and you have no choice to make anymore.' Oddly, I knew I would be relieved. No longer having to think about the choice would mean I could just go back to how I was before: disappointed but unburdened. I had already spent years being aware of transition but thinking I couldn't pursue it. It was not ideal, but I survived and made the best of those years to get where I was. I knew that if I had to, I could carry on pretending that I was male. But I then flipped the question around. 'I would prefer knowing I was going to transition,' I began, following my still evolving thought process as I spoke. 'If I knew for certain that I was going to do it, like if I was destined to transition, I'd just do it and stop delaying.' Knowing it was inevitable would be freeing. My life would be about managing the task and not questioning if it was necessary. I could meet my fate at full speed with no regrets. Of course, transition would produce problems; but if I had no other choice, then I would simply focus on solving them and getting on with living my life.

Evidently, the question had unearthed a mass of queries and emotions. I left that session feeling like I was closing in on an answer, that I was getting closer to understanding what was going on in my head.

When I got home that day, I decided to do something I hadn't done for a long time. I wanted to meditate. Like exercise, healthy eating, and going to bed early, meditation was one of those activities that I knew had positive effects, but I often put it off in favour of fun things like snacks, video games, and trashy, late-night television. Yet the past had taught me that whenever I did meditate, I always saw a positive result in some form. The most common effect of meditation was a calmer and more relaxed state of mind, but I'd also found it very useful for answering tricky questions or untangling complicated emotions.

I'll remember that afternoon for the rest of my life. I closed the bedroom door, clambered onto my bed, and crossed my legs. I started to listen to my breathing and focused in on the question that was ruling my entire life: 'Should I transition, change my name, change my presentation, and embrace being a woman? Or should I abandon that path, live as I do now, and pretend to be male?' I felt the frantic nipping of other thoughts but tried to let them wash over me, guiding my mind back to the key question.

After a few minutes, I started to visualise the choice before me. Through an imaginary window into my possible future, I saw a reflection form of a much more feminine version of myself. With softer features and wearing a summery dress, she was laughing with friends. This was the person I would aim to be if I pursued transition. She was me, but happier and free, unburdened by the weight of people's expectations and self-inflicted guilty suppression. Next to her I pictured another window, one showing the current masculine version of myself, but without the baggage and stress that I'd been carrying around. This was someone free to focus on life without my eternal doubt and discomfort. I saw two happy people, two people who'd left this lingering question long behind them. In clothes and presentation they were opposites, but still recognisably me. I knew this was the perfect representation of the two paths ahead of me – staying still was no longer an option, I had to become one of these people. I focused on the masculine image that had abandoned transition, seeing myself with painted fingernails but shaggy facial hair. 'This is easier,' I thought to myself clearly. This path was safe, predictable, and familiar. I could shift my presentation to be a little more outgoing without transitioning or doing anything openly extravagant. I didn't even have to take a new name or even tell people anything, I could just exclusively disclose my queer identity to those close to me. My body would continue to grow more masculine, but there'd be predictable safety in what I could rely on. Furthermore, there'd be no risk of abandonment by family and friends. I felt myself settling on this decision, my new choice solidifying as my feminine alternative faded. Then I was struck with maniacal panic. 'But I don't want this.' I knew it was a sensible choice not to transition, I could feel myself accepting it, yet the knowledge filled me with intense horror and dread. My flailing thoughts grasped at the alternative choice: a future of being unashamedly feminine and living openly as a woman. It was risky and rash, but overwhelmingly I wanted it. I wanted to become that person more than I'd ever wanted anything. I opened my eyes, shaken and relieved. I had been asking the wrong question all along. It didn't matter what the 'right' choice was or what I 'should' do. It only mattered what I wanted, and I'd always wanted to transition.

Without even realising it, I'd been secretly seeking the encouragement of everyone I had spoken to. I knew it was nonsensical to throw away my comfortable life and transition, so I had been craving justification to do it anyway. I wanted an irrefutable excuse, something to throw back in the face of common sense, but such a revelatory riposte was impossible to make. Nobody would ever write a decree that told me I was trans enough, that it was time to go seek HRT and change my name, yet that's what I'd been looking for. I'd failed to find my answer by measuring up practicalities because transition is not logical. The choice to go ahead with it can only be made as a deeply personal one, by listening to your gut and ignoring everything else. Transition made no sense, but I was going to do it anyway because it was what I wanted to do.

Chapter 8

COMING OUT

When I was a teenager, all of the transition advice I came across about blending in was instructing me to put as much effort into 'passing' as possible. For those not aware, 'passing' in this context means to be perceived as cisgender despite being trans. The idea behind it is that upon meeting someone, they will subconsciously prescribe a gender for you, which is something you can influence the result of. Stereotypical indicators, such as hairstyle, clothing, height, jewellery, vocal range, and even body language, can all change what gender someone assumes you are. These websites explained that if I couldn't pass and be perceived as a cisgender girl, perhaps because of having too much of a masculine face or frame, then I would be miserable; if I wasn't being seen as a girl, then I would be left as the dreaded 'man in a dress', a humiliating result that carried a high probability of harassment. When I came back around to exploring my gender identity again, I was still carrying that messy mind-set with me. Even now that I had embraced my identity as transgender, I still wanted to be seen by the public as a mundane cisgender woman, for vanity and safety. But it was a desire that was leaving me tense and miserable.

Even before I had started to attend counselling, I'd continued to purchase more feminine clothes in my spare time. Despite not knowing if I was going to transition or not back then, I knew that dressing up in private was still something I was going to do. As such, I had now built up enough outfits to actually have some choice in what to wear. As I'd been slowly inching forwards and making more and more progress, I knew the next step was to start going outside to run errands and visit the shops. It was something that I felt was well beyond my comfort level, but I knew I'd have to grow used to it if I was going to survive my transition. It was impractical to expect that I could just cocoon myself indoors.

One evening, I decided that it was time. I was going to head outside in a dress and full makeup. Loretta and I lived in an area that was just on the outskirts of the city centre. I had a loose idea what times of day were busy and I specifically wanted to head out when it was quiet. I didn't want to wait too late and stroll around a ghost town, but equally I wanted it to be a little later in the day so there wouldn't be too many people around. As we were deep into a brisk winter, advantageously it would be dark and I could take a coat. I decided that if I felt too anxious then I could just zip up the coat, pop up the hood, and totter away into the darkness. As for my outfit, I picked a dark purple dress that was a little on the gothic side, matched with black leggings and a new white coat I had picked up. I also threw on a blue scarf, because back then my sense of style could still be summed up as 'enthusiastic rainbow' and I saw no issue with clashing colours.

There's a joke in the trans community, especially among trans women, that the first few outfits you buy for everyday wear will be hideous crimes against taste. I was certainly not an exception to that rule. At this point, I was stepping into a new comfort level in terms of buying clothes. No longer was I picking a single rare flashy item that had caught my eye, I was building a wardrobe. But I was still going overboard, enjoying the fact that I was now shopping from the opposite end of the shop with playful glee. I grabbed outfits in every style, with no thought to what matched my hair, body type, or even age. Grandma-chic floral? Goth-girl lace? Office-lady pencil skirts? I bought and combined them all. Thanks to second-hand shops and budget end-of-line clearance boutiques, I didn't bankrupt myself with these purchases but I did burn through a lot of outfits that were quickly banished to the back of the wardrobe.

As I stepped out of the door for the very first time and onto the street, I was struck by adrenaline. Here I was, in public, somewhere I had longed to be while dressed like this but had previously dismissed the idea as some impossible fantasy. I was assaulted with frantic thoughts: 'How should I move my arms?' 'How are women supposed to carry themselves?' 'What about my legs?' 'Should I walk normally?' Thankfully, this surge of questions evaporated as I took my first few steps into the cold air. I reminded myself that this wasn't a performance, I wasn't in disguise, and I was just out for a walk. Still, I was nervous about how other people might react. All the news articles I had read of transphobic violence were rattling around in my head. I recalled one recent story of a trans woman who was constantly besieged with harassment every time she shopped for groceries. She had explained that she couldn't even walk to the shops without being openly laughed at. Was that my fate if I continued on this path? Would every trip outside be as stressful as this one?

Walking beside the road I couldn't help but imagine how drivers might perceive me. Were they seeing a woman walking along? Was I 'passing' or were they seeing some guy wearing a dress? More than likely I supposed they were probably busy concentrating on driving in dark, wet conditions and ignoring me entirely.

As I approached the first group of people, a cluster of local students, I tried to ignore my urge to clamber into the nearest hedge. Yet they didn't bat an eyelid at me, continuing to talk amongst themselves as I went by. The next couple of people similarly didn't react at all. I then started to loosen up. This was going pretty well, I thought. By the time I was on my way back towards the flat, having done a circuit of the local area, I had even relaxed. I walked past more and more people and it really started to sink in that all the hyperbole I had internalised about my appearance being scandalous was an anxious exaggeration. In reality, the average person just didn't care. Nobody was treating me any differently and nobody was gawking at me. Everyone was busy just hanging out or doing their own thing. It made me feel free and relaxed in a way I couldn't remember feeling before.

Looking back on that walk, I find it a little amusing that I built it up so much in my mind, but it's something that we often do. Trans people know we're breaking the invisible rules of society and many of us are very nervous to take that first public step. A big reason for that is the worry of who we'll bump into. Stories of transphobic violence are everywhere, it's very frightening to know you're part of a small marginalised group which sees such misdirected and unjustified hate. To reiterate an earlier point, as a white person who's of a slim build and stands on the modest side of tall at 5 feet 9 inches, I'm privileged when it comes to the topic of transphobia, and transmisogyny in particular (the brand of hate specifically targeting trans women). Sadly, the more a trans woman differs from society's hegemonic ideal of the small, submissive, pretty, white woman, the more of a target they become. If you match that description, you have a notably better chance of going under the radar. This is one reason why 'passing' is such a complex idea. Many have no choice but to pursue it for safety, whether because of where they live or the colour of their skin. Our society is painfully racist, sexist, classist, and heteronormative. These issues bleed over into how trans people are treated and it's one reason why transphobia isn't a simple concept to grasp. Regardless of the risk, being transgender can be scary. The fact that there are people out there who would hurt me, just because I'm trans, is something I've had to learn to live with.

I returned from that walk feeling fantastic. It was like I'd just hit a personal milestone and I had proved to myself that I was still making progress with my transition. But when it came time to get changed for bed, it was like being slapped hard enough to lose a tooth. I caught my reflection as I slipped off my dress, and instantly all the joy of the situation was gone, replaced by ice-cold disappointment. It was the first time in a very, very long time that I'd had this feeling to this degree. I knew exactly what it was: textbook gender dysphoria.

I sat down and started to digest it. I'd always felt blessed that my dysphoria was bearable and easy to manage, but this felt utterly horrible. I concluded that it must have been brought on by the whiplash of going back to normal after doing something new that had felt so good. Nail polish, long hair, and even a touch of makeup had all already become ordinary to me, but going outside in a dress wasn't. I'd been wandering the area long enough that it had started to feel normal, it felt right. I was used to strangers thinking of me as a girly-looking guy, but never a girl. Yet minutes earlier I'd been strolling past people who presumably were making the assumption that I was a woman. Even if I wouldn't have gotten through any close inspection, my silhouette had said female. Seeing my brightly lit reflection was like being violently shoved back to reality. It was a reminder that I didn't have the body I wanted. I was a flat and boringly rectangular shape, and owned a tired masculine face. I had inadvertently tricked my mind into expecting something else, something that my subconscious was certain was true. I felt like the mirror had just snorted at my happiness and rudely reminded me, 'No, you're a guy. Look, see? Welcome back to reality!'

As well as controllable, I'd always seen my dysphoria as something slow and creeping. I visualised it as dark cloudy tendrils, dragging me down into misery and disappointment. It always rose slowly and engulfed me gradually, pulling me into depression with painful patience. But this new experience had been something different. Upon seeing my body, it was instantaneous and gut-wrenching. A fast flash of ready-made misery.

My newfound happiness had come with a cost, but I knew it was one I was willing to pay. I didn't want to stop this momentum, even if these moments were going to become more frequent. It was a painful but worthwhile trade-off to have felt so comfortable and free. Over the next few weeks I repeated my initial walk, sometimes in the middle of the day and sometimes in dim frosty evenings. Loretta would often accompany me as we'd get some fresh air and pop to the local shop or the library. My confidence remained shaky. Although I became used to stepping out in my dresses and skirts, I still worried how other people would react when they saw the truth. I avoided people's gaze when I could and stuck to quieter routes through the city, still paranoid that being seen as who I was meant disaster. If we ever took a taxi, I refused to even speak, knowing my voice would invite scrutiny. My long hair helped, but I was depressingly aware that my face still looked masculine. I wasn't going to get the result I wanted.

Once, when in the local library, Loretta wanted to momentarily use one of the computers. It was stiflingly warm inside, which had left me carrying my coat and feeling very exposed in my black dress. When I saw how many people were by the computer banks, I whispered to Loretta that I'd wait nearby and ducked into an aisle of books. Alone between a narrow stack of bookshelves, I pretended to be interested in the selection of geography textbooks, without actually taking anything in. A young woman around my own age turned into the same aisle and suddenly I didn't know what to do. If I followed my instinct and fled from her, I knew I'd draw more attention to myself, but the idea of being so close to someone else in a tight, bright space made me intensely nervous. Would she laugh at me if she saw how I really looked? While fidgeting and deciding what to do, we caught each other's gaze. She said nothing, simply shifting by me and moving on to another set of books. Despite how uneventful the encounter had been, I left that day with a strange mixture of shame and embarrassment that I wasn't sure how to process.

After I'd made a few more trips out, I was growing exhausted. Each venture required hyping myself up in advance and then carefully constructing an outfit just to get out the door. As a release, I started to vent about my feelings in a private diary, which accidentally became less private than I'd intended. Over the last few months, since just before I entered counselling, I'd been writing about my experiences on an anonymous online blog. I'd found it helpful to write up what was going on in my life and share my thoughts and fears about the idea of transition. At first it was an entirely solitary exercise, but by using simple keywords like 'transgender' and 'transition' I eventually drew in a handful of readers who also used the same blogging platform. Although initially alarming, I quickly realised there was a comfort to the company and even started to engage with my readers. One evening I updated my blog with my newest worries and received a comment which had a devastating impact. An elderly trans woman, someone who had transitioned before I was even born, blasted my behaviour as pathetic and disgustingly whiney. This was a surprising blow from someone I had expected to trust. I had spent time bracing myself for toxicity from outside of the trans community but I was unprepared to find it inside too.

That night I entered a slippery spiral as this stranger's rant unlocked the worst of my fears and frustrations. I started to think again about how difficult transition was going to be and couldn't stop myself from dwelling on scaremongering stories and media reports of shocking violence. Was there really a point in this if everybody was going to hate me? Should I bother wearing my favourite outfits if they made me jump at every incoming shadow? Why was I even doing all of this in the first place? I opened up a blank document on my laptop and began furiously typing a new blog post. It began with the words 'I quit.'

I typed for an hour, rambling and raving about how tired and angry I was that our society was so hostile to trans people. I detested that I was expected to accept fear and vulnerability as worthy of trading. That wasn't a deal I wanted any part of anymore. I declared that I was tapping out, refusing to play. I was quitting before I had begun and wasted even more time. I would live knowing that I was really a woman within but exploiting my ability to live a safer and uncomplicated life by never revealing the truth. All the while I'd be internally fuming at the cultural intolerance that had driven me away from my transition, my chance to be myself. I would be dead inside but safe. Finishing the draft entry late at night, I scheduled it to post automatically the following evening, leaving myself enough time to edit it with fresh eyes. I then went to sleep, not even telling Loretta what I'd written.

I awoke alone, with Loretta having already run off to attend an early morning lecture while I slept in. Sleepily, and still grumpy from the night before, I dragged myself out to the high-street to find some breakfast. Unlike recent days, I didn't wear a dress or even my new coat, choosing an old hoodie with ancient worn-out jeans. After picking up a cheap pastry, I drifted to the local square and hoisted myself onto a wall to sit. As I ate, I watched people walking by: men and women, and maybe other genders for all I knew. Everybody looked so mundane, so comfortable. I especially focused on the men, thinking about how I'd written a resignation from my transition and a promise to blend in as one of them. For the rest of my life, people would continue to see me as a man. It wasn't quite funny enough to laugh at but it sure felt like a joke. I wasn't a man. No matter how much I wanted to pretend I was one for an easier life, I knew there was no point. It wouldn't work. I had already spent years trying to settle and had felt wonderfully relieved when I'd made the ultimate call to transition instead. Who was I kidding, trying to quit? I didn't know where transition was going, but choosing to avoid it wasn't going to end in happiness.

In the end, my decision not to transition lasted less than 12 hours. After daydreaming on that wall, I returned to the flat and deleted the blog post I had written. Nobody needed to know that I'd had such a massive blip in confidence. I decided to keep the whole ordeal to myself.

Although a single grumpy comment had brought on my temporary crisis of confidence, that night did teach me a worthwhile lesson. Specifically, I inevitably learnt that not every trans person shares the same politics or the same concept of transition that I did. In hindsight, I know now that it's important as a trans person to develop your own sense of what your transition is and what it means to you. By choosing to transition, you need to be prepared to ignore anybody who says you're doing it wrong, or not going fast or slow enough. Each trans person is an authority on their own gender and transition but not anybody else's. I do feel compelled to say though that coming across that level of rudeness from a trans person has been exceedingly rare for me. The vast majority of trans people I've met have been wonderfully lovely. But it's perhaps not a surprise when you consider the level of intolerance and fear that many of us face – it's bound to give us a healthy dollop of empathy.

I was still in counselling at the time, but at Holly's suggestion I had dialled back the appointments to twice a month rather than every week. As it was a pressing topic on my mind, I would often talk about my fears of going outside. When I pointed out that I never arrived for her appointments in a dress or anything beyond a touch of makeup as I was still too afraid to travel that far away from the safety of the flat, she dismissed my disappointment. In response, she clarified that she remembered me arriving for my first few appointments in baggy jeans and old t-shirts, but now I often added a floral scarf, wore flattering skinny jeans, brightly coloured nails, and plenty of jewellery. It may not have been my ideal outfit, but I had made progress and was visibly more comfortable in my evolving presentation. Cheerfully, I acknowledged that she was right, but I still felt constrained by my bleak expectations of what others might think or do to me.

An opportunity to step out of my comfort zone arrived when, thanks to social media, I heard about a local comic book convention taking place the next month. Being the pair of nerdy people we were, Loretta and I decided we might as well attend it. It would take so little travel time to get there we could even walk to it. Although we suspected it would merely be an entertaining way to kill time on a Saturday, it turned out to be an incredibly significant day with long-lasting consequences.

Personal experience had taught me long ago that if you want to feel safe and experiment with your appearance, any sort of comic book convention is perfect for that. When Sailor Moon, Superman, and a giant bipedal cat are strolling around nearby, you can kind of get away with practically anything as an outfit. Therefore, I knew I should take advantage and really dress up to present myself how I've always wanted to, for the whole day without fear of criticism or harassment.

I pictured myself arriving at the convention in a wild outfit and extravagant makeup. The only problem was that I really couldn't be bothered with any of that. That day I awoke late, feeling groggy and lazy. I wasn't in the mood to inspect my appearance and carefully apply makeup, or put together a loud and audacious outfit like I'd planned. I barely even wanted to go to the convention anymore. So I thought to myself, what would I wear if I could wear anything today and not worry about what people would say? That was easy. I wanted to put on some leggings and a black denim skirt, but then I just wanted to pair them with a big Spider-Man t-shirt and a comfortable open hoodie. So I did.

I was nervous leaving the house that day, but not in the way I usually was. It was the first time in weeks that I wasn't actively trying to look like a cisgender woman. In terms of makeup, all I had bothered with was some mascara, as my eyelashes were a little disappointingly light otherwise. I knew I looked blatantly trans, or at least I looked like I was someone messing with socially acceptable gender presentations. There was very little chance I'd be seen as a woman, I certainly wasn't 'passing' today, but undeniably the skirt and painted nails would stand out as unusual. As I walked towards the convention and was busy chatting with Loretta, all thoughts of what I looked like to others melted away. I wasn't actively hoping people would view me as a woman because I accepted that I couldn't realistically expect that with how I'd chosen to dress. As a result, I didn't care what people did or didn't see me as. I had no expectations. Yet I still felt like myself. I felt like a woman anyway.

As we arrived and began mingling with the crowds, I felt great, precisely because I was dressing for myself, not for other people. Nobody had the power to invalidate how I felt because I wasn't basing my happiness, or the validity of my gender, on what they thought. As the convention environment was safe, my fear of harassment was removed from the equation, freeing me to think about how I wanted to look and who I wanted to be on my own terms. That's when it clicked: I shouldn't care if strangers saw me as trans, a woman, or a man, either now or in the future. Trying to 'pass' had pointlessly complicated my life with little pay-off. By just being myself at the convention and knowing that my female gender was mine alone to define, I was truly and utterly happy.

When we got home that evening, I walked into the bathroom to take off my makeup and undress. I was looking forward to slipping into my pyjamas and settling down, still riding the high of having had such a good day. But when I slipped out of my skirt and saw my body in the mirror, it was like having a bucket of ice emptied over me. My body looked fundamentally wrong, worse than it had ever looked. I felt an overwhelming sense of disappointment and despair, despite knowing that I looked no different than I did every day. It was my dysphoria again, but somehow even more painful than last time. I theorised that since I'd been so comfortable in my skin that day, and for such a long time, my subconscious had been tricked into expecting to see a cis woman's body. Instead, what I saw in the mirror startlingly disconnected me from my blissful fantasy. It seemed that the more I progressed into transition the more I risked these awful bolts of dysphoria. Walking away, I got changed and slumped back onto the bed, thoughtful. I still had a long way to go, but I wasn't going to give up. I reminded myself that the gender euphoria of presenting myself how I wanted to, and of embracing my real gender, was worth every bit of pain so far. Today had been the confirmation I needed to keep going.

As I became more and more comfortable with the idea of being a transgender woman, it became more difficult to keep everything a secret. Logistically, it was effortless. When with Loretta, I was myself. When visiting my parents or friends, I fell back into that old role, with old clothes, pronouns and a forced, easy-going attitude. But secretly I detested having to feign apathy at being that old persona. I abhorred hearing masculine pronouns and had to bite my tongue not to correct everyone. Meanwhile, my old clothes now felt like an awkward costume. Every time I had to go back to pretending, my mood would plummet. The effort I put into covering up the truth withered into weak flimsy gestures as I became so disinterested in keeping this charade going. On a rare visit to my grandmother, she noted my coloured nails and asked if Loretta had painted them. I simply shrugged and said I'd painted them myself as I liked how they looked; likewise, I now wore jewellery for the same reason. In the past, I'd have scrambled for the opportunity to blame someone else. But now I didn't want anyone to think I was being pressured into changing my presentation. This was all me. Admitting that truth among family felt like an angsty act of rebellion against how deeply I was still closeted. I knew soon I'd have to come out to everyone, if for no other reason than to alleviate my own mental health, but the thought still made me abundantly anxious.

The concept of coming out is inherently a clunky one. Unfortunately, many people assume that everybody is heterosexual and cisgender until proven queer. This puts the pressure on said queer person to inform their social circle that they don't actually fit into that box. Some people come up with very detailed plans for how they're going to come out to people, drawing up timelines and carefully firing off coming out messages with timed precision. Being the disorganised person that I was, I started to come out to people simply when it felt convenient to do so and I couldn't bear tiptoeing around it anymore.

The first new person I decided to tell about my gender was my old university lecturer. I planned to visit her office on my way to counselling and explain during a friendly chat. It was an easy decision to make, having remembered that she'd spoken out in support of trans rights before. Of course, that was the same occasion which had awkwardly sent me into a panic attack, but I decided I'd leave that part out. Ultimately, I knew she was a safe person to approach and someone I could trust. Often when queer people are looking at who to come out to, we have a loose idea of who's safe, based on someone's history and politics. If you're not openly queer yourself but you're unknowingly talking to someone who's wondering about their sexuality or gender identity, I can guarantee that every fast and flippant comment you make about queer people will be carefully catalogued and remembered. What can be meant as an innocent joke also acts as an important clue. We then deduce whether you're more likely to lean in with a supportive hug or lunge in to choke us once you learn the secret that we're sitting on. I've also heard of the same frame of mind being used in reverse. If you think a certain friend or family member is queer, dropping a seemingly innocuous comment about supporting whoever the newest celebrity to come out is could give them the green light that you're a safe person to confide in.

The reaction from my former lecturer turned out to be exactly what I'd been hoping for: warm and friendly delight. When I explained that I'd recently realised I was a trans woman, she cheerfully said that if she could do anything to help, she happily would. All I would need to do was e-mail her. I thanked her and then hoped that this might be the start of a positive trend. I had faith that the majority of the people I had to tell would react similarly but I knew it was no guarantee. Awareness of trans issues was still relatively low. It was depressingly possible I was going to lose some friends over this. However, it felt good to have brought one more person into the tiny team who knew the truth, and to have shrunk the circle of remaining people in my life who still didn't know.

Over the following weeks I steadily told other friends and acquaintances, discreetly inviting them to learn my longest held secret, something I never thought I would share with them. Practically nobody cared, which left me ecstatic. My fears of mass desertion were unfounded as most friends congratulated me and accepted my new identity. The worst reaction I got, if you can call it that, was from Ruben. As the years had gone by we'd remained in intermittent contact, checking up on each other two or three times a year. Since last speaking, we'd both successfully graduated from university. Outside of our degrees we were both in ongoing successful relationships and had found new passions and interests independently. We'd each come a long way from the two self-loathing teenagers who ignored their problems by immersing themselves in anime and video games. I explained that a lot of my attitude during and after those school years had been a result of my gender dysphoria, even though I didn't know that at the time. He accepted the explanation, and even shared his own personal revelations of what had caused his own apathy and self-loathing all those years ago. But he didn't quite understand what I was telling him. He'd only ever met one trans person before – a trans man who he had recently started working with. He was still struggling to get his head around the concepts of dysphoria and transition, and especially the fact that I wasn't a man. But even with his hesitation, there was no anger or dismissal, and we promised to talk again soon.

When I saw Ruben next, later meeting him in a small village within travelling distance of us both, he was distant and still visibly uncomfortable with my news. We didn't know it then, but it turned out to be the last time we saw each other. Further attempts to catch up online were stunted and awkward; the relaxed and unbridled conversation we used to share had been lost. Years later, when I told him I'd be near his home and was happy to meet and catch up, he said he'd consider it and let me know the following day. But he never messaged me back. One day we might reconnect, but I've had to accept that among those who refuse to accept my transition, sometimes giving them extra time still isn't enough to bring them around.

Of the positive responses that I got to coming out, my favourite was when someone told me they had already figured it out and were excited I was now being open about it. Apparently, being visibly gender nonconforming and often talking about trans rights had planted the idea that I was probably trans in many people's minds long ago. In a way, I found it strangely affirming that my gender had been obvious enough to pick up on. However, in all the success I still had yet to tell my family – they were the main event that I was building towards and who I dreaded the most.

It felt like an ongoing joke that I would begin each counselling session with 'Well, I've still not told my parents.' This even escalated to the point where after another repeated proclamation that I had still yet to come out, Holly tenderly reminded me that she had no expectations of what I should or shouldn't do between sessions. She then explained that she was growing concerned that I felt I was letting her down and failing to follow her predicted schedule. I laughed and explained that it wasn't her schedule I was worried about but my own. Months had passed since I had admitted to myself I was transgender, but without telling my parents I felt like I was still stealthily tiptoeing around. The prospect of telling them and finally strutting into the spotlight was terrifying. I hoped that my family would be able to accept it with ease, perhaps just chuckling it off and asking if I was doing okay. Although that was how most people had reacted so far, I knew it was delusionary optimism in this case.

My dad came from a family that kept all of its personal thoughts, feelings, and memories buried out of sight. When his own father died, for the first time I learnt about my grandad's history and interests in a five-minute eulogy delivered by a stranger. That tight-lipped nature had passed down to my dad, and although he'd evidently worked on being more open in recent years, serious personal discussions were still an extreme rarity. My mother on the other hand was someone who usually reacted to family news with nothing less than apocalyptic alarm. I knew in time things would probably cool off, but that initial bombshell would surely be so difficult to endure for everybody, I was in no hurry to detonate it.

Countless times I picked a date, planned to come out, but then backed down minutes before I was due to tell them. It never felt like the right time in the moment. There was always some other family news going off or some stressful project that I felt too guilty to interrupt. I came close to just blurting out, 'Look at me! I'm transgender!' more than once, just out of the growing frustration of having to keep hiding it and hearing the wrong pronouns. I'm still surprised Loretta was able to flip-flop between them so easily when in different company, protecting myself and my parents by using what they expected to hear. I was still living two lives, but with almost everyone I was a newly out trans woman beginning her transition and vocally queer. Only when visiting my parents was I pretending to be a son, and covering up all signs of what had been going on.

When I told Holly about my continuing troubles and endless thoughts about my parents, she suggested that perhaps I was hesitating so much because I was seeking a specific response I felt unable to achieve. She was right. I wanted to tell them that I was their daughter and to be met with love and acceptance, maybe even a group hug, but instead I predicted only rejection and confusion. With Holly's help I realised that I had been picturing my coming out as an imbalanced exchange, a game rigged against me and doomed to fail. I'd been playing scenarios where I was practically asking their permission and wincing in preparation for the backlash. But I was an adult, engaging in a sensitive conversation with two other adults. I wasn't responsible for their reaction and I wouldn't be asking for permission either, I'd be informing them of the truth. This stuck with me as a useful perspective and granted me an extra surge of confidence.

Unfortunately, shortly after that conversation I inevitably had to say goodbye to Holly for the final time. She explained that it felt like our sessions had reached their endpoint, something she had indicated was soon coming several weeks earlier. I had admitted to her that in an ideal world I never wanted to stop seeing her, as she had been indescribably helpful. But I understood entirely that we were already overdue to end. I no longer even had a valid student card at the university, having technically graduated months ago and with my account now closed. Yet for that entire time Holly had insisted that I was still welcome to see her and continue to schedule sessions. When I'd aired my apprehension and guilt over taking advantage of a service intended for current students, she had defended her decision. Each time, she said that we were still in the process of working through this issue and demonstrably I needed the help; it would have been unprofessional to allow a logistical detail to justify abandoning me.

In our last session, affectionately but firmly Holly pointed out that I had made a lot of progress over our time together and I should be proud of myself. She felt that it was appropriate to conclude here as I was moving forward into a new chapter with new confidence and growing momentum. My initial worries over who I was and what I should do had been resolved. She had faith that I would be okay. As I got up to leave on that final day, I felt sentimental and unsure of what to say. I'd never step into this room again, this small special space where I had poured out my deepest secrets and grown into someone new. Simply saying goodbye felt like a hollow and weak gesture for someone who had cracked open my insecurities and helped me truly understand myself. Lingering in the doorway, I repeatedly thanked her and pointed out that without her I wouldn't have gotten here, something she gently refuted by downplaying her part. I wanted to say more, to hug her, to gush that talking to her had been truly life-changing, but I didn't trust myself to keep my composure. As she nodded with a warm smile, I was certain I caught the beginning of tears in her eyes as I felt them grow in my own. I knew if I stayed a second longer it'd only be harder to walk away, so with a sense of bittersweet accomplishment I turned and walked down that corridor for the last time.

A handful of weeks after my final counselling session, I thought I had highlighted the perfect time to come out to my parents. My dad had a few days off work coming up, which then ended in a holiday abroad. I decided that if I told them just before those first days off, they would have time to process it, and would then be off for a relaxing holiday once the news had settled. However, the flaw in my plan was the realisation that I was never going to be able to come out to my parents in person. I just couldn't even fathom a scenario where I sat down to tell them and didn't abort in panic and dread. The only way I could ensure I didn't back out would be to write a letter and launch it from a safe distance. The awkward similarity between this method and how I came out as a teenager was something I probably should have paid attention to, as it went about as disastrously as it had the first time.

I kept my coming out letter short and to the point. I placed extra emphasis on the fact that I was still the same person, eager to pre-emptively bat down any accusations that I was melodramatically morphing into a stranger. Calmly, I stuck to the basics: I am transgender; I am going to transition; this is something I have known for a long time; I have made peace with this decision and would like your support; however, without your support I am still going ahead with this as it's something I need to do. As a final note, I explained that I'd be by the phone and ready to talk as soon as they wanted to.

I sent the e-mail. In a rapid painful gesture, it was done. I couldn't take it back. Although I felt awful for coming out in such an impersonal manner, my immediate sense of mild panic and foreboding confirmed that this was probably the best way to do it. After what felt like about three hours, but in reality was about 15 minutes, I got a text message saying that they were in deep shock and, rather than talk to me, they were both going straight to bed. I was disappointed but not surprised. I even started laughing, finding their message absurd and far worse than my low expectations had predicted. Loretta was very upset, having hoped for a warmer reaction, and was left deeply disappointed, but I felt empty and detached. After comfort eating my weight in chocolate ice cream, I went to bed too.

The next day I had a messy conversation with my mother as she explained via text messages that the news had shaken them to their core. They were considering cancelling their upcoming holiday. I was accused of being heartless and cruel for coming out to them when they were soon to be going abroad, as if the news was so horrific they couldn't even function. I didn't know what to say beyond stressing that nothing dramatic had changed and this was, for me, a very positive thing and a step towards happiness. She aggressively disagreed, stating that she couldn't believe that I was acting as if things could ever return to normal after this. As far as she was concerned, I had done something abhorrent and should be ashamed of myself.

Eventually, I decided I needed to turn my phone off and just unwind, I had done nothing but think about them for 24 hours and I wanted to lose myself in some TV. With perfect timing, *Sense8* had just popped onto Netflix, a show that looked ideal to binge-watch. I had been curious about it because I was a fan of the Wachowskis and J. Michael Straczynski, the three creatives behind it. But I was especially interested as it starred a trans woman actor, portraying a trans woman character, from a writing team that involved a trans woman. Specifically, Jamie Clayton was playing a character called Nomi, a queer woman with a rocky relationship with her mother and a heroic character arc that was nothing to do with her gender. It was an example of that representation which had felt so lacking in my teens, a trans character who was treated as a serious and respected member of the cast.

I adored *Sense8*. Sitting with Loretta, I happily watched episode after episode. Nomi's scenes were brilliant, if sometimes a little hard to watch, and I continued to be sucked in by the whole charming cast and sci-fi storyline. That evening, we were moving towards the back half of the series and came across a scene that gave me chills: Nomi, when speaking with another queer character on the show named Lito, was recounting her story of being a young teenager. She talked about the locker rooms and what it was like to be pressured into hanging around with teenage boys in such a masculine environment; that pressure coming from parents who were disappointed in how feminine she was. I'd seen familiar bullying scenes in fiction before, but never one showing what it was like to be a young targeted trans girl. In awe, I watched this scene continue, witnessing my own story reflected back at me for the first time in my life. Nomi had been bullied for precisely the reason I had at that same age. I had never experienced this before, never seen such deeply personal memories and feelings shown as part of a protagonist's story. My secret history was being shown as sympathetic, something that had been survived. At the time, my bullies had been the confident and happy kids, supported by teachers and hailed as popular. I had felt weak and pathetic by comparison, but here those archetypal bullies were villains. In this framing I was the hero, someone to root for and a survivor of an unnecessarily difficult ordeal. The bullying was wrong, needless, and cruel. When Nomi explained the extent of the bullying she had experienced – trauma hauntingly like what I had been through – Lito snapped back with astonished anger. He called them monsters, with tears in his eyes, utterly incredulous that people could be so heartless. It broke me. I exploded in tears.

It wasn't just experiencing my past that had caused my outburst; it was the anger and sympathy that it was designed to induce, the sympathy I had been denied, the anger that nobody had ever summoned for me. I had never felt that my true feelings deserved to be protected, respected, or loved, but watching that scene made me realise how very wrong I'd been. All this time I had just wanted to be myself, to be open about my personality, my emotions, and the way

I wanted to present myself. Yet I had faced an onslaught of rejection and bullying that had convinced me that I was fundamentally wrong. I'd spent my life in shameful guilt, blaming myself for being too emotional, too different, and never enough of anything that mattered. I'd still feared the possibility of being pressured back into denial because I felt unworthy of help, undeserving of the right to be myself. Yet this episode had just explicitly told me that I always deserved to be me, I'd always been enough. It wasn't my fault.

While crying harder than I ever had in my life, the scene continued. Nomi gently explained that what had been done to her was nothing compared to how it felt having to repress herself. The true violence wasn't the physical pain but the torture of hiding who she was. With that powerful line, I was hurled into a hurricane of emotions. The foundational beliefs of my life crumbled as I processed everything that I had just realised. All the self-loathing and guilt that I had built my identity around was finally revealed as poison. Embodying these toxic feelings and suppressing myself in every facet of my life had been agonising. It was an exhausting pain brought on by living against the expectations and standards of other people, needless rules that had never been built to accommodate someone like me: someone who was still valid, someone who should have been accepted all along.

The rejection from my parents finally crashed into me. I felt the longing to be seen and loved for who I was, something I had been denied my entire life. Now that they knew the truth, I wanted them to be happy for me, to ask what it was like growing up with this secret, to ask me if I was okay. I wasn't okay, I was tired of pretending I was. I just wanted to be me. Through sobs I announced that this was the end, declaring that I wouldn't let myself feel guilty for being this way ever again. In a wave of relief, I released the last of my shame, self-loathing, and fear in a declaration of self-love.

That scene remains the most memorable and deeply upsetting piece of television I have seen in my entire life, but it also gave me renewed strength. Whenever anyone says that media representation isn't important, I think about that scene. If I could have watched it as a teenager, it would have been revolutionary – not just because of how it would have made me feel, but knowing that I could present it to other people. I believe that pop culture has the power to open minds and force people to re-examine their own prejudices. The best substitute for learning about trans issues without knowing a transgender person is seeing a well-portrayed one on television. It sounds silly, but when you consider how many people don't make the effort to learn about other groups or hear the stories of people outside of their community, fiction is the only place they're going to come across people unlike themselves.

The fact that Nomi is portrayed by Jamie Clayton is a respectful and powerful gesture. There has been a disturbing trend lately of casting cis men as trans women, which damagingly reinforces the myth that trans women are men. Proponents of this type of casting defend it as more authentic when playing pre-HRT trans women, but this maddeningly ignores the fact that there is a widespread societal problem of trans women being judged, victimised, and outright harassed due to the belief that they are men. By casting trans women as women, it demonstrates the truth of what gender we are and is simply the accurate way to portray the character. Otherwise, trans actors deserve to be cast because they know precisely what it is like to be trans. You know when Jamie Clayton is delivering those lines in *Sense8* that she knows exactly what it's like to feel dysphoric and afraid by growing up trans. It also shows the audience what a trans woman looks like, which is enormously important in the face of such misinformation campaigns in the media. Although they didn't say it, when I came out to my parents, I knew they had no context for trans women beyond damaging stereotypes, and thus that's what they were imagining I would become too. Showing authentic experiences gives context for the families and friends of trans people, as well as giving themselves hope that they too can have fulfilling careers. After coming out, I certainly wished my parents had seen *Sense8* so they could have understood even that small snapshot of what I had been through, and who I was aiming to become.

As the pain faded that night, I went to sleep with a sense of calm acceptance. I now had a resolute certainty that I would never feel ashamed of being myself ever again. Transitioning was going to be difficult, but it was my right to do it. I deserved it. All I had to do was power ahead.

Chapter 9

GROWING PAINS

A week after I had come out, I still hadn't seen my parents. There was no contact taking place as we hadn't phoned each other or sent any new messages. However, they were soon to be going on the aforementioned holiday, and I presumed they still wanted me and Loretta to house-sit. The day before they were due to leave, I got in touch via a text message and asked my dad what time we should come by the house, unsure if he was even going to respond. He replied by offering to pick us up directly from the flat within an hour. I suggested that we could stop for something to eat on the way. He agreed. I wasn't hungry, but I wanted to stall in a neutral place and get a feel for where we stood. At the very least, I figured I hadn't been completely disowned, because we were talking again. That was something.

Refreshingly, I realised that I didn't have to deliberately dress down to meet my parents' mundane expectations of me, but I didn't want to flaunt the truth in their faces either. That day I wore skinny jeans, a fitted t-shirt and ankle boots, with light makeup and pink-painted fingernails. I completed my outfit with an unnecessary number of rings and a silver necklace in the shape of a large heart. It was important to me that I looked different from the lazy masculine uniform I usually maintained in their presence, but I wasn't quite comfortable enough to wear a dress or a skirt. Although it wouldn't have been intended as one, I suspected an overtly feminine outfit would have been read as an aggressive gesture, considering how they'd taken things so far.

My dad arrived on time and I got into the car ready to talk properly for the first time about being transgender. If he thought anything about my appearance, he didn't say it. Ridiculously, neither of us alluded to my recent coming out in any way. As the car pulled away and we set off, I froze. Instead of bringing up the topic that was undoubtedly on both our minds, I sat and made small talk about recent TV shows I'd seen, and how cold the weather looked for the next week. I simply couldn't think of how to bring it up without sounding absurd. Days ago, he had indicated he was going to cancel his entire holiday because of what I had revealed; now we were sat side by side as if nothing had been said. Evidently, he wanted to have this conversation as much as I did.

After driving to the nearest fast-food restaurant, we sat down across from each other and the awkward, inevitable conversation began. It was my dad who finally said something, by breaking into an unsurprising confession of how much he'd hated hearing that I was transgender. But he had accepted it as the truth. He knew he couldn't change my mind. I took that as a vast improvement after my low expectations. I then apologised for coming out via a letter, in an attempt to concede something and compromise. I elaborated that even if it had been clumsy, I had done so as I was worried about how bad the reaction might be. Solemnly, my dad answered that it was one of the worst days of his life. He seemed to gain a small level of self-awareness when I pointed out that it was a thunderously dramatic thing to say compared to what the news was and how others had reacted. I was transitioning, not dying. He defended his response by reminding me that he had come from a very traditional family; furthermore, he was now having to accept that he would never have the macho 'man's man' son that he'd always wanted. I boisterously laughed and pointed out that long ago he should have figured out that I was not exactly a very masculine person and was never going to grow into that role. Thankfully, he saw the humour in this too and laughed, reluctantly agreeing.

The conversation became a relaxed but uncomfortable game of give-and-take. Neither of us was pleased with what the other one was saying, but we both tried to listen and give each other ground in the name of reconciliation. Unfortunately, I continued to get the vibe that my dad believed I was choosing to be trans. In his mind, it was as if I was actually cisgender but had been lured in by pretty dresses and makeup. I explained that this had been on my mind for over a decade, that it had been a cause of anxiety and depression for as long as I could remember. Apprehensively, he admitted that he'd learnt recently that I'd come out as trans to my mother as a teenager, which seemed to have been a factor in him realising how serious this was. On the topic of my mother, he then asked me not to talk to her until after the holiday. I found this request odd but I wasn't in any rush to speak to her either so I agreed. After almost an hour of talking, we reached a natural end and both decided to head home.

Once we got back to the house, it turned out that I didn't even need to try keeping my word about speaking to my mother as she had become a ghost. I heard murmurs and saw signs of her presence but I never physically saw any hard evidence that she was staying in the house with us. The next morning, I awoke and both parents had already left. The house was now free for me to lounge around in, wearing whatever I pleased.

It was profoundly liberating to spend a week openly dressing in feminine clothes in the house I had spent my teenage years in. No longer was I bolting the door in paranoia or carefully listening out for returning cars. I simply enjoyed a relaxing week working from my laptop and spending time with Loretta. Once the week was over and my parents returned, I promptly left for the flat, and the frosty silence between us resumed.

Although there was still no real resolution with my parents, I did find a reprieve from the situation in a short mini-holiday away. Only weeks before it began, Loretta and I decided that we were going to attend 'Nine Worlds' for the first time. A convention in London described as being an inclusive, long weekend for all geeky interests, it sounded like the perfect little escape from the recent stress and drama. Incidentally, I also knew it would provide an opportunity to meet new people and introduce myself with my new name, one I had just recently settled on.

I had never liked my birth name. It's not difficult to unearth what my old name was as I've not been overly concerned with burying it. But I'm not going to mention it here – it's entirely irrelevant. Trans people will often refer to their old name as their 'dead name', to underline how completely inert and abandoned that name has become. Although some trans people will freely elaborate on what their old name was, many of us greatly dislike hearing it. It's incredibly rude to ask a trans person about what they used to be called, or to tell anybody else about it if you already know. Our old names are more than simply what we used to go by. They can often become representative of our years of pain and denial, or all the time spent trying to fit somebody else's idea of us. Otherwise, they can be a reminder of the people in our lives who may disrespectfully insist on still using that name.

Hurling our old name back at us is a common abusive tactic of transphobes, who'll often insist that whatever name you're given at birth is your 'real name', although it's revealing I've never seen those people argue that cis people like Elton John and Michael Caine must be credited as Reginald Dwight and Maurice Micklewhite. It's simply another lazy and hollow attempt to dehumanise trans people and hurt us. Thankfully, having my old name used as a weapon against me isn't something I worry about much. Many of my friends are well aware of it and that doesn't really distress me. But I can't deny that if I had the choice I'd prefer that people don't know it, and instead only ever know me as the name that I settled upon.

I look at my current name with a sense of personal accomplishment and pride. It's a reminder that I changed it to begin living for myself, but it certainly wasn't easy picking it. As someone who's extraordinarily indecisive at the best of times, I expected to be flip-flopping for months. I couldn't even name my fictional World of Warcraft characters without agonising deliberations, so how was I going to name myself? When I spoke to my trans friends, they shared stories of choosing names from inspiring historical figures or their favourite literary characters. Other people took a name from their family or even adopted the one their parents had almost called them. Meanwhile, I found myself scouring databases of names, breezing through endless options and jotting down any that gave me a little spark of inspiration. I ended up with a huge sprawling list, vowing to narrow it down until one remained. Oddly, in all of this I never considered Rebecca. The name I had taken on as a teen didn't feel right anymore. It felt like somebody else's name, even though I had once excitedly, if secretly, taken it for myself. I pegged it as being down to how much my personality had shifted over the years. I was bound to have different tastes than I'd had in my teens, right? But I suspect in hindsight that my apathy about the name Rebecca was partially fuelled by how I had yet to properly unpack those memories. I still hadn't reconciled my hazy acknowledgement of those years with the reality that I had suffered through a very difficult and depressing time. There were also the painful implications of how close I had come to transition. Those revelations were brewing, but it would be another year before those walls came down with emotionally explosive clarity.

Early on in my cataloguing of names, Mia, Amelia, and Violet were three that I had homed in on almost immediately. I just couldn't let them go – they were the bar I measured all other possibilities against. I felt especially torn between Mia and Amelia, figuring I had to pick just one, while Violet made a nice accompanying name. In the end, I decided to be greedy and take them all. I planned on having Mia as a nickname, while Amelia Violet would be my formal full name. At this point you've probably figured out what happened, due to the name on the book cover. Amelia only lasted a few months. When I arrived at Nine Worlds, I was invited to write down my name on my convention badge. Right away I knew Mia was the right name, not Amelia, it was simply what I wanted to be called. From that moment onwards, I knew my real name was Mia Violet.

On the first day of Nine Worlds, I was nervous. Away from my familiar town I was now down in London, somewhere I had never presented openly in feminine clothes. I had brought a huge selection of outfits with me, lugged down the country in two giant suitcases. Looking at my luggage, you'd think I'd left home and was permanently moving into the hotel. I brought so many clothes because I knew I'd never be able to choose, but nervous doubt pushed me to play it safe too. I had outfits for the full spectrum of my confidence, from bold dresses to androgynous t-shirts. For that first day, I settled on a pair of skinny jeans and a brightly coloured t-shirt. I wore minimal makeup – just some foundation to even out my skin and some mascara to give my eyes an extra pop. Truthfully, it wasn't the outfit I wanted to wear, it was a compromise. Although the convention took place in a hotel, it wasn't the same hotel we were staying in. Having booked last minute, we could only get a room up the road. This meant we had a 15-minute walk every morning just to get to the convention hotel. The idea of walking the entire way in the morning sun, being so blatantly and visibly trans in a place I had never been before, was just too far outside of my comfort level. I was disappointed in myself, worried that I was going backwards, but I also reminded myself that there was still time to try again tomorrow.

Nine Worlds is a convention that prides itself on its inclusivity, and from the moment I walked in it really showed. In a sign of thoughtful trans inclusion, pronoun badges were offered for free, a small white circle taken up with a giant single pronoun. I happily scooped up a 'She' badge and felt for the first time that I was in a truly safe environment. I'd never been anywhere that had made special considerations to make trans people feel welcome, rather than either ignoring our existence altogether or expecting us to fend for ourselves. Across the day I attended discussion panels on comic books, TV and video games, all the while chatting freely to other attendees. Nobody blinked when I introduced myself as Mia, or when I casually mentioned that I was transgender. Here it was unremarkable and accepted.

As the second day started, I was now rethinking my outfit choice. I was tempted to wear a dress and go overtly feminine. When I had worn dresses in the past, I had always brought a coat with me. Having a long baggy jacket around my shoulders helped me feel a little more protected – something to zip up and hide in if I became too self-conscious – except that plan wasn't going to work this time. The hotel may have been cool and air-conditioned, but outside it was scorching hot. We were in the middle of a classic British heatwave, the kind where paddling pools are brought into back gardens and family barbecues are hastily arranged. There was no way I was going to walk across London for a quarter of an hour in a heavy coat, not unless I was prepared to arrive delirious with heatstroke. So I was left with two choices: play it safe yet again with a t-shirt, or wear what I really wanted and embrace the exposure. I picked the dress.

I could pretend my outfit choice was driven by courage but in reality it was the knowledge that I would regret this opportunity otherwise. I guilt-tripped myself into wearing it, figuring that if I had come all this way I might as well go all in. Making up for my lost youth of longing to be a melodramatic goth girl, I reached for the dusty purple lipstick, eyeliner, silvery jewellery, and black lace dress. Coupled with my purple-sheened black hair, recently dyed for the trip, I looked comfortably like an extended member of the Addams Family.

Stepping into the hotel lift, I felt a bubble of nerves as a family squeezed inside with us. They looked stereotypically ordinary – the type of respectable-looking people who could either turn out to be lovely or who would utter hushed homophobic remarks. While the father gave me a cursory glance, he went back to talking to his two kids about breakfast. Waiting for the doors to open, I gaped at a woman's reflection in the vividly lit mirrored walls. She amazed me. Looking incredibly comfortable, there was an otherworldly level of confidence about her, like she was born to wear her witchy outfit and command the attention of everybody around her. I grinned when I reminded myself that she was me. When the doors slid aside, my nervous energy had evaporated. I strutted across the hotel lobby with a soaring sense of invulnerability. As I walked out into the summer sun, I finally felt like myself, in a profoundly fulfilling way. My new presentation had quieted my dysphoria and replaced it with euphoric confidence.

The following two days were another significant step for my transition. The last of my reluctance fell away as I embraced the freedom of walking around in precisely what I wanted to wear. Visiting the surrounding shops, pub, and restaurants with other Nine Worlds patrons without feeling on edge was extraordinary. I knew that I stood out but I didn't feel like that was a negative thing. Why should I care what people were thinking when I felt this good? Better still, my new confidence helped me forge new friendships with other queer attendees. I spent my evenings in hotel rooms playing party games until the early hours of the morning and excitedly sharing stories. Significantly, it felt like a preview of what my life could be if my transition went well: blissful, social, and proud.

Across the long weekend, I was reminded of attending the comic book convention several months prior, where I had wandered around visibly not conforming to gendered expectations. But this time was very different. Here I was able to forget that being transgender was taboo, and I never felt out of place or any more notable than everybody else. The Nine Worlds organisers knew that it wasn't enough to just verbally provide a safe place for transgender people, they had to do more with practical solutions. Steps were taken to ensure we were as protected and comfortable as the cisgender attendees. For instance, on top of a strict anti-harassment policy, the convention had dedicated gender neutral toilets for those who felt uncomfortable or unwelcome in an exclusively male or female space. A common excuse against the development of gender neutral toilets is the practical feasibility of building them in existing spaces. Yet at Nine Worlds they simply used the toilets that were already there, specifying that both were gender neutral but one had urinals, and one had a sanitary towel bin. Whichever one you wanted to use was left up to you. It was surreal to realise that I was able to walk into a toilet, touch up my makeup, and walk out without any sense of urgency or underlying nervousness that I was about to be called a fraud or a danger to someone.

The topic of transgender people and public toilets is one drenched in hyperbole and behaviour reminiscent of a stereotypical moral panic. It goes without saying but trans people are not a threat to anybody in toilets. A laughably obvious counter to this argument, which often flies over the heads of those ready to stand on toilet duty, is that Caitlyn Jenner did not usher in our arrival – trans people have been here all along. You have very likely shared a public toilet with a trans person before in your life without noticing. It's not as if we only recently developed the need to pee. There is no logic or reality to the idea that trans people are a danger to anyone, and history backs that up entirely.

The softer argument against us using public facilities agrees that trans people are not predators but positions our rights as a zero-sum game. It's claimed that by accommodating us, nefarious creeps could slip into female toilets, pretending to be transgender women. The most obvious reason that this excuse is baseless is that nobody with evil intentions is currently holding themselves back because they're struggling for a sufficient scapegoat. Monsters barging into private places don't plan their outfit around an excuse for when they're later caught.

The fundamental problem with all of these arguments is that even if they did have validity, their supporters are asking trans people to accept that our lives are simply worth less than those of cis people; that our own genuine endangerment and discomfort, by being pushed into the wrong facilities, is a worthy cost to pay to uphold a status quo of ignorance. We're being told to lie down and accept that we're not welcome to partake in everyday life. This is the root of so much transphobia in our society, the fact that many people do not like the fact that trans people exist and would rather we just didn't. To them we're not really people who deserve the same rights and considerations as them, so hurting us or risking our safety is theoretically fine. To many that's an easier mind-set to adopt than to extend compassion and empathy and to realise we're people too. It sounds like a stunningly obvious statement to make – that trans people are people – but the horror stories heard internationally and domestically support the depressing truth that we're not considered people by everybody.

I'm not particularly interested in unearthing precisely why so many people are transphobic – I think energy is better spent elsewhere – but there are a few potential explanations. One I find most plausible is that we force people to confront the idea that gender is flexible, something that many find scary and uncomfortable. Our society rigidly depends on a gender binary in virtually all aspects of life. On the surface it affects what clothes we're expected to wear, how we're supposed to style our hair, how we should smell, and even what colour razor or toothbrush we should buy. But expectations also go much deeper than that. How we react to certain situations, what role we occupy in a family unit, and what career is suitable for us are all things that carry assumptions according to what gender we are. When trans people transition, we move between these roles, revealing how fragile the gender binary really is.

Things become increasingly disturbing for transphobes when sexuality is considered. Although my transition has nothing to do with my sexuality, it has allowed me to understand my own preferences with clarity. Prior to transition, I considered myself exclusively attracted to women, but now I identify as bisexual. It's a term I use to mean attraction to two or more genders, rather than just to men and women. I began using it when I realised I was attracted to people regardless of gender. My theory as to why I was never able to face up to this in the past is that I was always reluctantly viewing myself as male. The idea of being in a relationship with a man was awkward and off-putting – due to the way I identified then, I imagined it as a relationship between two men, with no women involved. Essentially, the idea made me dysphoric. Yet now I know that I am a woman, I'm comfortable with who I am, and as a result a relationship with a man, or non-binary person, sounds peachy.

I'm a believer that genitals really only concern how you and your partner are going to have sex, and they don't factor into attraction whatsoever. I consider attraction based on gender presentation much more believable. The gendered cues that someone uses in their outfit and their overall aesthetic are natural things to be attracted to, based on your pre-existing preferences. But surely, when you see someone you're attracted to, it's not the idea of what's in their underwear that summons that feeling of attraction and affinity. With trans people, not all of us can access or want genital surgery. This means that trans people do not fit into the rigid worldview of anyone who has inflexible ideas of heteronormative sexuality and still anxiously considers reproductive organs as the ultimate gender markers. Of course, we do not fit because such a view is inherently built on transphobia and warped homophobia. As much as we've moulded our society to think that we have just two opposing genders, each with its own identifying genitalia, it's simply not a reflection of reality.

The ideological clashes that we're seeing centred on trans people and their relation to toilets, clothes, and relationships are representative of the growing pains our society is going through with trans acceptance. We have a mainstream culture that was built without any thought or care about trans people whatsoever. As such, some are now working to make changes to accommodate trans people, while others actively want to live in ignorance. This is a mind-set we see being adopted on a political stage where trans people are left hurting because somebody with the power to help would rather look away and hope we just disappear back into obscurity. Meanwhile, the same type of thinking happens in families and social circles, where instead of embracing the truth they go into their own version of denial. Unfortunately, I encountered a similar perspective from my parents when I returned home from Nine Worlds, as they were still struggling to accept the result of what I'd told them.

I was dreading the inevitable follow-up conversation with my parents but I knew I couldn't avoid talking to them forever. My weekend in London had been a tantalising hint at what my future held. I wanted to fast-forward to that time where I could openly use my new name and identity without the drama or questions that I faced back home. But to get there I still needed to work out a lot of logistics and face the fact that my parents still wanted more answers. With their holiday behind them and the news now fully settled, they wanted to sit down and to talk together to fully hash out and explore what I meant when I'd said I was trans. Loretta insisted that if any conversation was going to take place, she was going to be there to back me up. I really appreciated that offer, as I certainly wasn't looking forward to facing this alone. One afternoon, shortly after we returned from Nine Worlds, we all gathered in the living room of my parents' home to have the longest talk we'd ever had.

To call what happened that day a 'conversation' would be generous – it was more of a cross-examination. My parents played at being prosecutors, with probing questions and accusations, while Loretta served as my protective lawyer, jumping in with objections and ensuring I didn't have to handle my defence alone. One of the first topics to come up was Loretta herself. With a scrunched, confused face, my dad slowly explained that he didn't understand how Loretta could be fine with the idea of me transitioning. As she'd had no idea about this secret when we became a couple, why wasn't she now fleeing from the relationship? 'I'm bi,' Loretta responded, as if it was the most obvious answer on the planet. She casually went on to explain that she loved me for who I was, not because of the way I presented in public or the name that I used, and especially not for what was in my pants. That promptly shut down that line of questioning.

The next thing my parents wanted to know was why there weren't more signs. If I really was trans, then there should be a pile of clues left behind me, yet they hadn't detected anything. If you've gotten this far in the book, you can probably imagine what my amused response to this was. I reeled off all the things I had been hiding for years, putting extra emphasis on how I'd been buying dresses and makeup since I had my own money. I also explained how I'd felt out of place and lost since I was a child, that this idea was always rattling around but shame had caused me to cover it up. The fact that all this felt like new information to them was a testament to how well I'd worked to hide everything.

The elephant in the room, which I decided to casually throw a spotlight on, is that I told my mother I was transgender as a teenager. She couldn't innocently claim this came out of nowhere when I had blatantly revealed it to her earlier in my life. I asked her if she remembered, and as expected she'd never forgotten the day I had written that letter. Her explanation for why she had never brought it up since was that she thought it was a 'sick joke' that I had played on her. Apparently, she had assumed I'd come out to her at 14 as a hilarious prank in a bizarrely cruel and out-of-character attempt to distress her. I found this reasoning obscenely odd, but decided not to press how she could possibly have come to that conclusion. Rather than sit there discussing mistakes, I reminded myself that this chat was about the future and an attempt to drag my parents aboard the transition train; because, like it or not, we were setting off imminently.

If one thing especially distressed my parents, it was the rapidity of my timescale. I carefully reminded them that by coming out to them I had been giving them notice that I was going to transition now – my period of hiding was finished. Their reaction to learning that there would be no cooling-off period was as if they'd just learnt I was joining a cannibalistic cult. They wanted me to slam the brakes on and slowly rethink the entire thing. This is a request that I've noticed often pops up from people who are new to transition. I can understand the altruistic origin of asking someone to slow down, even if it's also laced with a hope that everything will be called off, because it is a big change to make. But transition is nobody's first idea, or second, or third; it's usually the last resort. Until a trans person comes out, we're assumed to be cis, and that means we grow up in the same society as everyone else and absorb the same cisnormative messages. We know full well that trans people are stigmatised and that transition can bring social exclusion. More than that, we know we're joining a community whose members are disproportionately harassed, rejected, and murdered. We do it anyway because we have no choice. When every other option has been exhausted and we still don't feel right, that's when we give in and transition. One thing I often find myself saying, like in the Introduction of this book, is that only trans people genuinely consider transition, because we're the only ones who still think it sounds exciting and enticing despite all the side-effects. Warning someone who's decided to transition that they should think it through is like asking someone if they're sure they want to be released from prison.

If a trans person is coming out to you, chances are they've already spent countless hours stewing about whether to go through with it and if they can avoid having this conversation with you. They'll have imagined this moment and fantasised about how you might react. It's very unlikely you're being told this in a flippant or thoughtless manner; it's the result of seriously weighing up all the possible ramifications. What this means is that person is probably eager to get started. With my parents, I was no different. I stressed that I had already tried to talk myself out of this for years, yet I'd come right back to the same solution. I had finally stopped lying to myself and admitted that I wasn't happy, that I needed to do this. If I could never talk myself out of this, there was no chance anybody else would be able to.

It dawned on my parents that a horrifying implication of my plan to transition so soon was that my extended family would soon know. Not being particularly close to them, I didn't see this as any sort of concern. But to my parents this was a deeply frightening threat. Admittedly, I did understand that some were likely to react with confusion or disappointment, due to their own heteronormative bubbles, but inconveniencing family was better than lying to them until they inevitably died in ignorance. According to my mother, I wouldn't have to wait for that eventuality very long, as she believed the news would be so shocking that my remaining living grandparents could drop dead with disbelief. I can fairly confidently say that this was ignorant melodrama – no trans person has ever murdered someone by simply being too outrageous for the human mind to comprehend. Some of us may rock an otherworldly level of fabulousness, but certainly not to a lethal degree. Still, it's a line I hear a lot from panicking parents when first confronted with the thought of their child coming out. Ironically, I've seen grandparents often be the most understanding family members, possibly from accumulating enough wisdom in their time on Earth to know that being happy is more important than adhering to expectations.

I don't think I have to point it out, but it's a fairly horrible thing to do to tell any person that they have to hide themselves to preserve the ignorant bliss of their family. Even if we trans people were mind-shatteringly scandalous, it would hardly be fair to tell us to maintain a forced facade just in case we accidentally hurt someone by existing. It reminded me of something Holly had said to me when trying to guide me into understanding my issues with validation and permission. When explaining my anxiety about revealing myself to my parents, she asked me to imagine a world where people were only ever responsible for their own wellbeing. In this fantasy land, everyone had an understanding that everybody else was to protect their own mental health regardless of consequences, guilt-free. The contrast between what I knew I would do in that place and what I was actually doing in reality illuminated how I'd been trying to protect people from myself. Of course, it's true that we do indeed have to be responsible for our own mental health. It's simply unhealthy and unsustainable to expect that we can ignore our own needs forever. For trans people it can be hard to admit, but how other people react to us coming out is not our responsibility. We deserve to be us and to stop pretending, even if we shatter some formerly comfortable perceptions of ourselves when we do.

The conversation with my parents stumbled onwards for hours in an exhausting spiral. I continued to try to justify and convince them of the legitimacy of my emotions, while they offered doubts and questions. Finally, in frustration I pointed out that I had done a lot to cushion their comfort level and was feeling like my wellbeing had been entirely ignored. I had previously delayed coming out, specifically in order to find a time where it would impact them the least, while also going out of my way to make it as painless as possible for them. When I underlined the fact that I had worn no dresses, skirts, or makeup when returning to visit them, and that wearing my old drab masculine clothing was enormously uncomfortable for me, I had expected my parents to say that they were sorry I had felt pressured to dress like this. Instead, my dad nodded and thanked me for protecting them both from seeing me with an overtly feminine presentation. I almost asked him to repeat himself because I was so flabbergasted by that response. More than anything else, that one gesture drove home the reality of the situation: my parents saw my transition as an ugly imposition; the fact that it was the path to my happiness was entirely irrelevant.

As if the conversation couldn't get any worse, it ended with a firm instruction to move out. Days earlier, Loretta and I had lost the flat as our tenancy had come to an end. My parents had previously assured us that we had their home to fall back on in emergencies and could stay while we saved up to move out. But now we were being told to leave. Surprised, I asked if we were really being kicked out over me being trans. My dad was quick to assure me that there was a difference between being kicked out and being told to leave. Upsettingly, I didn't see much of a difference. It felt like my parents were protecting their self-image through semantics. Regardless of the language, the intent was clear. Loretta and I now had nowhere to go just at the time when we needed support the most.

Over the previous year, as I had been exploring and learning more about my own identity, I had built up a new bubble of Twitter friends via a new account. I was writing under the handle I still use today: @OhMiaGod. I had been chronicling my transition for the entire time – everything from counselling visits to my rambling thoughts about coming out were popped online, 140 characters at a time. With an open (some might say over-sharing) attitude, I had picked up a set of friends who were used to me spilling details about whatever had just happened. So, of course, after the uncomfortably disastrous conversation with my parents, I anxiously aired how upset I was and elaborated on the trouble that Loretta and I had just been dropped into. Almost immediately, two queer friends we had made at Nine Worlds – a fellow trans woman named Laura and her partner Tilley – reached out to suggest that this could be an opportunity.

I had met Laura before Nine Worlds – actually around 18 months earlier – but we hadn't spoken much. While I was starting my postgraduate degree, she was invited to give a talk to second-year undergraduates about video games. I wouldn't have known about the talk had I not bumped into my old course tutor, the very same one who I would eventually come out to as trans. We got to talking about guest speakers for that particular module and the diversity of this year's line-up, compared to the problems with repetition and drop-outs when I had been taking that module myself in earlier years. Happily, she invited me to attend the talks if I wanted to, explaining that they were open to all postgraduate students (although hardly any of us ever found the time to head on over). As I was interested in the topic of this particular talk and wanted to support my former tutor's offer, I agreed to go. When the day came, I got talking with Laura afterwards and headed out to lunch with her and my former tutor. I vividly recall one particular moment that afternoon when a playful jest was made about the stereotypical behaviour of men around us, with a jokey apology extended to me. At that moment I debated blurting out, 'It's okay, I don't mind.

I don't identify as a man anyway.' However, as I had yet to come out to anybody beyond Loretta, and still wasn't even sure what the hell the deal was with my gender back then, I let the moment pass. Jumping forward to Nine Worlds, I coincidentally was stood next to Laura in the queue to collect our name badges. Figuring she might also enjoy the funny coincidence, I reintroduced myself and explained we had met back at my old university. As we chatted, I casually mentioned I now went by Mia, and was in the process of coming out to everybody as trans. Across the rest of the convention we hung out together a few times and left as friends.

As Laura and Tilley wanted to move out of their tiny flat, they suggested that we could help each other out by pooling resources and renting a house together. This was an incredibly enticing opportunity. We needed a place to go to as soon as possible, as the atmosphere in the family home had become suffocatingly tense. We had no idea how long we could sit around before we'd be nudged out the door. Beyond the need to get out quickly, it was significant that this opportunity could lead to living with queer women too. I couldn't possibly ask for more understanding housemates.

What made the whole idea of living with Laura and Tilley irresistible was that they lived down on the south coast of the country. Although I grew up in the rainy North, surrounded by small towns, former industrial cities, and endless fields on all sides, I adored the sea. Thinking about the possibility of taking regular walks to the beach, and being a little closer to the equator, was enough to make me giddy with excitement. Incredibly, they even lived in the exact same town that Loretta and I had talked about wanting to move to two years ago. That serendipitous detail further fuelled our belief that this was something that was meant to happen. In the space of just a few hours, I had gone from being anxiously distraught about the future to excited that we were on the verge of exactly the type of break we needed. One way or another, this was going to be a new beginning.

The following weeks were tense, to put it lightly. While we tried to gather up as much money as we could, Laura and Tilley were down at the bottom of the country visiting prospective homes and feeding the information back to us. As the days ticked by, my mood continued to plummet. I didn't like being stuck back in that house, but I also knew that having a relatively safe and warm home wasn't something I had any right to complain about, even if my parents were soon to yank the rug away. Many trans people are disowned by family and friends immediately. I had at least been granted some time to find a new home. If I didn't rock the boat, then it could give me the security I needed until we found somewhere on the coast. But I couldn't shake off the knowledge that I was still deeply unhappy with the situation. I wanted to begin my transition at full speed, but until I could get out of my hometown again, I knew it wasn't going to happen without constant pressure and judgement.

One morning I made a conscious choice to stop suppressing my presentation and picked a black dress to wear, forgoing the hoodies and jeans that I'd fallen back on. But when I passed through the living room at lunch time, my mother pulled me aside and in hushed tones demanded that I warn her in future. She stated that she needed to know when I'd be wearing clothes like this, in case a neighbour or relative was planning a visit. If they ever spotted me, she'd be forced to address why I looked this way. At first, I found the whole exchange amusing in its melodrama. I pointed out that she should feel free to tell them the truth if anybody did see me. But quickly I began to get agitated. Already in a sensitive state, I felt that I was being told that my comfort was irrelevant to her compared to maintaining feigned familial normalcy. I tried to defend myself and stress how important this was for me, but I didn't have the energy to continue, so I simply went back to working in my old bedroom, defeated and exhausted.

In a way, this whole situation was embarrassing. I was getting older and had found who I was, yet I had gone backwards. I was now in my parents' house and suppressing how I wanted to dress again, to keep them from getting too upset. I considered using every bit of money I had to move out that instant, to take everything I had made from my freelance web development and spend it securing any alternative, but the allure of being able to move to an entirely new part of the country kept me still. If I could just hold on a bit longer, that money would be vital in helping me settle on the coast.

Although it was a very long time before we sat down as a family again, later that month I did go to my mother and tried to talk to her one last time. She was still fixating on the sudden nature of my coming out, claiming that she was reeling from the revelation and couldn't move beyond the shock. I pointed out that she had recently admitted that she did remember me coming out to her as a teenager, so this wasn't entirely uncharacteristic. With that topic raised, I continued and admitted that I was upset by the fact she was acting the same way as she had over ten years ago. She was making it about herself and telling me I couldn't be trans, denying what I knew about myself. I told her that I'd been disappointed, that I had come to her for help as a teenager and it hurt that she had tried to reject my confession. In response, my mother defended her reaction as normal. I explained how I had wanted her to be my mother and look out for me; surely she could understand why that memory was still so touchy. In response, she scoffed and said that I couldn't shift the responsibility to her. It had been my fault that I was so helpless as a teen and my fault that I had gone back into the closet; at 14 I should have had the maturity and drive to stick by my conviction. I didn't have any retort or comeback to this. I walked quietly back into my childhood bedroom, closed the door, and started to cry. She was right. If I had persevered as a teen, I would have never strayed from this path. Although my mother didn't know it, I'd been struggling with that regret all year.

I've written about how dysphoria is a slippery and personal beast to wrestle with. After speaking with countless trans people, there is one thing almost all of us have thought at one point or another: 'I wish I had transitioned earlier.' At this point, I felt that more strongly than I ever had. Browsing online transgender communities I found that things had thankfully moved on somewhat from where they had been in my teens. Despite this, I still saw plenty of people warning that younger was better and anything beyond 25 meant you should considerably lower your expectations. I was now 26, just on the wrong side of the cut-off. But unlike my teenage self, it wasn't so much the diminished effects of HRT that concerned me, but the lost time. Being in my mid-20s I had forever lost the chance to enjoy a young adulthood without the spectre of dysphoria dulling every experience. I thought about how university might had gone if I had been allowed to arrive as a young woman instead of someone who had routinely wrestled with a sense of wasting the best years of my life.

I had lost much of my youth in a dead-end relationship, using it to fill me with a sense of worth. Had I not gone back into the closet, perhaps those years would have been spent building happy memories and enjoying myself with much healthier pursuits. Speaking to other trans friends, I found that they all more or less felt the same way. Even those who had transitioned as young as 19 carried regrets for not beginning before puberty.

It's heart-breaking, but time is a strange concept to many trans people like myself. It's easy to feel like we've been cheated, with fate requiring many of us to spend years transitioning in order to find comfort. We can never get those earlier years back. Some of us try to make up for lost time, living life in fast-forward once we finally unlock the truth of who we are. But the knowledge that we were robbed of childhood never goes away. I hasten to add a reminder that I can't, and would never claim to, speak for all binary trans women. I can only share my own thoughts and feelings. I have met trans people who are entirely ambivalent about their past, with no longing or concerns for those years they spent in the dark. It affects us all in different ways, but I've met a depressing number of people who share the belief that I held quite tightly back then: that I was trying and failing to catch up with my own lost potential.

The truth stung. I knew that with my current momentum I could expect to be finished with transition around the time I hit 30 – meaning, if I was lucky, I had over half my life left without any sort of transition shenanigans in the way. Thanks to Twitter, I was acquainted with trans people who hadn't started transition until they had their own adult children. The knowledge that I was still relatively young humbled me. Yes, this situation was painful and clumsy, but

I was still relatively lucky. For now, all I had to do was hang on and focus on the future.

The search for a house down on the coast was hitting dead end after dead end. We were either putting in offers too late, or only finding dangerously dingy and rundown homes that we weren't comfortable committing to. Having an escape so close was agonising. Since the beginning, I had insisted to myself that I couldn't get too excited or relieved, because it could fall apart at any moment. Moving to the other side of the country felt like a dream outcome – what I wanted and needed more than anything. I knew I wouldn't be able to handle the disappointment if I let myself think that this was locked in and then it all fell apart. Mentally, I had prepared myself for a message from Laura saying that she thought we all should give up. My plan for that outcome was to immediately move somewhere close, to have that necessary space away from my family but resign myself to still being in fairly familiar surroundings. Although it wouldn't be ideal, it was far more practical and cheaper than trying to arrange moving somewhere radically different with limited resources.

After almost three months of looking, when it felt like the plan might need to be scrapped altogether, we were suddenly on the verge of having a home. There was a house not too far from the beach and situated within walking distance of the local shops. It was detached and had enough bedrooms for all of us, as well as a nice cosy living room. Laura and Tilley had visited the place that morning and reported back that it got their thumbs up, passing on a set of photographs as proof. Loretta and I immediately gave them the go-ahead to get back in touch and explain that we wanted it. The next few hours were torture, as the letting agency left to liaise with the landlord and pass on our offer.

So far we had reached this stage three times, but this time it felt different. The house had only been available for a single day, and we had been the first group to visit. Time dragged on until that afternoon we finally heard what we'd been waiting for: We'd been accepted, we had a new home.

Chapter 10

HOME

Moving day arrived, and thanks to three train rides and two taxi trips, fatigued but vibrating with nervous anticipation, we successfully arrived on the coast. Structurally, our new house was a mess and riddled with quirks. It was draughty, had a bizarrely placed, temperamental boiler, a bathroom door without a lock, not a single bit of carpeting, a couple of damaged windows that wouldn't close, a perpetually leaking pipe, and one wall decorated entirely in a dizzying collage of Marilyn Monroe pictures, which we were forbidden to remove or cover up. But despite it all, it was ours, it was home and it was hundreds of miles away from all of my old memories. That made it perfect.

You might think that when I arrived, I'd immediately start looking for a new job – that would certainly have been the sensible thing to do. Instead, I treated those first two weeks like a holiday. The returned freedom to dress and act however I liked without judgement was electrifying. As it was the last month of the year, daylight was scarce, but I still couldn't resist visiting the beach almost immediately. With tourist shops boarded up for the holidays, and few people braving the cold that day, I practically had the beach to myself. The sand stretched on forever, inviting me to explore and leave the city behind. I wandered down to the sea and stared at the water, listening to the hush of the waves. My hands were growing numb, my hair was being whipped into my face by the wind, and my shoes were itching with sand. But I was happy. This place was magical. Instead of retracing my steps and marching off towards the bus home, I started walking along the shore and enjoying how hypnotically peaceful the beach was. When I later made it to a cafe for lunch, I struck up a conversation with the owner and explained I had just moved here. At that she grew animated and assured me that I'd adore the friendly atmosphere and lovely weather once summer rolled around. I didn't disagree, but I was already having such a wonderful time I didn't care if things were never going to change.

With Christmas approaching, Loretta and I decided that we'd stay down here on the coast, rather than travel back for potentially awkward family gatherings. Save for one year that I'd spent snowed in with Nicole and her mother, I had spent every single Christmas with my family. Although we had prepared ourselves for a quiet and secluded holiday, Laura's mother Jenny extended an invitation for us to attend their family Christmas party. We happily accepted. The party provided me an excuse to dress up in glamorous clothes and fancy makeup for the first time ever. Unsurprisingly, I ended up running late as I worried about what dress to wear and what was the most appropriate lipstick. Laura had assured me that her family had learnt the basics and etiquette of talking with a trans person, since they had one in the family, therefore there wasn't a need for me to brace myself for any probing questions or collateral transphobia. True to her word, we walked into a modestly large house filled with smiling strangers. As we walked through the building making small talk and being introduced to various relatives, friends, and cats, I was struck by how profound it was to be here and feel so pleasingly unremarkable. I knew if I dared wear an outfit like this to any family function back in my hometown, I'd be tackled out of the room by one of my parents before anyone else could see me in my party dress. I wondered if perhaps this evening could be seen as a preview, an example of what could happen with my own family, given time.

As the party went on and I met even more of Laura's relatives, it further highlighted how ridiculous and painfully unnecessary it is for anyone to reject someone for coming out as trans. From my appearance and my voice it was blatantly obvious that I was transgender, but everyone understood that it wasn't what defined me, nor was it something that needed to be addressed in conversation. I may not have looked like a cisgender woman, but I was a woman. Everybody there respected that. I almost felt like sending a passive aggressive photo to my parents, showing off how I was enjoying myself around so many people, despite how impossibly scandalous this scenario was to them.

When the new year started, my honeymoon phase fizzled out. Dysphoria crashed back into my life, bringing with it a band of various nasty feelings. As the days ticked by, I felt progressively worse until I was confined to my bed, without any drive or desire to face up to any of my problems. I was so overwhelmed with dread and disgust, I didn't even open the curtains or consider getting up. Physically I felt clumsy, ugly, and masculine, while emotionally I was scared. There now was so much to do to get my life on track, I wasn't sure I was strong enough to do it all. The sheer scope of my transition, and the thought of how visible and vulnerable I was going to be throughout it all, was petrifying. Outside of Christmas parties, happy housemates, and geeky conventions, this society wasn't accepting of people who looked like me. It was doubtful I was even being seen as a woman by anyone else yet. My dysphoria relentlessly reminded me of those facts. Yet as they always did, these feelings gave way to a second wind. Yes, this was going to be a challenge, but moping in bed wasn't going to achieve anything. I had to get up. By moving here, I had found a way to start again. It was time to make that work.

Reluctantly, I had realised that I was struggling to make the rent. So far, I'd been relying on my savings, which were steadily being reduced to dust, as well as unpredictable freelance web development. I'd recently been wrestling with the choice of what to do about my job. Self-employed work was not bringing in enough to last me in the long term; it was only enough to keep me going for the immediate future. I knew that normally in this situation I would simply apply for any job at all that would take me, but now I had to think about how being trans had changed that. I imagined taking a retail job and having to encounter people misgendering me every hour, or ending up in a hostile workplace with casual transphobia and an ambivalent human resources (HR) department. They were both situations that friends across the country had landed in, and I dreaded having to endure them too. The size of my wage didn't matter to me as long as I had enough to survive. What I really wanted to find was a supportive workplace. I craved somewhere that would respect the fact I was trans, and make the minor adjustments needed to support me, while also not expecting it to define me. However, before I could even send off an application, I had to figure out who was going to apply.

At the time, I was in the bizarre situation of still being partially closeted. The vast majority of my social circle now knew me as Mia, but I had no form of identification, qualifications, or references in that name. Since moving, I had never introduced myself to anyone as anything other than Mia. My old name was a logistical leftover. I'd hesitated to change it formally because I was worried about how it would impact my job prospects. I imagined a scenario where I'd apply for a job as Mia, then arrive and wince as it became clear I didn't look or sound like the woman they'd expected to show up at the interview. As I still hadn't started HRT, I was depending entirely on clothes and makeup to project what gender I was. But outside of my hair, everything else about me was leading unsuspecting strangers to see me as something I wasn't. I felt stuck, held back by my own physicality. But the only alternative to knowing I'd be taking people off guard was a detestable one: applying under the guise of being a man. The idea of using my old name, and then having to pretend to be male with new colleagues, was repellent. It would result in becoming closeted to new people, further muddling my confusing state of gender limbo and forcing me to uncomfortably pretend once again that I was okay being seen as a man.

I begrudgingly decided that the easiest thing to do was to apply under my old name anyway. My chances felt maximised by not having to explain why my documents looked like someone else's. Meanwhile, this way I could apply for jobs that instant and not delay while I went around updating everything and waiting for the change to be processed. I vowed that if I was brought in for an interview, I would come out as transgender before leaving the room. That way I would make it very clear that if offered the job I would be walking in as Mia on Day 1.

In hindsight, I think that whole plan was a messy mistake. It wouldn't have been terribly difficult to update my documents and name first, and if anyone had a problem with me being trans then it would have been a warning not to accept a job there anyway. But at the time I was intensely anxious that I might end up with no ID and miss opportunities while wrestling with inconsistencies. More than anything, I was afraid that I'd soon have to leave my new home behind if this didn't work, because I wouldn't have the money needed to stay.

Meanwhile, it was rapidly closing in on one year since I had first talked to a doctor about my GIC referral. Going by their initial projection, I was due to be seen there fairly soon. The fact I now lived 250 miles away from the clinic I had signed up for was a problem I decided I would worry about later. In the short term, I wanted to gamble the last of my money on trying to go private to start HRT right away. During the previous summer, I had hoarded money, intending to use it either for moving or for HRT. I desperately wanted HRT so I could stop my body from growing in the wrong direction and start 'feminising' instead. Yet I'd understood the importance of getting somewhere safe to live first, especially after my parents reacted so poorly to me coming out. Now that I had successfully moved away, the only thing that was stopping me from pursuing HRT was the knowledge that it would sterilise me.

It's something the media often overlook, but when trans people take HRT it can severely affect fertility, depending on what gender you are and what dose you take. For trans women, wiping out testosterone and raising oestrogen will render us infertile, first temporarily and eventually permanently. Being in my 20s, parenthood wasn't exactly something actively on my mind, but it was there in the background – a little nervous voice reminding me that if I cared about becoming infertile, now was the time to do something about it. But did I really want to 'father' a child? I could barely even look after myself and I'd never been any good with children. Like everything else with my transition, the knowledge of the next step's consequences caused me to overthink and hesitate, before finally deciding to charge ahead.

Although not widely discussed, many countries still demand trans people be sterilised before they're allowed to change their legally recognised gender. This has its roots in Sweden, which, as the first country to allow someone to undergo 'gender reassignment', defined the terms and conditions. Barbarically, sterilisation was demanded because trans people were seen as mentally ill and unfit parents by default. Rightly so, this was finally deemed a violation of human rights by the European Council, yet in 2018 it still remains law in various countries worldwide. It's another example of trans people routinely having our agency denied to us. Although sterilisation is an extreme example, it's common for medical practitioners and government bodies to require trans people to complete certain needless processes before we're given the recognition we need. Even in the UK, everything from changing the gender on our passports to starting HRT requires we first get the permission of a professional – our own word isn't enough.

Although I knew it was a long shot, I decided I'd ask my new GP if they were willing to prescribe HRT for me. Technically, any local GP can prescribe a trans person the hormones that they need; it's just exceedingly rare that any will do it. A lack of training on how transition works is a common reason to refuse, but I've also heard of doctors insisting that only GICs can prescribe, firmly believing that trans patients are just someone else's problem. The end result is that the majority of trans people in the UK are told that they need to keep waiting, despite the long queues.

My main motivation for asking my GP for hormones wasn't just to cut short the waiting time, it was also to save myself money by not going private. I'd now committed to the idea that I was going to start HRT any way I could. I was laser-focused. Although hormones are relatively cheap, the actual appointments to see private specialists are not. Therefore, I wanted to give this unlikely shortcut a chance before I opened up my purse for another significant expense.

Considerably less nervous than the last time I had visited a doctor to come out as transgender, I arrived at the new surgery feeling quite at ease. Once I was inside for my appointment, I introduced myself to the stoic, bearded doctor and explained right away that I was transgender. I added that I was on the cusp of social transition, with a formal name change planned imminently. I mentioned that I had been referred to the GIC almost a year ago, which he then confirmed with the help of my newly delivered notes. Then I asked if he'd prescribe me hormones. 'No. None of us have the experience to do that,' he replied. Disappointed, but not even remotely surprised, I went back to my original plan of going private.

Although I knew of two private clinics located in London – now blessedly nearby – I had also heard rumours of a new online-only doctor. According to their website, it was a fairly routine and straightforward process to be approved for HRT, at least as straightforward as it could get with life-changing medical care. It would require signing some forms, answering some questions, and being assessed over a telephone appointment. Best of all, it was cheaper than I'd expected. Although I was cautious about the potential instability and shady nature of an online clinic, I couldn't resist the incredible possibility of accessing hormones so easily.

I saw HRT as the vital oncoming kick-start for my transition. Many friends in the USA had been on HRT for a year or more before they had come out as transgender, allowing their bodies to change while they went about their life as if nothing was happening. When they felt comfortable enough, and that they had made enough physical progress, only then would they come out. Everything I found on English GICs indicated that they required transgender patients to come out to everybody in their life first. Not only that, they insisted that all trans people presented openly as their true gender for several months. Only after both conditions were fulfilled would the person be approved for HRT. These conditions sounded awful. Therefore, going private not only meant that I would be able to start early, it would also give me the freedom to transition according to my own timeline and not have to dance to the GIC's tune first.

Outside of the NHS and private clinics, there was of course one other way to obtain HRT, but it was a route I had specifically not allowed myself to explore. Personally, I knew of many people who had begun their transition through self-medication, with the help of grey-market drugs imported in bulk from dubious-looking websites. Whenever I lamented my lack of hormones on social media, I would occasionally receive a message from someone offering to help me get my hands on them through this technically legal, but arguably dangerous, alternative means. This is something that is very often discussed in the community as a possible pathway for trans women, since oestrogen is a fairly common drug with loose restrictions, making it much easier to acquire compared to something like testosterone, which is tightly controlled. When you couple that with the giant waiting times to even see the GIC, and how potent dysphoria can be, I was certainly sympathetic to those who caved in to the temptation and bought their HRT without a doctor's involvement. But for everyone willing to assist with under-the-table hormones, there were plenty who warded me away with sobering reminders. For instance, there would be no evidence that these sites were consistently providing the correct dose, or even the correct drug. The price for a head-start on my transition in this way was to gamble with my own health.

What drove me away from considering self-medication wasn't the thought of buying lethal pills or unstable doses; rather it was the knowledge that nobody would be monitoring my hormone levels. When beginning HRT under an informed doctor's supervision, their job is to monitor your levels via regular blood tests. They can then make recommendations based on what you need to bump up or dial back on to get your oestrogen and testosterone in the ideal range. Hormonal transition is tricky in that there really is no one-size-fits-all approach to doses. What your body does with what you put in it isn't guaranteed. I could have decided to take an identical dose to that of a friend but ended up with dangerously high oestrogen, while her levels could have been fine. Without a doctor's help, I wouldn't be able to find out what was going on with my body or be prescribed a more suitable dose. As someone who was naturally anxious about many things at that time, especially anything medical, I knew it was just simply too risky for me to consider. The sensible option was undeniably private care.

Even with the obstacles that I had to clamber over, the fact that I was able to contact a private clinic at all was a result of luck and privilege. It was pure chance that the online clinic had opened right at the very same time I was ready to pursue HRT. Meanwhile, the money that I had left to spend on my healthcare was certainly a humble amount, but it was still something that not everybody has access to.

After making contact with the online clinic, and giving a brief history of my gender dysphoria and mental wellbeing, I was sent the initial consent forms for HRT. Browsing through them, they didn't tell me anything I didn't already know from previous research. They detailed how I would become sterile, experience mood swings, my sex drive would implode, and I would also be opening the door to a crop of new health risks that came with taking lifelong medication off-label. Although it might be a surprise to some, there is no medication specifically created for transgender people. None whatsoever. Instead, all trans people who transition take medication devised for other purposes. This means we end up taking tablets for blood pressure or even prostate issues, specifically so we can access their 'side-effects'. In other words, for us, the effects of the medication are reversed – that is, the side-effects are what help us to transition, whereas the intended effects of the medication (to treat various medical conditions) are something we have to put up with. As I was given a choice of what medication to choose, I picked oestrogen patches, and a daily finasteride tablet to lower my testosterone levels. The tablet is also used for countering hair loss, but as I was still lucky enough to have a long, thick mane of dyed purple locks, thankfully I didn't need it for that. Still, it was nice to know that it would intercept any risk of me going bald.

Before I could actually purchase HRT, I had to be assessed and approved. At a pre-arranged date and time, I tapped in the number I'd been given for the assessment therapist and began dialling. Although counselling had previously done a lot to ease my nerves about sharing my life story, I was still quite antsy about the significance of this phone call. If it went well, I could have my hormones within days. If it went badly, it could add more delays to my fragile timeline.

Everything I had read about trans healthcare had warned me that caregivers could often work from insultingly outdated information. I'd been told unnerving stories of doctors demanding trans women wear dresses or skirts to prove themselves, while trans men were criticised for wearing anything colourful at all. With this in mind, I braced myself for a conversation where not adhering to stereotypes and clichés could undo this whole plan.

The therapist was a patient but pragmatic woman, who listened as I recited my history of gender dysphoria on cue. I talked about being a child and wanting to be grouped with the girls, while I selectively ignored my love of Batman and video games. I explained that I went to counselling and how I'd had the 'eureka' moment of realising I needed to transition, but I decided not to elaborate about that intense fear I'd felt over what transition might bring me. On the topic of my family, I explained the technical truth that they were fully aware and were coming to accept the reality. I didn't bother to add that they had reacted with extravagantly overboard disappointment and that our relationship was in tatters. 'So they've met Mia?' the therapist asked, referring to my parents. 'Yes, they have,' I replied, and was glad she couldn't see me roll my eyes at the bizarre wording of the question. That had been another thing I'd been warned about: that caregivers can expect us to see ourselves as two people, the old person and the new one we're transitioning into. I found this idea baffling, though I had encountered more than one trans person who did conform to this outlook. I would never criticise another trans person for the language and perspectives that work for them. We're all unique and dealing with our own personal conflict, but that was one viewpoint that was very far from my own. From my perspective, I had always been me, always Mia, always a girl. What had changed was my perception of myself, and the information I'd divulged to those around me.

With a few brief questions about my support network, the call concluded with a note that the therapist would speak with the doctor and get back to me with their decision soon. Dropping my phone, I slumped face first onto the bed. Done. Now all I had to do was wait. The following few hours I spent frantically refreshing my inbox, as if I could summon forth the e-mail that would bring about the next phase of my life. It was a day later when I got a response, which said the doctor and counsellor had discussed my session and thought that I should re-enter counselling for extra support. I hastily responded that I would happily go back to counselling and that it was an excellent idea. Although I was motivated by being salivatingly close to hormones, I did agree that counselling was a good idea. In an ideal world, I knew I'd return to seeing Holly. I made an attempt to find out if she gave online sessions but couldn't find any trace of her on the Internet. As far as I could tell, I had been talking to someone who didn't exist. Disappointed, I looked for alternatives and stumbled across a counselling directory website. Bizarrely, it was laid out like some sort of strange therapeutic dating website, and I browsed profiles of nearby counsellors, complete with photos of the many comfortable couches and cramped offices that each of them operated out of. I filtered my search by 'gender dysphoria' and that narrowed down my results to two possibilities. I fired off e-mails to both of them, introducing myself and explaining my situation. I said that I wanted to talk to someone about issues resulting from being trans, but not necessarily about *being* trans. I pictured myself blathering on about my parents or the anxiety of looking for a job, but my worries over whether I should transition or not were long over (or so I thought).

With counsellors contacted, I returned to the online doctor and assured her I had made some enquiries. With all the subtlety of an erupting volcano, I hinted that I was in great mental health and was feeling very supported. Two days went by, and then the doctor responded with a question: 'Would you like to start hormones now, or wait?' I felt like I was chained to the bottom of the ocean and while I was drowning someone had just casually asked if I'd like some help. I responded and, trying to hide my electrified eagerness, stated that I would certainly like to begin HRT right now.

One morning, a few days later, my hormones arrived – except they didn't arrive at my house, they popped through the letterbox of my parents' house, 250 miles away. You're probably thinking that this ridiculous snafu was my mistake, and I accept it would have been entirely in character, but it was actually down to the online chemist that had processed my prescription. Double-checking my order, I saw that they'd processed it and dispatched it to my invoice address, not my delivery address. As I had just moved and not updated my bank details, I had invoiced my old address, not wanting to cause any issues by putting an address where my card wasn't registered. I would have laughed if the disappointment wasn't crushing. Cautiously, I sent a text message to my mother and asked if anything had arrived addressed to me. She said that there was a small box. I told her the order had been sent there by mistake and, if she could, I would appreciate her sending the box to me. She said she would do it the next day. During the whole exchange, I was dreading a very simple, very understandable question: 'What's in the box?' yet she didn't ask. I told Laura what was going on and she suggested it was possible my mother suspected but didn't want to know the answer. Meanwhile, I thought they probably had no clue, considering how stunned they'd been by my initial coming out. I doubted they were thinking about the fact I was about to take body-changing drugs.

Yet again I waited, and then at last my hormones arrived. Years had led up to this moment: the chance to shift my body towards who and what I wanted to be. This would be the first monumental dose, one that I'd continue for the rest of my life. My body would undergo changes that would soon become permanent. I began to cry – not with happiness but with outright panic. I started to babble incoherently to Loretta, who calmly listened to me fret about how I might change my mind or regret this later. Was I making a huge mistake? I was about to change my future. The whole direction of my life became represented and defined by these drugs sat in my hands. I couldn't do it. I was too afraid. My mind reeled with all of the worst-case scenarios I could conjure up as a result of HRT, everything from devastating depression and regret, right up to tragic illness and death.

Unusually for me, I didn't go to Twitter with my conundrum and I didn't speak to friends. This felt wrong, like something I shouldn't be feeling. It clashed with everything I had been working towards. I knew logically that I should just take the HRT, but the weight of the decision was overwhelming. Instead I decided to put them aside and sleep on it. That way I could delay the decision. Once I awoke, I felt refreshed, relaxed, and reassured. I looked at the square box of patches and long silver strip of pills. It was like being back in my counsellor's office, realising that my doubts and apprehensions were nothing but fear. It was inevitable that I was going to do this. So I did. I started HRT that morning, with a reassuring note to myself that I could always slam the brakes on if I changed my mind.

When I tell people that I was overcome with fear and indecision over whether to start HRT, my friends are often surprised. Transition has been such a powerfully positive influence on my life, the idea that even as far along as receiving HRT I was still not sure seems strange and out of character. Yet I've met a lot of trans people who had their own mini-meltdowns when faced with Day 1. Just like transition as a whole, starting hormones is something that we're warned away from by the media, society, and sometimes friends and family. It's hard to press on and do it anyway, knowing that it comes with health risks and consequences.

Twenty-four hours after starting HRT, I felt sick. Mentally I felt great, but physically I was feeling a little dizzy. My immediate thought was that my body must be adjusting to the hormones, but then I quickly realised this was probably down to my unhealthy lifestyle more than anything else. It's a cliché in trans circles to measure every effect of HRT, looking for the tiniest changes and cataloguing them with daily photos or an extensive diary. I knew I would drive myself into a ditch of over-analytical nonsense if I tried to do the same for myself but I was very tempted by the idea of logging my changes for future reference. With a lot of my transition so far, I had left behind blog posts and diary entries, which I knew would make entertaining reading one day, or at the very least they'd make turning this time period into a book much easier. With those things in mind, I decided to start keeping a short, private log.

Every few days I would jot down in my diary how I was feeling and what I had noticed. For the first two weeks, all I had to report were feelings of calm contentedness. However, I knew that it was likely that these feelings were the result of peace of mind from finally having hormones, rather than due to any physical changes in my body. After three weeks, I noticed the very first change: my smell. Surprised, I Googled how quickly HRT could change my smell. Sure enough, within the first month it was possible to notice a change in aroma. It was odd to realise that although I couldn't see it, my body was transforming. The next change I noticed came a week later and was much less subtle. While hastily scooping up my handbag from the floor, I accidentally swung it into my chest. It hurt. I had a type of pain that I'd never felt there before. I gasped with glee as I realised what it meant. I didn't want to get too excited, so I forced myself to lower my expectations and tell myself that it might have just been a fluke. A week went by and I awoke one morning lying on my front, with an aching, tender pain in my chest. I was growing breasts. For trans women, breast growth takes a lot of time. As with everything else, the younger you start, the higher your chances are of significant changes. As I come from a long line of flat-chested women, I didn't have high expectations, but I sure had high hopes. Although it wasn't unusual to start breast growth early on, it would take up to five years until I'd see what the final result was going to be.

With this development, it sunk in that I really was transitioning, at last. The wait for HRT was over. My body would no longer be changing in the wrong direction; it was being realigned and becoming what I wanted it to be. Now I just needed to find a job safe enough to transition in, where I could ride out the rest of these changes and enjoy evolving into this new version of myself.

Chapter 11

WORK

One afternoon I checked my e-mails to find an interview invitation. The job opening was in IT – not a field known for being particularly diverse and accepting, but something that matched my skills. Growing up on computers, I had a mishmash of generalised IT skills, so I'd fallen back on them when sending out job applications. As a bonus, this interview was with a company that I had heard good things about in terms of their employee satisfaction and protections. I had applied for it but mostly forgotten about it as I didn't think my chances were good. It was specifically a graduate position at their entry-level pay, so I knew there would be lots of competition. I was also worried I might be considered over-qualified, considering that I had a Master's degree. But an interview was closer than I'd got to any other opening in a while. I couldn't deny it was a good opportunity.

Just as I got the interview invitation, I also got a devastating message from Loretta. She was being tested for cancer. While visiting her mother, she had gone to see her GP after finding a strange lump on her breast. Her doctor had inspected it himself and considered it concerning enough to send her for extra tests immediately. The interview now felt worthless. I told her I'd travel up to be with her right away. 'No,' she said, 'you need to attend that interview.' She was adamant that the interview was important; it was a chance to carve out some security. 'You being here won't change the results,' she insisted. 'You're not skipping this interview because of me.' She was right, but I hated that she was. The interview was too big an opportunity. Loretta insisted that she would be fine navigating this on her own, with her mother for backup. If she ended up needing a referral or treatment, she would ensure it was arranged near our new home, where she would reunite with me soon. That was her job; mine was to give this interview my best shot.

The morning of my interview was a difficult one. I didn't feel particularly stressed about the interview itself but I felt horrible about my presentation and especially worried about Loretta. After sending her a message of support, she reminded me to focus on the interview and that we'd catch up that evening. Staring at my wardrobe, I agonised over what to wear. I debated the idea of walking into the reception area in a dress and just asking everyone to roll with it. Although I'd felt confident that my plan to apply under my old name was sensible, I now regretted it. Enormously. I wasn't a man, I certainly didn't want to pretend to be one, and yet now I had to. I ended up picking my go-to androgynous outfit of skinny jeans, a patterned shirt, and some smart ankle boots. I tied my hair into a ponytail, knowing that it looked a little messy when left loose. My long, straight hairstyle was considered mundane for a woman, but lazy and borderline silly for a man. As I was trying to build a good first impression, I figured I had to endure the expectations of being seen as male. I remember snapping a photo of the outfit, intending to send it to Loretta. I'd wanted to ask her if she thought the outfit was suitable, but from my expression I looked like I was on my way to a funeral. I deleted it, knowing I'd not want to remember it.

On the way to the interview, I caught my reflection in a glass building, I looked miserable. My dysphoria was a swirling mess, telling me I was an ugly man who had been playing at pretend, and now I was back wearing what I deserved. I brushed the thoughts away as best I could, reminding myself there was a lot riding on this. If I didn't find a job soon, then I'd be heading back north, having to beg my parents to let me move in while I scrounged enough money to move out again. That idea was so unappealing, I wondered what it'd be like to live on the beach instead. Maybe I could spend my days collecting shells and singing sad songs to crabs. It would certainly be preferable to going back to my old life.

Once I arrived at the company, I begrudgingly introduced myself under my old name, knowing that it felt so horrible I certainly wouldn't be doing this at any future interviews. I was then directed to sit nearby and wait my turn. Crossing my legs and whipping my phone out of my handbag, I pondered on how I would appear. Expectations of gender and sexuality are so muddled, it was probably much more likely that I'd be perceived as a gay guy rather than as a trans woman. When a stranger sees someone who doesn't blend into cisnormative expectations, it seems homosexuality is usually their first lazy assumption. My mannerisms and appearance had been progressively mocked for being feminine over the years, but ironically I was now uncomfortable that I didn't appear feminine enough. I wanted to be wearing my makeup or one of my dresses, a presentation that made me feel at home. I had once called wearing outfits like that 'dressing up', but now they were my everyday look and this masculine presentation was the costume. Plucking me out of my daydream, a young woman invited me to follow her into the lift for a ride to the interview room. 'So, have you lived here a long time?' she asked, likely having picked up on my accent. I'd gotten used to people questioning where I was from or asking about my hometown and found it a useful way to spark up conversation. I explained the truth, but left out the part about being trans. 'I wanted something new. Since some friends live here already, it was a good opportunity to all move in together,' I said. Before we could chat more, we arrived and I was gestured to step inside the interview room.

Although I'd been expecting to sit across from an interviewer, I was unprepared to find myself seated in front of four people. Thankfully, they were all dressed casually and introduced themselves in a very relaxed and friendly manner. After introductions had taken place, they dived into questioning me. The interview involved questions about the workplace and my skills, and technical queries to test my alleged expertise. Most of it felt fairly routine. The only question that almost tripped me up was when I was asked to explain why I wanted this job. They noted that it seemed a little simplistic for my qualifications. I answered that I was looking for something that would give me valuable workplace experience and help me to hone foundational IT skills, as well as providing opportunities to pick up some new ones. It wasn't a lie, but I neglected to mention that I wanted something straightforward while I transitioned. With a round of nods in response, I figured I had assured them I wasn't going to bail early if offered the job.

At the end of the interview the panel asked if I had any questions for them. I knew if I was going to do it, then this was the time to come out. 'Well,' I began, momentarily pausing for time as I always did before dropping the truth, 'I'm transgender, and I'm about to transition.' Before starting the next sentence, I quickly glanced between the panel members and was relieved to find that nobody had flinched, swallowed, moved, or reacted in any way whatsoever. They were all staring with a kind of curious expectation. 'So, if I'm offered the job, I'll be presenting as myself: female. I'm currently on hormones to change my body. The name I actually go by is Mia. I'll be changing my name formally this week.' I hadn't actually planned to change it this week. That declaration had slipped out on its own, but I decided to roll with it and pretend I had more of a plan than I did. 'Would that be an issue at all?' I raised my eyebrows and looked around, not sure what to expect. 'No, that's fine,' the panel erupted into casual nods and shrugs, indicating that it was a complete non-issue. The oldest member of the panel, a woman with grey hair and a soft voice, began to explain that they were a very equality-focused employer, and that they did everything they could to make sure they had a supportive environment for marginalised people. Continuing, she elaborated that they had equality teams and even held regular meetings specifically to strive endlessly to improve the company and accommodate those who needed extra help. The other panellists supported this claim with more nods and other comments about how safe and secure this place was. Amusingly, I felt like the dynamics of the room had become flipped. Suddenly they were pleading their case to me, convincing me that the company and I were a good fit. 'That honestly sounds great,' I admitted, truly surprised by how many measures were in place. With no other questions to ask, I explained that I was happy and headed out.

I got to the bus stop, released my hair from its ponytail, and let out a sigh. I replayed what had happened, analysing my interview performance. I didn't want to get my hopes up, but it seemed like a positive experience. When I had told friends about my upcoming interview and my dilemma of whether to come out or not, I'd once again been told a string of uncomfortable stories about when things had gone wrong. I heard about employers who had failed to hide their disapproving surprise upon seeing a trans person walk into the room, how interviews had been cut short, and even how one employer had erupted into a rant about never employing someone like that, when they believed they were out of earshot. The epidemic of poverty in the trans community speaks to the issues we can have with employment. Although the media is fond of showing glamorous transgender personalities in sparkling formal wear, for most of us, coming out is a career-crippling gamble that severely limits our options and slashes our income. If you're not already well established in your field, it can be tough to find someone willing to hire you, especially in those early years.

The next day, I was sat watching TV when I got a phone call from an unknown number. Cautiously, I answered, expecting another automated message about PPI or a request to hand over my bank details. Instead, it was one of the panellists from my interview the day before. 'Oh hello!' I said shooting to my feet. They explained that they wanted to offer me the job and were really happy with my interview. 'Oh! Thank you. Well, in that case, I would certainly like to accept your kind offer,' I replied, cringing at my nervous wording, as he gave a friendly chuckle. After being told about some logistics of the job, and how my contract would be mailed to me, I hastily reminded him that I would be starting the job under my new name, Mia. He reiterated that it was absolutely fine, and if I wanted to get in touch with HR to talk to them prior to joining, that would be fine too. And that was it. I no longer had any reason to ever use my old name again.

Surprisingly, in the UK there is no such thing as a legal name. Instead, we have a name that is generally understood to be ours and what we use, but we're not legally required to use it in our life. Although in the USA trans people often have to go to court just to change their name, in the UK we use deed polls. They're as simple as printing out a declaration of your intent to immediately change your name, then signing it with a witness or two. My deed poll was signed the morning after I was offered my job. Feeling no hesitation at abandoning all ownership of my old name, I was ecstatic to officially become Mia Violet. The next step was to begin the long and tedious process of changing my name everywhere I could think of.

The first place I went to was the bank. I was a little nervous that they might insist on seeing a deed poll that had been signed by a solicitor – something that is technically not required but often mistakenly assumed. After walking in, I explained to the door attendant that I was looking to change the name on my account. I was led into a small side-room where I was joined by a different woman. I explained that I was trans and thus had just changed my name. With a smile, she took my details and even passed on her own e-mail address, explaining that I could contact her directly if my new card didn't arrive or if there were any problems in the future. Although things went wonderfully smoothly for me, I've heard plenty of nightmare tales about bank staff asking for doctors' notes or a passport as evidence. Most of the time, there's so little training given that staff are left to guess. Yet even once names have been changed on the account, it's often not the end of the issues that trans people face with banks. I know of people who've had their cards cancelled when cashiers have marked them as potentially stolen, not believing that the name on the card could match the person in front of them. Elsewhere, someone told me of having their card suspended by their own bank, when their voice was deemed deceptive and inauthentic on the phone. I've even had to lend friends money before because their bank locked them out on a Saturday evening, leaving them with no cash until they could visit a branch and unlock it on the Monday morning. It's just another of the many minor risks and annoyances that come with being trans.

Until you've changed your name, it's hard to realise just how many places you have to actually contact to get it altered. Besides the obvious ones like the bank and your GP, there are online shopping accounts, student loans, your phone company, the local council, the landlord, your internet service provider, and of course, iTunes. Altogether, it took quite a while to do a trip around every place I needed to touch base with, but finally I felt like I had taken care of everything.

While double-checking there was nothing I'd missed, I got a phone call from Loretta with an update on her health. She was fine. The hospital had taken a biopsy and found the lump benign. She didn't have cancer. I nearly cried with relief, realising in that moment how much the spectre of that possibility had been following me around. She announced she'd be heading home that day so we could be reunited and keep moving forward.

A few weeks prior to starting my new job, I arranged a meeting with the company's HR department. I did this more to ease my own nerves than anything else – to get an idea of what sort of support existed and what type of office I was walking into. I had imagined melodramatically apocalyptic scenarios of walking into the office on the first day and being leered at like I was in a circus. As I'd be working in an open office, I couldn't help but wonder what I would do if people were mean. What if I felt really uncomfortable and exposed every minute I was there? Worst of all, what if my panic attacks came back? Having walked up a long, winding staircase, I arrived at the HR department and was ushered into a small, bright office for a secluded chat. Right away, I said that I was happy to talk about basically anything and everything, and if there was anything the HR member was curious about, I was happy to answer it. It is normally risky to give someone free rein to question a trans person. When I did this with a cis male friend, his first question was, unsurprisingly, about my genitals. As an HR manager I suspected she wouldn't choose that topic. Curiously, she did ask how my transition worked in terms of healthcare logistics. I explained about the NHS's GIC system, and how I still had to travel to the original clinic I had signed up for but had no idea when that would actually happen. I mentioned that I was on hormones now, having started very recently, and that I was paying privately for this treatment. When I explained about the waiting lists, she was surprised. 'Really? Eighteen months for an appointment?' she gasped. She could see why I'd chosen to pay for my own treatment.

The most significant question from the meeting was when I was asked what I wanted to have happen before I joined the company. I said I wanted some sort of message to be sent out to my department, briefly letting them know that I was trans and what that meant. I didn't want anything too serious or too dramatic. It's not like I came from another planet, but I did want it to be very well established that I was a woman and that misgendering and such would not be tolerated.

She said that was entirely fine, and produced a handful of documents she had prepared that she wanted my opinion on. Flicking through, there were dry explanations of what being trans meant and quotes from the clumsily worded Gender Recognition Act, which was now over ten years old. I pointed out that a lot of the sources were quite dated, while not wanting to seem ungrateful for the time she'd spent on research. As an alternative, I suggested just linking to the GLAAD guide to being transgender, which was my personal favourite at the time in terms of the many trans factsheets available. Knowing that nobody would read anything if they were bombarded with information, I thought providing a single link would increase the chance people might peruse it out of curiosity if nothing else. Promising to send it over, and a draft message announcing my employment to the team, the meeting concluded and I headed home.

As I sat at the bus stop, fidgeting on my phone, I was approached by a young man who asked me if I knew when the next bus was coming. I gestured to the timetable with an apology and admitted I had no idea as I'd only been here twice before. With a 'Thanks anyway', he glanced at the listings, then wandered off. I broke into a grin. I was sat on a bench in a dress with full makeup on and I'd just had a one-on-one conversation with a stranger, alone. I had thought nothing of it, yet a year ago being outside in these clothes was enough to make me seize up and avoid all human contact at any cost. I was making real progress. My life was changing right in front of me and things were going well. I now just had to cross my fingers and hope that this job worked out too.

By the time I came to start my new job, it had been almost two months since I'd accepted the position. My start date had been pushed back twice, prolonging my new state of increasing anxiety. Laughing, I said to Loretta that I half-expected to come home after the first day and insist that I was never going back. Entirely straight-faced, she replied that it wouldn't surprise her, considering how averse I had recently become to the idea of working there. Though I'd originally felt assured and comfortable about accepting the job, my mind had run rampant and developed a list of worst-case scenarios. The more my first day was delayed, the better I felt about the excuse to hibernate indoors and panic about what was to come.

Despite my anxiety, I had done everything I could think of to prepare for the job. I had stocked up on makeup, purchased a number of new business-appropriate outfits (all dresses, to deter misgendering), and even bought a new handbag with extra room for snacks. With a ping from my phone, I received one final task to do: take a photo for my employee card and e-mail it back over. Standing in our hallway, the only place in the house with a blank backdrop, I held my smartphone out and snapped a photo of myself smiling softly. I hated it. I looked tired, stressed out, frazzled, and worst of all I looked like a man. I stood there and took at least 100 photos, constantly checking the results and grumbling angrily that nothing looked good. I had taken photos of myself before that I had liked, but they were rare and usually heavily filtered. For a work photo, I concluded I had to use something unfiltered and professional. It meant using a photo of how I really looked, but seeing my appearance always left me hollowed out and disappointed. In the end, I chose the least horrifying photo from the set and sent it away. I reassured myself with the knowledge that everybody hates their staff photo, although I doubted that most people worry it makes them look like a different gender.

On the first day of work I awoke exceedingly early, determined that I wouldn't be late. I wore a black dress with a floral-patterned blouse under it, carefully choosing one of the most stereotypically feminine professional outfits that I had. To get there, I had to ride on the bus. As I arrived at the bus stop, I noticed with trepidation that there were a number of teenagers waiting around too. Disturbing flashbacks reminded me that I didn't have a glowing record when it came to taking the morning bus with a bunch of school kids. I told myself this was not a big deal, that I hadn't encountered any sort of abuse from teenagers since I'd moved here, so maybe these kids would leave me be. I also reassured myself that I was no longer that awkward and weird kid who used to get bullied. I was now a proud, awkward, and weird adult, who also stood a head taller than most of the tiny, uniformed teens. Once the bus arrived, by instinct I sauntered to the very back and dropped into the seat furthest from the front. The teenagers sat beside me, of course. Amusingly, I ended up surrounded by them, as they all took to the back of the bus too. The rest of the commuters sensibly stayed out of their way at the front. I thought about how I had been stared at, and even yelled at, by teenagers in my hometown just for having long hair, yet so far nobody cared. The journey progressed and the kids were too preoccupied with each other and their smartphones to even bat an eye at the trans woman sat next to them. Apparently, down here teenagers were either politer, more open-minded, or I just wasn't as much of a spectacle as I thought.

I could feel the nerves bubbling up once I arrived at work. I tried to remind myself that I had been known back at university for having grown into someone preternaturally relaxed under pressure. I certainly didn't feel like that person right then but I tried to channel that old confident mindset. People did generally seem to like me, and surely my new colleagues would at least tolerate me. HR had notified the team and nobody had even flinched when I came out in my interview, so I had no logical reason to worry. I was just letting stress get the better of my common sense. Everything would be fine. Probably.

After getting to the reception area, I was met by my new line manager. As he was one of the people who had interviewed me, I awkwardly hoped he wouldn't make any comment about being re-introduced to me. Last time we had met I hadn't even been using the same name, and here I was in radically different clothing. Thankfully, he made no indication that my complete presentation change was anything out of the ordinary, and led me to the office where I'd be working. I walked into a long, open space filled with computers and men. Other than myself there were no women in the office whatsoever. Working in this branch of IT, it was quite possible there wouldn't be many women – I'd heard plenty of stories of the disappointing gender ratio in this sector. I'd still held out hope that there might be someone like me, but there wasn't even anyone in my age bracket. Being introduced to the department manager, a warm and friendly man, we figured out that when he started working here I was two years old. It was a similar story for the rest of the department – most of them had children and were floating around either side of 40. Still, despite the differences in demographics, everyone was pleasant and greeted me quite warmly. I was given some simple tasks to do to settle into the role and told I should feel free to stretch my legs and explore whenever I needed to. At lunchtime I ate alone, choosing to sit at an empty table in the canteen and catch up on my Twitter feed.

I excitedly updated friends and told them everything was going well. After an uneventful afternoon, I went home and told a relieved Loretta that the job went well. I was actually looking forward to going back.

Days turned into weeks and soon I was settled in nicely. My job involved an element of tech support and therefore I was often dispatched to other departments and met lots of new faces. It was at this point that I realised that when you're a transgender employee of a fairly large company, you quickly become memorable. I got used to being greeted with friendly waves and warm smiles whenever I passed a colleague in the corridor. Admittedly, my awful memory meant I embarrassingly struggled to recognise who I was waving at a lot of the time. I became an expert at feigning delight while I made small talk with someone who may as well have been a polite stranger. I was terrible at remembering faces at the best of times, but working in a new company with hundreds of employees left me constantly improvising and avoiding using anyone's name. Often, I would later guiltily use the internal staff directory to track down who I'd just been speaking with, relying on outdated company photographs to make the best educated guess.

For whatever reason, I found women were by far the friendliest of my colleagues. Most men in the company ignored me, but women would often stop to chat or even compliment my outfit or hair. I got the vibe that some may have been trying to go out of their way to make me feel welcome, compensating for the fact I was obviously different and maybe even a little novel. As I'd talked to HR, I'd learnt that there had never been an openly transgender employee at the company. I wasn't just the new girl, I was a new type of girl altogether. I wondered if I was occasionally inspiring lunchtime talk – perhaps the reason so many people seemed to eagerly go out of their way to say hello. 'Have you met Mia yet? She's trans you know', someone in the finance department said, maybe. 'Oh, I saw a documentary about trans people. They're cool', their colleague could have replied. On the other hand, it could just have been that I was instantly recognisable, especially with my dark purple hair, and my colleagues were lovely, friendly people.

There was only one introduction that gave me a very peculiar vibe, a sense that this woman was very much not happy with my hiring. When being introduced to a small department nearby my own, a blonde-haired older woman narrowed her eyes as if I was deeply suspect. I gave her my most disarming smile but was led away by a colleague before I could say anything else. A week later, I was stood beside her as I filled up a bottle of water in the staff kitchen. 'Hello!' I said, with the same warm giddiness I had trained myself to use. Without a word back, she walked away. I was perplexed as I had seen her cackling and chatting gleefully with other colleagues. From observation, she had seemed like an approachable and cheery woman, apart from when she saw I was around. Another week went by and I found myself walking towards her, as she came from the other direction along a narrow corridor. Once again, I smiled as warmly as I could, as if I'd spotted a beloved old friend. This time I didn't get ignored. She visibly scowled before rolling her eyes and brushing by me. I couldn't help but lift an eyebrow and watch her strut away from me as I processed such an obvious snub. The first two instances I could dismiss as coincidences, but three out of three felt like a deliberate pattern. I went back to my desk and thought about what I could do. One option was to make it my mission to befriend her, to prove to her that I was a nice person. If she had a problem with me being trans, then I could accept the responsibility of being an ambassador for my people and show how tolerant and kind we were. Or I could report her to HR for thinly veiled harassment. In the end, I decided that neither option felt right, and instead I descended to her level, answering pettiness with my own brand of unnecessary spite. Whenever I saw her coming, I adopted the bitchiest face I could and ignored her existence. If she ever visited our office, I snubbed her back and struck up animated conversation with someone else, feigning I was having the greatest day of my life. I didn't tell anyone else how she was treating me; instead I just continued to wage a silent, vengeful war. It was absolutely not the mature or sensible thing to do but it sure made me feel better!

After a few weeks at the job, I was invited to take part in one of the equality meetings that I had heard about in my interview. This wasn't actually anything to do with the fact I was trans but just a general invitation. I arrived that afternoon to find a gigantic table ringed with people from all different parts of the company. As I quietly took a seat at the back, the meeting began. Across the hour, different equality-related topics were presented by the chairwoman and discussed, but none were to do with trans people. I had kept silent the whole time, feeling a little out of my depth as I was still getting to grips with how the company worked, but there was something relevant I had noticed. 'Our gender identity policy sucks,' I said. The whole room turned towards me, waiting for me to elaborate. I suddenly felt like there were a million eyeballs focused on me. 'It's really old fashioned and you can tell no trans person has ever looked at it. I think it needs to be simplified,' I continued. I had found the policy while snooping around on the company intranet, curious as to what protections I technically had by transitioning here. I'd been dismayed to find it full of bizarre suggestions and vague declarations. Although well meaning, it contained overly complicated recommended timeframes for how to inform people about transition, in what order to tell them, and when to return to work with a new identity. When it came to the topic of toilets, the wording implied surgery would be needed before access could be granted to the correct facility, which was especially maddening. It then ended with an awkward glossary of queer terms, half of which were now considered ancient, unsuitable, or offensive. After my outburst, a woman I didn't recognise thanked me for alerting her and implied she would take a look at it herself. I realised too late that it was perhaps not the best idea to have blurted out my opinion in such a blunt manner, but I hoped it might trigger a change down the line.

Just a day after the meeting I got an e-mail from the company's equality manager, inviting me to help her craft a completely new gender identity policy. When I showed her the state of the current one, she agreed that it was a mess. Together, we stripped out all references to surgery and unnecessary rules, replacing them with a simple and clear decree that an employee's transition, new pronouns, and choice of appropriate toilet would be respected and supported immediately. Although I hadn't encountered any issues at work due to being trans, I now knew exactly what my protections were, as I'd suggested them myself.

One thing that starting a job had necessitated was daily shaving. I had never been any good at growing a beard, sporting rather wispy and pathetic bristles in my university years, but I still had to shave every day if I wanted to avoid a stubbly face. Annoyingly, HRT does not stop facial hair growing for trans women – once puberty fires up those hair follicles, they won't stop producing. The solution is either laser hair removal or electrolysis. Laser is considered the faster and more efficient method of clearing up facial hair. However, it only works on dark hairs, ignoring white ones altogether. After weighing up my options and asking my Twitter support team for advice, I decided to pursue laser hair removal.

Among the many, many benefits of giving trans teenagers puberty blockers, one for trans girls is certainly the prevention of facial hair. It's a slog to get rid of it, both time consuming and expensive. If facial hair can be avoided in the first place, it saves countless hours and the need for pricey procedures. As there was a private hospital nearby that offered laser, I got in touch with them directly and explained my situation. They responded promptly and invited me for a patch test, where they would zap my skin and ensure that I wasn't going to have any adverse reactions. With the stories I had heard about laser, I was afraid of what was going to happen. I'd been told worrisome tales of trans women taking powerful opioid painkillers just to get through a session, while others had openly wept from the unbearable agony. I had always considered myself to have the pain tolerance of a three-year-old, panicking at the most mundane and mildly irritating discomfort. I suspected laser might be too much for me and that I'd have to just grow used to running a razor over my sensitive skin every morning.

The day of my patch test came and I arrived at a hospital far fancier than I had anticipated. Instead of sterile decor and outdated architecture, I walked down a lavish driveway and into a converted manor house. Stepping across plush carpet and passing polished oak furniture, I was directed to head to up to the next floor, with the receptionist explaining the nurse would collect me when it was time for my appointment. I then ascended a staircase so grand it felt like it belonged in a period drama, before arriving in a waiting room full of glass displays and arty posters advertising the clinic's services. My phone signal was entirely dead, cutting me off from Twitter, my go-to digital playground where I expended my nervous energy. I felt strangely isolated, knowing I was out of reach from my friends. I'd grown used to airing my anxieties there and depending on familiar faces to help assure me nothing too disastrous was going to happen. With nowhere to vent, I realised I was supposed to remove my makeup yet still hadn't done so. Without a mirror, I hunched in front of a glass cabinet and started to frantically wipe away foundation. 'Mia?' I looked to the doorway to see a young woman in a white nurse's outfit. 'Hello!' I said, as usual trying to remember to elevate my voice to a higher and softer pitch. She introduced herself as Rita, the woman who'd be doing my patch test and my monthly sessions if I decided to continue.

With a large, intimidating-looking machine in the corner, and an adjustable chair beside it, the treatment room doubled as an office. The first thing we did was to sit down and discuss the basics of the treatment. Rita explained that laser was very effective but would take 8–12 sessions to fully clear the area, due to the way that hair grew in cycles. Additionally, I wouldn't see any effect until around two weeks after the session, as that's when the hair would finally fall out, with new hair beneath to replace it. The worst part was that my face would have bubbled up with redness by the next morning, and it would be a week or so until the inflammation went away. As someone who was already self-conscious about her appearance, this felt like a particularly annoying side-effect. Apparently I had to look worse before I could look better.

When everything had been discussed, I hopped onto the chair and was handed a pair of blacked-out goggles to wear. Already unable to see anything, I closed my eyes and leant back, preparing myself for what was about to happen. 'Okay, here we go,' Rita said. In a flash of light, I felt a sharp, hot pain akin to being stabbed with a scalding hot needle. Surprised, I yelped in pain, prompting her to ask if I was ready for her to continue. 'Mmm-hmm,' I murmured, through clenched teeth. The light and pain flared again, and again, and again, as the nurse selectively picked a few small areas to test the laser's strength against my skin. The pain was bad. Surprisingly, it wasn't quite as horrific as I had steeled myself for, but it wasn't like anything I was used to feeling. I didn't cry, but a string of colourful curses passed through my mind as I waited for the steady stabbing session to end. 'And that's it,' Rita said, as she lifted the goggles from my eyes. 'That wasn't so bad,' I lied, as I shuffled over to collect my bag and check on my reflection. I had patches of bright red skin already, as well as comically smudged makeup where my eyes had watered while being held tightly shut. After arranging a follow-up session to check on the result, I headed for the bus stop and told Twitter the account of my awful and borderline traumatic evening.

As soon as I got home, I decided I was going to have a bath. I had heard it wasn't the wisest idea to grab a hot bath after laser, but since I'd only had a small session I decided to just risk it and let myself unwind. Slipping into the hot water, I started to think about the last few weeks. Relatively speaking, this new job had gone well. With the exception of one person, people seemed to like me, the work wasn't too hard, and I hadn't missed any time yet through illness or appointments. It was starting to take its toll a little though.

I was adjusting to the sudden loss of free time, while my body was craving extra sleep and all the food it could find. I had little time to myself anymore. My blog and personal projects had been halted altogether, with work and recovery taking up all my time. Laser presented a brand-new time sink, one that also put me in borderline agony. There'd once been a time when I considered trying to do PhD research alongside transition. Now that seemed laughably optimistic. The stress of transition was difficult enough by itself. In fact, I hadn't stopped to think about it, but transition was turning out to be extra difficult in ways I had overlooked. Surprising myself, I started to cry. I was overcome with a deep sense of helplessness. Transition suddenly felt like too much. Starting a job was stressful enough, but I was doing it with all the added quirks of being a newly out trans woman. Navigating all these problems was impossible.

After lying there in tears for what must have been at least a quarter of an hour, I heard a knock at the door. 'Yes?' I answered. To my own ears my voice sounded confident, successfully suppressing the emotional tremble beneath it. 'Mia? What's wrong? Can I come in?' It was Loretta, and apparently I wasn't as good at hiding my emotions as I thought. I made an affirmative hum and watched the door open to reveal Loretta's worried face. Her expression snapped into panic as she saw me laid there, submerged from the neck down and with bloodshot, teary eyes. She asked why I was upset, to which I stumbled into an overflowing explanation, a list of everything that had been building up. I talked about how work was stressing me out, that I hated how tired I felt all the time, how I was scared transition wasn't going to work, that living payslip to payslip was awful, and how laser had really, really hurt. Retreating to the bedroom, I curled into a ball and cried, again.

While munching on pizza later that evening, and watching one of my favourite superhero TV shows, I started to finally feel a little better. My mind was clearer – less scattered and foggy than it had been for days. Crying had been cathartic, a necessary release of building pressure. 'I guess that was also the hormones,' I said, looking to Loretta with an apologetic look. She laughed and reminded me that my body was undergoing a pretty radical change. Thanks to HRT, my second puberty had started. This emotional mood swing was just the first of many to come. 'Oh God,' I uttered with realisation. 'I'm a 27-year-old teenage girl.'

Chapter 12

PUBERTY, PART TWO

My first go at puberty wasn't very successful. Angsty music had just about got me through it, as a body I was ambivalent about became even more awkward and unfamiliar. It felt like I would spend my entire life in that awful school, forever surrounded by cruel bullies and apathetic teachers. Now that my hormone levels were shifting towards the cis female range, inverting from what they'd been my entire adult life, those same feelings of grumpy misanthropy returned. I found myself listening to moody and pessimistic music again, gravitating towards the theatrically gloomy lyrics of Black Sabbath and other bleak artists I'd drawn comfort from as a teenager. On the bright side, I had enough self-awareness this time to routinely find the entire thing quite hilarious. Although when in a self-pitying mood swing I had no patience for anyone who tried to assure me I was just being hormonal, afterwards I would be able to laugh off the absurdity of being in an angsty strop in my 20s.

Outside of my mood, other puberty stereotypes returned for a second act too. Namely, I couldn't stop eating. My appetite ballooned as I gobbled down high-calorie foods as if they were light snacks. I began bulk-buying sugary shortbread and munching through at least half a packet of it as my daily morning snack, but I was still unable to stop my greedy hunger from demanding I keep eating. Sick of always sneaking off to the canteen, I cleared my middle desk drawer at work and turned it into a dedicated snack drawer, filling it with biscuits and cheap chocolate. Getting through the day without a junk food fix was impossible. Meanwhile, if I wasn't eating I was busy sleeping. Although I'd been able to survive on a solid eight hours a night for most of my life, I now happily slept up to 12 hours if left undisturbed. This meant a significant portion of my weekends was spent recharging from the work week.

My post-laser crying session had opened the door for more emotional outbursts. I cried while watching movies, reading books, talking to friends, and even watching adverts on TV. When I watched *The Good Dinosaur*, a children's movie about talking dinosaurs that Loretta had bought for me as a gift, I spent approximately 80 percent of the film in tears. But crying was no longer an explosive and painful event; it was a satisfying and liberating experience. It was like I had grown up with a limiter on my emotions, blocking me from feeling anything too deeply – positive or negative – but finally it had been taken off. I was feeling things profoundly and meaningfully for the first time in my life, and I loved it.

It wasn't just my emotional state that was altering; physical changes took place too. I had begun to wear a bra as soon as I'd felt my first ache of chest pain, and although breast growth continued exceedingly slowly, it was a reminder that my body was moving towards what I had always wanted. Elsewhere I found that my butt had begun to pad out. I had always been someone who was particularly bony, and suddenly finding myself with a soft cushion beneath me was a welcome surprise. No longer did I fear the firmness of solid wooden chairs; every seat became a comfortable rest stop, thanks to my permanent pillow.

When I first started hormones, I tried to temper my expectations about changes to my face. Of course, I wanted to look more feminine. I also wanted to be pretty and for my reflection to match that idealised image of the soft and happy woman that I felt like inside. But I knew that expecting this result was dangerous. The trans community is full of divided opinions on the effects of HRT, and I especially noticed two different camps of thought. The first camp was one of positivity, celebration, and hope. People with that outlook proclaimed that HRT was a wonder drug; it would guarantee fantastic results and turn even the most masculine and grizzled-looking trans woman into a squishy and elegant woman. On the other hand, the opposing camp was much smaller but no less vocal. They were all about warnings and pessimism. I saw claims that HRT was vastly overrated, that going in with any expectations was setting yourself up for disappointment. I was scared of getting my hopes up too high and finding myself longing for something out of my reach. I'd learnt through experience that youth wasn't the sole important factor regarding HRT's effectiveness – that was a myth. The real key factor was luck. Those who had more traditionally feminine features to begin with seemed to have a much easier time reaching a result that made them happy. This, of course, made sense – oestrogen won't shave down bone or reshape a brow. Testosterone seemed to be a moderately safer bet for trans men, while the trans women I knew had a far wider range of results and satisfaction. Thus, when I started HRT, I found myself somewhere in the middle of those two camps, hoping for good results, but not expecting my idealised fantasy.

I decided that I would simply wait, and that I would do my best to accept whatever result I found myself with.

After six months of slapping on patches and popping anti-androgens, I was flicking through old photos after finding a cache on a forgotten USB stick. They'd been taken back when I'd started to explore my gender in private. My scratchy beard had gone by that point, but my dyed purple hair had just arrived, as well as a more notably feminine fashion sense. The oldest photo was barely two years old, yet I looked wrong. I couldn't point out exactly why I looked wrong but I knew that the person looking back wasn't quite me, not anymore anyway. My face looked longer and sharper in these photos. I'd grown used to the mirror showing me softer features and a different shape to my face altogether. I tried to contain my excitement as I realised what this meant: my face was changing; I was starting to look more feminine. I hesitated to celebrate this fact with friends, even on Twitter. I felt like this news was personal and special. I didn't want to risk being discredited and shot down by those who might disagree. Yet I still wanted a second opinion, albeit a gentle one. I asked Loretta to come look at the photos I had been poring over, doing my best to downplay why they were interesting. 'Wow!' her eyes widened at the photos of us from back before we headed south. With joy, she explained that she hadn't noticed how much I had changed until she had this before-and-after comparison in front of her. The changes weren't spectacularly dramatic but they were enough to have notably changed how I looked. It was enough to give me hope.

With time, the changes to my appearance only became more and more obvious. I began to take selfies on a near-daily basis, usually on my way into work. This wasn't for any cataloguing purposes or anything else beyond the fact that I now loved taking photos and sharing them with friends on social media. Where once I had loathed my appearance, I was now excited to show off how I looked that day.

Although selfies have a bad reputation among some – often demonised as being silly and self-indulgent – for trans people they're especially powerful tools of affirmation. When you grow up with dysphoria and a muddled sense of who you are, it's easy to have a natural aversion to photographs. But selfies put us in control, letting us carefully pose and pick how we're seen. When a trans person shares a selfie, they're saying they've found a way to appreciate how they look, and they're happy enough to make it public. It's a form of self-expression. Although I had grown up hating having my photo taken, I fell in love with selfies as my appearance continued to change into something that felt like my own. Sharing a regular photo became more than just a momentary celebration; it became a visual reminder that I had made personal progress. Unexpectedly, selfies became the most powerful tool for my self-confidence that I had ever had.

As I walked into work every morning, like clockwork I would glance at my reflection in that same glass building I had encountered when I came for my interview. Unlike that first time, where I was disheartened and demoralised, seeing myself in a swishing dress and with a feminine silhouette always boosted my mood and got my day started on a happy note. It was months into my job when I realised that the sense of satisfaction that I had every morning was actually pride, something I had rarely ever felt. In my young adulthood, I'd struggled with a disassociated sense of detachment from everybody else, I felt like a nebulous shape, undefined and expendable. But now I was grounded. My identity was tangible and real. I was Mia, a colleague, a friend, a partner, and a woman.

After I'd grown up struggling to make friends, always feeling like the shy and awkward kid, I had found that transition was turning me into someone sociable and outgoing. This had begun during my first summer on HRT, when I accepted offers to speak on panels at that year's Nine Worlds. In doing so, I became a part of the same convention that had significantly boosted my confidence and given me a safe place to express myself a year earlier. Speaking to an audience of fellow attendees, I was electrified by the rewarding sensation of making them laugh or seeing them turn into a sea of smiles and nodding heads. After finishing my third panel, where I'd talked about queer representation in pop culture, a young woman walked up to me and giggled nervously. I smiled at her and cheerily gave her a 'Hello', which prompted her to gush about how she thought I was 'really cool' and had loved the comments I'd made. I was so delighted to be praised like that, I felt like I was going to float off the ground. Before the panel I'd been terrified of having nothing to say, or of looking ridiculous next to the other panellists, but somehow people actually liked me. After the young woman had left, a middle-aged man stepped over and asked, 'What do you do?' I had to ask him to repeat the question as I had no idea what he meant. It turned out he wanted to know more about me and if I had a website or podcast he could check out. To say I was blown away would be an understatement. I'd struggled my whole life to shake off the feeling that I was failing to live up to everyone's expectations. Being different had left me ignored, afraid, and ostracised, but now what had made me an outcast in my youth was drawing people to me, and handing me new friends and opportunities.

This is one of the ironies I've noticed in how trans people are depicted versus how we actually live. The media delights in presenting trans people as shut-ins or strange outcasts. Although coming out as trans can undeniably damage our social lives and introduce new challenges, it also opens the door to a welcoming community of fellow queer people. Concurrently, presenting ourselves in a manner that finally feels authentic can often amplify our confidence. This makes it far easier to form new bonds, or repair old ones, than ever before.

While still at Nine Worlds, I was taking a break in the vendor room – a large hall full of stalls selling all kinds of geeky merchandise – when I spotted a familiar face. It was Andrea, a woman I hadn't seen for about three years. Andrea had been the manager of my local comic book shop around the time Loretta and I first met. Often, after university finished for the day, I would take a short train ride over to the next city. There I'd spend the rest of the afternoon chatting about Star Wars and superheroes, as Andrea sold action figures and comic books to people of all ages. We lost touch when she left the shop to find a job closer to home, and the last I'd heard she was working in a bank. I had actually spotted Andrea at my first Nine Worlds, back when I was still closeted to all but a handful of people. I had been torn between rushing over to tell her the exciting news about my gender, and hiding under a table. In the end I hadn't said anything, promising myself that I would catch her before the end of the convention, but ultimately missing my chance. This time I was determined to reintroduce myself.

Excitedly I approached Andrea's table and got her attention by calling her name. 'Hi Andrea! Do you remember me?' I asked with a nervous smile, unsure what was about to happen. She hesitated, clearly a little uncomfortable at not being able to place who I was. I told her what name

I used to go by and reminded her that I used to visit her comic book shop every week and that we often chatted about the newest Marvel releases. 'Oh!' delight exploded onto her features like a firework as she skipped around the table and wrapped me in a hug. I grinned and asked her how she was doing, to which she told me she'd left her stuffy office job and gone right back to managing a comic book shop. I gestured to my outfit and playfully told her I'd obviously made some changes too. I ended up missing the next round of panels as I spent the afternoon catching up with Andrea and trading excited thoughts on Star Wars tie-ins and recent comic book movies.

I would love to end this chapter now and imply that everything about my first six months on hormones was positive, but that wouldn't be honest. With these changes came new vulnerabilities too, from outside and from within. When chatting one evening on Twitter, I talked about the fact I used to be part of a collective of trans teenagers back on Gaia. To my shock, an acquaintance who I had followed and respected for years explained that she had been part of it too. Stunned, we traded information and confirmed that although never close friends, we had been part of the same community and likely interacted there over ten years ago. The next day that revelation was still swirling around my head. Memories were trickling back of that time, of how heavily I had depended on that community to combat the suffocating loneliness of being a closeted trans teenager. I acutely remembered being that scared girl, logging in every night to trade worries and reassurances with friends just like me. What I'd wanted more than anything was to transition, but in the end things worked out worse than I feared. Silently I got up from my desk, walked rapidly to the toilets, locked myself in a cubicle, and collapsed into tears.

Sitting in that cubicle I felt a crash of regret and longing at the unearthed revelation of what had happened. For years I'd fearfully and shamefully suppressed those memories for my own protection. I'd come to think of trans teenager Rebecca as a character, one that I vaguely remembered in a story I'd willingly forgotten. But she was me. I was Rebecca. I had gone through that time of intense anxiety, of being tantalisingly close to transition but still entirely out of its reach. I'd somehow endured the isolation of being separated from those friends, and the quashing rejection from my mother that had led to severing that lifeline. I'd never faced up to the full reality of what I'd been through until now, and it left me lost as to how to feel. The regret was undeniable. Knowing that perseverance would have led to a much earlier transition is something I'd already been struggling with. But I'd been reminded that it wasn't my fault; it was never something in my hands to begin with. For a young trans teenager to find a way to transition in that year, at that young age, and with the confused and unsupportive family that I had, it would have been a miracle. I might not even have survived the attempt. By transitioning now as an adult, one who had cast off insecurities along the way and discovered newfound confidence, I had assured I was stable and supported enough to finally transition on my own terms. I couldn't deny that, despite everything, I was proud of myself for making it here, even if my teenage self would have been hurt to learn the truth of how far away her transition was.

I've heard a few older trans people say that they're jealous of trans teenagers, specifically the ones with the clarity to know what gender they are when still in school or even before puberty hits. The implication is that they have an advantage in getting their transition over with early. But whenever I hear that claim, I always think of my own experience, and that of the other teenagers back on Gaia. In many ways, knowing I was trans made my life much harder. The ignorance of being the weird outcast kid was far preferable to the loaded knowledge that I needed to transition. Being trans is difficult at any age, but when you're under the control and watchful gaze of a rigid school system and parents who may outright disown you for being queer, it's a special kind of hell. Transitioning as an adult comes with its own extra challenges, but chances are you're much more emotionally and logistically equipped to handle them. Knowingly navigating the wrong puberty as a trans teenager is harrowing. I can't agree that it's universally better or worse to know at a younger age, because the consequences are radically different based on easch person's situation.

Although at this stage in my transition I now felt surer of myself than ever before, the general public often had no idea what to do with me. This first became clear while purchasing some new makeup on the high street one morning. While serving me, one cashier was asked to help fetch some more stock by a colleague. In response, with a gesture towards me, she explained 'I'll be there in a minute, I'm just helping this...' and paused. After a few awkward seconds of staring blankly at my face she finished with 'customer', and quickly looked away. I finished paying, stepped outside, and slumped into a fit of giggles. I realised what had happened. She'd hesitated on what noun to use as she'd been left unsure about what gender I was. Even in the unflattering and boring weekend clothes I'd stepped out in, I didn't look reassuringly enough like a man anymore. Soon this became a recurring trend, as cashiers and waitresses across the city deliberately avoided gendering me, never sure what the mixed signals of my appearance and voice were adding up to.

This is one reason I'm in favour of more trans visibility. Sympathetically, I do understand the viewpoint of some in the community who have expressed nostalgia for the earlier years of ignorance and invisibility, when the general public had little idea that transition was even a concept. But in those moments when I saw people generally unsure of what gender I was, I became grateful that some surely correctly concluded that I was transgender. I took comfort in knowing that since I presented myself in a traditionally feminine manner, it could be deemed likely I was a trans woman. Still, this wasn't a plan with any guaranteed success. Not long after the makeup incident, I walked to the reception desk of my doctor's clinic and was referred to as 'this gentleman' while wearing a black dress, colourful scarf, and pink lipstick. I found this much less funny. In the receptionist's defence, her fidgeting body language and hasty retreat afterwards at least allowed me to assume she might have reconsidered. But sometimes if people heard my voice before they saw me it was enough for them to assume I was male, and then whatever I was wearing couldn't always swing them back to the right answer.

Misgendering is a complicated topic to trans people as it intersects with so many other issues. Innocent misgendering by the general public can still be painful, as it's often taken as a sign that no matter the effort we may have put in, we're still seen as that old persona we're trying to leave behind. Someone in the street could innocently ruin a trans person's day by reading them as the wrong gender and openly using the wrong pronoun. By trying to keep my expectations low, I felt that I was minimising the hurt that misgendering was causing, but I'd be lying to say that it wasn't still disappointing.

Another memorable time was when I went to have my eyes tested. I'd worn a belted shirtdress over black leggings, but hadn't bothered with makeup beyond my foundation as I wasn't sure what type of tests were going to be done. I didn't think it'd be fair, or a good look for me, if I was going to end up smudging mascara all over testing apparatus. When I arrived, I was asked my name so the attendant could write it onto my eye-test form. Afterwards she handed me and the form over to a second attendant to perform the tests. The good news was at the end of the tests it was revealed I didn't need glasses. The bad news was the attendant had taken it upon themselves to fill out the rest of the form for me, where they had listed my gender as male. The effortlessness with which they had done so, with no thought to ask me or to leave it for myself to complete, was utterly depressing. Although I felt much happier with my appearance, evidently to many I still looked unambiguously male.

Out of everybody who misgendered me, it was children who could hurt me the most. Lacking manners and any social awareness, kids often gave rather obvious reactions to my appearance, showing zero tact. Over a period of a few months I was openly gawked at, became the subject of delighted laughter, and even once caused a child to grab his mother in frantic excitement and loudly exclaim that I looked like a boy, despite my lipstick and clothes. Those reactions from children were memorable because they were the most unfiltered. There was no agenda at play, they were just loudly speaking their minds and revealing that I didn't look how they believed a woman should. On good days, I was able to shrug these comments off, feeling like I was back at Nine Worlds and blissfully uninterested in what others saw. But on bad days they triggered dysphoria, scaring me into wondering if I'd ever look even remotely like I wanted to, and encouraging me to wear less attention-grabbing colours.

My apprehension about being misgendered made my first summer on HRT an occasionally awkward one. Although I dressed in pastel blouses, floral scarves, and smart dresses at work, on weekends I fell back on more casual outfits. I'd grown used to the gaggle of teenagers and sleepy commuters on my trips to and from work, but weekends were wild, with unfamiliar faces. I avoided wearing my loud weekday outfits out of apprehension that they would draw attention and invite ridicule. Instead, I wore buttoned dresses in muted greys and blacks. When I made my first trip to the beach in summer, planning a day of lying on the sand and enjoying the warm weather, I'd only been on HRT for four months. My intention was to wear a light cotton dress to keep cool, but that morning my dysphoria swept all my confidence away. I felt ridiculous when I saw my reflection. I didn't look like the cute woman that I'd wanted to see; I saw an awkward man. I took off my dress and instead wore a light, feminine t-shirt paired with a familiar pair of dark jeans. I was halfway to the beach when I started to feel silly and realised I'd let fear get the better of me. When I arrived, I saw people wearing all kinds of outfits. I even saw somebody playing football in their pyjamas. As I sat roasting in tight jeans, women in dresses and bathing suits splashed happily in the sea. I wondered how it would feel to not have this dysphoria or this fear of misgendering and attention always barging into my life like a rude guest.

The other type of misgendering I came across was when it was done maliciously online. This intentional misgendering was much more common, but thankfully had no sting to it whatsoever, because I knew it had no basis in reality. Being a trans woman with an online presence on social media, I became increasingly aware that there were a lot of people who wanted to take time out of their day specifically to hurt others. This usually entailed addressing me with the wrong pronouns on purpose, such as posting a link to something I'd said and then using the word 'he' as much as possible. I assumed the intention was that by misgendering me they'd cause me to remember in horror that I was trans and not a woman to them. Other tactics I saw claimed that I was simply a gay man in denial, despite the fact I was happily in a relationship with a woman. Elsewhere, I was mocked for wearing such an obvious wig in my photos, when they were talking about my real hair. I did find that one particularly amusing though, as I wondered who would buy a wig with roots so desperately in need of re-dyeing like mine regularly did.

More than anything, these people reminded me of school bullies – jerks out to lazily impress their peers and recite whatever cruel quip they had already preloaded in their arsenal from last time. As everything they said was clearly coming from a blanket-wide hate of all trans people, it was hard to be insulted and much easier to simply be bored of such harassment. The fact I had been afraid of being dogpiled by strangers now seemed ridiculous. It was simply dull background noise, something that could easily be ignored. The more my online profile grew, the greater the lengths these types of people went in their attempts to hurt me. I once found a profile of someone who was screenshotting the abusive messages they had sent me and was sharing them to their own followers as evidence, using me as a prop in their quest for kudos. Presumably he was trying to prove how edgy and controversial he could be. Another time someone left a ridiculously long, rambling comment on my personal blog, trying to use pseudo-science and techno-babble to goad me into debating them over whether trans people were actually just mentally ill. Instead, I didn't even bother to read the entire thing, deleting the comment after I'd skimmed enough to get the gist and never bothering to respond. Memorably, I was once aggressively accused of being a Russian spy, someone out to 'de-gender' the West through pro-trans propaganda. Although a lot of these messages can be laughed off, I have received some truly twisted ones over time. After posting an interconnected thread of messages promoting pride and self-love, I received a long set of replies back from a single person, promising that they were going to hunt down trans people and physically hurt them, to try and specifically counteract the positivity I was encouraging. Another time, someone said that if their young son turned out to be trans, they would 'beat it out of them' so they couldn't end up like me. Messages like that served as grim reminders that some people utterly despised trans people for absolutely no reason, and there was nothing I could do to change how they felt.

The moment I realised I had become truly desensitised to targeted hate was when I was messaged by a representative from the police, who had seen me discussing the type of abuse I'd recently received. They wanted to know if I'd like help to pursue lawful action against any of the originators. I explained that I appreciated the offer but I was used to abuse, and since most of it originated from international and anonymous throwaway accounts, I didn't see much point in trying to track them down. It would be like taking months to try and swat a single flea in a swarm of thousands of identical pests. I didn't want to expend any more energy on them than I'd already lost.

With everything I've said, I think it's important to explain that I do hesitate to talk so flippantly about online abuse. I've seen close friends become the target of much more organised harassment campaigns of disturbing intensity. A loose stream of angry and illiterate messages is easy to ignore, compared to a barrage of letters, phone calls, and explicit death threats. I was lucky in that the abuse against me remained online and never escalated to something I couldn't escape by shutting off my phone and stepping outside.

Encounters that left me feeling physically in danger in my daily life were rare, but unfortunately not entirely absent. Although the confusion around my gender identity could mildly amuse me in shops and restaurants, there was one incident in particular that reminded me that it had safety implications too. One weekend I had travelled to a nearby town to visit an animal sanctuary. After a fun afternoon taking photos of goats and pigs, I was on a silent rural train platform with Loretta and Tilley. The three of us were stood loosely together, each tapping away on our phones or taking photos of the scenic surroundings, when we were approached by a towering man with a cigarette in his hand. 'Got a lighter?' he asked, leaning in a little uncomfortably close to me. 'Sorry,' I responded, trying to sound as friendly and upbeat as possible. After also getting nothing but shaking heads from Loretta and Tilley, he sauntered back to the other side of the platform. Despite the smile I had forced on, I was feeling nervous. I'd got a strangely arrogant vibe from his body language and I hoped he was now going to stay away from us. Making things worse, there was nobody else around at all. The station itself was little more than a single platform amongst silent surroundings. The would-be smoker was so tall and stockily built, it looked like he could tear me in half as a warm-up stretch. I tried to hide the worry from my eyes as I noticed he was ambling right back towards me. 'Are you sure?' he asked, with a doubtful tone, clearly implying he suspected I was holding out on him and had a lighter hidden away somewhere. 'I've never smoked, sorry,' I shrugged, again trying to look pleasant and at ease. He narrowed his eyes at me with such intense suspicion that I prepared myself to be violently frisked. Leaning down to my level, so close I could smell the smoke on his clothes, he asked another question: 'Are you a boy or a girl?' It took me so completely off-guard, a nervous giggle was the only response I could muster. I had imagined this scenario before – being directly asked to my face what my gender was. I had always pictured myself theatrically announcing that I was transgender, before strutting away with pride. But now here I was, with someone twice my size staring me down. The only thought that entered my mind was an alarming desire to de-escalate the situation.

Admitting the truth to this stranger felt like a potentially dangerous idea, but I had no guarantee that a lie would solve the situation either, even if I could swallow my pride enough to tell one. 'Does it matter?' It was Tilley who responded, with brows narrowed enough to rival the smoker's own. Now it was his turn to laugh. After his rough bark of surprise, he shrugged, 'I guess not.' Seemingly satisfied, he left us alone. Discreetly, but with immense relief, I thanked Tilley for deflecting the question. It had been a small and fairly quick encounter but it had downright frightened me. I'd heard so many stories of trans people being violently assaulted by men, often arising from encounters that had started just like that one. I realised that all of my pride and courage over being transgender was essentially worthless. If I was attacked by someone of that stature when on my own, I'd be powerless to change the outcome.

One of the things I grew weary of, as my transition trucked on, was witnessing the breadth of male privilege. I don't just mean privilege in the obvious sense of higher pay and jeans with pockets, but the subtle advantages too. Later in this chapter I'll cover my more nuanced thoughts on gendered privilege in relation to trans people, but I'm happy stating now that trans women are definitely victims of male privilege too. The first time I worked as tech support for an event at work, I found myself helping someone higher than me on the corporate food chain. I saw what she was trying to do as she tinkered with the computer at the front of the huge speaker's room. As it was hooked up to a projector in the ceiling, everything she was doing was duplicated onto a huge cinema-sized screen covering the wall. As I inched over to this person who probably had the authority to sack me with ease, she spotted me and explained she was struggling with the video feed options. In response, I blurted out what the answer was, knowing it wasn't too complicated and I could quickly take care of it. Yet she eyed me with suspicion. 'Is Samuel coming?' she asked, referring to one of my male colleagues. 'I think so,' I replied, not quite sure what she was getting at. 'We should wait for him,' she decided, divisively. A few minutes later, Samuel arrived and received the same hasty explanation of the problem. He suggested the identical solution I had offered just moments ago. 'Good idea,' she said, as the two strode over to the computer to fix it together, leaving me staring at their backs. I was stunned. I'd been completely ignored and was given no credit whatsoever for suggesting the solution earlier. It was only when a male colleague brought it up that it was deemed a good idea. I thought this might be a one-off, but I saw it again in other ways, especially when running events. Regularly, I would be overlooked or second-guessed in favour of male colleagues. I was virtually invisible. While men were assumed to be technical masters, responsible for keeping everything running smoothly, attendees seemed to see me as a seat-filler or someone who had wandered in by mistake.

Elsewhere, I noticed my personal space had become worthless. As an adult, I'd never been touched against my will (except for the odd surprise hug from friends). It was like going around with an invisible force field on. But with transition I realised it'd been shut off. Colleagues, superiors, and strangers would touch my arm, tap my shoulder, or pat my back as a casual gesture in conversation. This gave me mixed feelings. I felt strangely validated and patronised at the same time. Elsewhere, there was less ambiguity; some strangers had no respect for my space whatsoever. When waiting for friends in a busy pub, a middle-aged man took me by the shoulders from behind and steered me out of his way, like a mannequin on wheels. It was bizarre to realise that this invisible bubble around me had gone, just from the perception of what gender I must be. Evidently, men were perceived to have valuable personal space, while women had none. The only advantage – if it can be considered that – is that suddenly everybody expected me to go ahead of them. Many times I stood awkwardly waiting for a man to hop onto a bus or into an elevator first, while he repeatedly insisted I precede him with a sweeping hand gesture and a smile. Once a middle-aged man bowed and signalled so dramatically, I wondered if he had mistaken me for a princess. After a while, I stopped waiting for men to go first and started to dart quickly ahead, if for no other reason than to avoid another stalemate of politeness.

As time went on, the novelty of noticing these little changes and affirmations started to wear thin. I still often felt that I was usually in a gender-dead zone. My worry was that I would be here forever, always seen as a confusing unknown, or even a man, unless I spent time fixing my makeup and wearing an overtly feminine outfit to unlock the correct reactions. But even that came with no guarantees as my facial structure was still quite masculine, something that HRT could only do so much for. Ironically, I had inherited my mother's wider, more masculine jaw, and not my dad's narrow feminine one. Had I taken after my male parent, I may have looked more feminine. Instead, it seemed like I had all the masculine features of both parents. I imagined my future if this was the end, if this was the extent of my changes. I'd always be correcting people, always having to expect to be seen as male by strangers. It would get exhausting.

Currently, options do exist for trans women who want to take more drastic steps to change their face. This is dubbed 'facial feminisation surgery', often shortened to the amusingly appropriate FFS. These procedures are intended to undo the effects of teenage puberty. What people specifically get done depends on their own face, but it includes options such as brow lifts, lip fillings, and even a trachea shave. The downside is that such surgery costs a small fortune. When looking into my options, I found that getting a round of changes done on my face would cost considerably more than I made in a year. Although it may be an option open to some trans women, many of us will never see that sort of money or get the opportunity to have that type of surgery.

I've said a few times over the last couple of years that I believe trans liberation means an end to 'passing', something that has received mixed responses from friends. But to clarify, I don't mean that no trans person should ever strive to be, or take joy from, looking like they're cisgender, I just mean that they shouldn't have to. If we can reach a place where nobody's gender is assumed based on a best fit guess, then it would do wonders for trans people. Until every one of us can walk down the street and not worry that people might harass or misgender us because of how we look, then we've not achieved trans acceptance. Anything less is only an agreement to accept trans people who fit within current cisnormative expectations of gender. That's not liberation; that's mandatory assimilation.

In terms of my clothes, I had recently been heading to work with a more conventionally 'girly' aesthetic than I'd ever had. One morning after applying soft pink lipstick, I put on my new pink coat, then with pink-painted fingernails I popped in my pink earbuds and grabbed a pair of cheap, pink, plastic sunglasses. I then saw my reflection and froze. When I had attended university, I had seen particular feminist friends rallying against pink in defiance of how everything from childhood toys to DIY tools would be drenched in it if marketed to women. Following their lead, I had adopted the same anti-pink point of view. Without realising it, I had clearly abandoned my aversion to pink along the way and entirely embraced it. That day, I was covered in pink. It wasn't the result of intentional coordination but simply arose from the laws of probability, given how many of my outfits now came in variations of it. Despite my conflicted thoughts, I liked how I looked. The ridiculous boldness of the outfit was part of the appeal. It was cute and silly, but I was suddenly self-conscious too. A little voice in my head, whether dysphoria or anxiety I wasn't sure, whispered that the average person would think the pink was overcompensation. I suddenly became worried that I was going to be judged as a caricature, someone dressing this way in an embarrassing attempt to look stereotypically feminine, to specifically outweigh my masculine features, and match a childish understanding of how women looked. Nevertheless, I was now running late for the morning bus and had no time to change. With doubts still rattling in my head, off I went.

Later that day, for the first time, I felt uncomfortable and exposed when walking back home. I'd made the same trek dozens and dozens of times, covering the short distance from the bus stop to my front door in dresses and skirts, never really caring that I stood out by virtue of being a trans woman. But that day I did care. I was still thinking about my presentation and how I was appearing to people. In the midst of my worries, a teenage boy passed me by. Behind my pink frames I saw him glance at me, quizzically. Immediately, I wondered what he thought, which made me continue to feel conspicuous. Eventually, I got home, flopped onto my bed, and thought a little bit about what just happened. Why, for the first time in a long while, had I felt so out of sorts with my presentation? Why was I noticing someone looking at me when I never usually bothered to pay attention? Was the outfit really too much? No. I realised pretty quickly that it was my own fault – not for what I'd chosen to wear, but because I'd doubted myself; because I had not only let myself care what others thought about me and my gender, I'd overanalysed my own outfit due to inherited transphobic thinking.

My anxiety over my outfit that day had come from something I was hearing at the time, and have continued to hear since: specifically, the claim that trans people's understanding of gender is inherently weaker than that of cis people, and that our gender is something we perform in conflict with the way we were raised and what came naturally to us. This is most evident when looking at how our culture chooses to show trans people in the media. Trans women are often shown slipping into high heels, pulling up tights, or putting on makeup. Meanwhile, trans men are presented as hyper-masculine, with the media focusing on them building muscles or growing facial hair. Documentaries in particular delight in showing trans women and men undergoing surgery as a final validation of gender. This all underlines a dehumanising belief that trans people are on a journey to become their 'desired gender', and the physical modifications to conform to stereotypes are what authenticate this. Worse still, the implicit meaning is that by design we're either actors or frauds, and remain the gender we were assigned at birth beneath these changes, or at least until their 'completion'. But that's all nonsense. These beliefs only exist because of the sensational lust for dramatic before-and-after demonstrations, ones that trans people can, incidentally, provide when you dilute our experiences down to surface changes and strip away the depth of our humanity and validity for a wider audience. It's much less scandalous to present the truth about us: that the genders of trans people are valid regardless of physicality. Likewise, how a trans person's gender matches or clashes with traditional expectations of masculinity and femininity is irrelevant, and varies from person to person.

Despite knowing that my identity as a woman wasn't ratified by my outfits or what other people thought of me, in the year before I started HRT it had still felt like a small victory that I had dressed in blacks and purples. It was an anxious 'gotcha' moment against the transphobes who I saw claiming that every single trans woman adorned herself in pinks, lace, and florals. There was a small twisted joy in having quietly proved them wrong. I had found a way to comfortably express myself as a trans woman without having followed their patronising allegations. But such a view had been inherently misogynistic on my part. By ignoring traditional 'girlish' femininity and specifically embracing its antithesis as if it was somehow superior, I had still been conforming to sexist beliefs that pink and other stereotypical aesthetics for women were inherently puerile. Now that I'd found myself with a surprising penchant for pink, I was forced to confront the remains of my former toxic belief. Naturally, I accepted that expressing traditional femininity was entirely valid in all its forms, even on me. It's our cisnormative society that demonises, discourages, and belittles certain expressions in particular contexts, but ultimately however anybody wants to express themselves should be considered worthwhile, regardless of whatever stereotypes they're working with or against.

The way that trans women in particular face scrutiny for their femininity is tied into the sexist beliefs that masculinity is inherently superior to femininity. To conventional society, a trans woman transitioning is considered an example of someone 'downgrading' and choosing to take up frivolous pursuits, instead of utilising the privilege and opportunities that being assigned male at birth provided. But the idea that trans women ever had male privilege is a lazy claim that ignores the nuance of our identities. Male privilege comes from traditional cisnormative understandings of binary gender; it is a concept that was never intended to account for what trans people experience. In my case, if I reaped the benefits of being seen as male, it was joyless and at the cost of my mental health. It's very difficult to look at all the time I lost in misery and denial as a time where I was rolling in privilege. I'd actually spent my life to date longing to express myself with femininity in ways that I was unable to, specifically because I was being perceived as male. Any advancements and accolades were utterly worthless to me; they were dwarfed by dysphoria.

All that said, did I benefit during my pre-transition years in terms of physical safety by being seen as male? Undeniably, at times, yes; it would be naive to think that there weren't times when I would have been in more danger had I been read as female. However, I was also bullied and the victim of violence specifically because it was socially acceptable to hurt me. I couldn't blend in with boys at school and they knew I was different, but not different enough to escape punishment. Had I been born a cisgender girl but retained the same personality, those boys wouldn't have treated me that way. However, I would have faced challenges, albeit different ones. Therefore, it's impossible for me to say whether I have experienced male privilege without contorting the context of my gender. Have I benefited from white privilege? Dyadic privilege? Able-bodied privilege? Yes, yes, and yes. As I wrote in the Introduction to this book, intersections of identity absolutely play a part and it's important for me to own up to the advantages I've had. But I find male privilege in particular a pointless lens in which to try and view the trans community, especially trans women. To fit its framework, you'd need to distil our diverse and complex experiences with simplistic assumptions, which invalidates the entire point of using this perspective to begin with as you'd no longer be looking at the truth.

A concept that is similar to male privilege and which is also routinely used as a weapon against trans women is 'male socialisation'. This claims that trans women cannot truly be women because of how they were raised. Making any sweeping allegation of what it's like to grow up as a trans woman, in a supportive or defamatory manner, is dangerous. Like cis girls, trans girls encounter all kinds of different upbringings as a result of everything from parental expectations to the natural diversity of childhood interests. But to use my history as one example of what it is like to be a trans girl who everyone was treating like a boy, you can see from earlier chapters that I did not exactly have the typical upbringing of a cisgender boy (granted, I did not experience my youth in the manner that cisgender girls do either). But to even make those statements I have to massively generalise and bundle the childhoods of every cis woman and every cis man into two distinct piles. It seems sloppy and silly to imply there's that much similarity while simultaneously that there's a notable distinction from everybody of the other gender. Furthermore, is the way we were raised really what defines our gender identity? Is a cis woman only the way she is because she was 'socialised' as a girl as a child? Of course not. Such a claim positions children as ignorant clay, moulded into their gender and passively unaware of what's going on around them or the context of their own actions.

The same socialisation theory is also touted as an example of how trans women have to perform femininity and cover up their natural inclinations that developed in childhood. But the only gendered expectations I have ever artificially performed are masculine ones, such as my attempt to fit in with boys and avoid criticism from my peers and teachers as a child. The parts of my behaviour that would have been deemed feminine, such as my enjoyment of princess stories and my high level of empathy, are the same things that came to me without any thought or effort. I knew I was supposed to avoid these feelings, even though I didn't want to, and I did so to survive. Throughout the rest of my pre-transition life, I continued to suppress the parts of myself deemed feminine and covered them with mimicked masculinity. I only openly exposed the interests and inclinations that meshed with the expectations upon me. The result was an exterior and presentation that didn't entirely reflect who I really was. The constant comic book t-shirts and the rock music persona I embraced were an exaggerated performance of a smaller part of myself, embellished to mask the multifaceted tastes I actually had. If there had been any performance in my personality, it was back there in the past where I pretended to be a man. Now that I was months into transition, I was peeling away these unnecessary forms of protection and discovering what the rest of my tastes really were, while expressing myself openly at last.

Essentially, the arguments that ask us to inspect the behaviour and tastes of trans women, and view them as inauthentic women or as men, are fundamentally flawed. They're drenched in transphobia. Their goal isn't to understand our lives, but to formulate an excuse to separate us from other women and define us as undeserving. Once I accepted that rebelling against these beliefs in my presentation was as pointless as it would've been to conform to them, I accepted that whatever my tastes turned out to be, they were valid. Because regardless of being transgender, I was a woman. I deserved to allow womanhood to exist outside of that context, and without analysing its origin to measure authenticity.

Chapter 13

HOMECOMING

If you're in Wales, then signing up for a GIC feeds you onto London's waiting list, as ridiculously there is no Welsh GIC at all. But in England you're free to sign up for whichever of the seven English clinics you want to attend. You're not funnelled into any by your postcode or region. Of course, they all generally have terrible waiting lists, so people often balance their projected waiting time against how far they will have to travel. It's not unusual for someone to skip their local GIC and try for something with a shorter queue. That's what I did when I asked for my original referral, choosing somewhere that was a little further away but with a much shorter waiting time. But that was before I moved across the country. Now I was approximately 250 miles away from that clinic.

As summer came to an end, I finally got the letter I had been waiting for. The GIC had arranged an appointment to see me the following month. At this point, I looked at the cost of pulling off the round trip with minimum time off work, and panicked. Earlier I had said I would worry about this issue later, and now that it was later I was indeed worrying. It was going to be very expensive and tricky to get up there – a city just a stone's throw from my hometown

– and straight back down here for work the next day. I then considered something I should have been asking about earlier: Could I transfer to a new GIC without losing my place in the queue? I wondered if by arriving at the front of the queue, I could now have my treatment rearranged at a nearby clinic. That would save me a lot of trouble. I asked the two nearest GICs if I could potentially see them instead, and both said no. Because GICs are isolated and independent, with their own method of care and even entirely different appointment processes, their waiting lists are considered entirely independent. People like me who've moved away by choice or circumstance during their time on the list have no choice but to make the trek back.

Since the last time I saw my parents, things had got worse. After I got my job and started to settle in, I sent them a message stressing that my transition was now properly underway. I made it clear that nobody in my life knew me as anything other than Mia and I was moving forwards, so it was important to me that they used the right name. I received a message back that they were struggling to deal with this, a revelation that I suspected meant they'd still been hoping I'd change my mind. Since that time, I had barely heard anything from them. Their phone calls had abruptly stopped and text messages were whittled down to nothing. Because of this, I didn't have high expectations, but perhaps foolishly I did hope they had slowly grown used to the idea of who I'd become while I was away. Staying with them when I went to my appointment felt too risky, while a hotel was an indulgence I couldn't afford. The remaining option was to stay a short train ride away from the clinic with Debi, Loretta's mother, who lived in a flat with her boyfriend.

With Debi's kind offer to take us in, I travelled back up the country with Loretta as we tried to turn the trip into a sort of mini-homecoming holiday. I was still worried about the time and money that would need to be sunk into these appointments, but I had convinced myself that there was no point in worrying about future consequences. I had one appointment, so for now I should just focus on attending it. In a way, it was just like everything else about my transition – I was only worrying about the step I was currently taking, and had decided I'd figure out what to do next when I had to. In terms of taking the time off work, I had hoarded holiday days in expectation of this very event. Now that it had arrived, I sprinkled extra days off on either side of the appointment, ensuring we had the time to travel without rushing up and down the country.

When the view out of the window turned from a rainy motorway into rolling northern hills and familiar urban landmarks, I felt sick. Although I could have blamed my uneasiness on travelling on a turbulent coach for eight hours, I knew it was the price of returning to the source of so many bad memories. Instinctively, I felt like I was going back in time, reverting to who I'd been. I had wanted to leave this place behind for good and focus on the future, but ironically it was my transition that had lured me back. Suddenly, having arranged to stay here extra days felt like an abominable idea, as all I wanted to do was flee back home to the coast.

I hadn't actually met Loretta's mother since coming out to her as trans, which had taken place over the phone some months previously. This meant that when we arrived at her flat it would be the first time she'd see me using my new name and presentation. I was a little bit nervous about her slipping up on pronouns or dropping my old name into conversation by mistake, but from the moment she greeted us at the door neither of those things happened. We arrived to an incredibly warm welcome. Debi seemed thrilled to have us staying with her and she'd even made up the guest bedroom especially for us, meaning we had our own space for the duration of the trip. Knowing there was a bedroom to retreat to, and someone ecstatic to see us, did a lot to ease my regret at returning, but I was still eager to get the appointment over with.

Although Loretta's mother lived relatively close to the GIC compared to us, it still required a very early start to get there on time. I rolled out of bed the next morning and into the first taxi of the day as the sun was still rising. I had expected to be nervous but I actually felt fairly relaxed. Having done so much reading on GIC appointments over the last two years I knew it was unlikely anything could surprise me. I'd also recited my history of 'gender variance' so many times to friends and doctors alike, I could confidently recite it in my sleep.

Next up was a train. I was travelling during commuting hours, so the carriage was full of formally dressed workers looking just as sleepy as me. The train itself was so rundown it was practically a glorified tin can. While I retreated into my familiar classic rock albums, courtesy of noise-cancelling headphones, I caught the eye of a man staring directly at me. He had that same curious but judging look that I'd seen before, an expression that said I looked just a little too queer for his liking. I braced myself for another awkward interaction, but the train thankfully arrived at his stop before he had a chance to say anything. Being back up here in this part of the North I felt more exposed and less safe than I had at home by the sea. I wasn't sure whether that was based on an accurate assessment, and this really was a more intolerant part of the country, or if it was an imagined danger summoned by bad memories of growing up nearby. Either way, I avoided eye contact with anyone else for the rest of the journey, keeping my nose pointed down at my Twitter feed as the train zipped through the countryside.

After taking the train, I had another taxi to grab before I arrived at the GIC itself. The clinic was situated in the suburbs as part of a bigger hospital – just one of many specialist clinics there. Once I'd navigated the maze-like layout, I tried the GIC door handle and found it locked. I was early but I wasn't that early, surely. Beside the door was a button, which I presumed must be linked to an intercom. After a moment, a voice responded and asked what I wanted. Suddenly very self-conscious of the pitch of my voice, I leaned down to the speaker and explained that I had an appointment soon. The door clicked upon and I walked inside to an empty but spacious waiting room. Covering the walls were pictures of smiling trans people with feel-good slogans and messages of support beneath. I popped down on a seat and settled in for what was probably going to be a long wait. I had imagined myself sitting shoulder to shoulder with other trans people, but there was nobody else in the waiting room. You wouldn't think from the empty halls and a dozen vacant seats that this place had a waiting list of well over a year. As I'd been trying to counteract my natural inclination to always arrive late, I'd shown up an hour before my appointment. So not only was there nobody to chat to, I had a lot of time to fill. Thankfully, Twitter once again provided me with something to do until the doctor collected me.

This appointment had been 18 months in the waiting, but the result was very anti-climactic. I was led to a small doctor's office, where I was asked to give a rundown of my situation. I explained who I was, that I was already on HRT, had changed my name early that year, and had come prepared with a letter from my last doctor. The letter specifically stated that after being assessed it was very evident that I was trans and in good mental health. The doctor scanned the letter while I waited patiently for her reaction. My hope was that all my preparation would help me cut through some of the upcoming hurdles and get right to the treatment part. However, the doctor sympathetically explained that although the letter was useful, and she trusted the doctor's opinion, it wouldn't change what would happen next. Regardless of my situation, I was to be assessed, multiple times. After two different doctors had heard my story, I was to meet a nurse for a physical examination. The three of them would then meet to discuss my case. In doing so, they'd determine whether I should be diagnosed with gender dysphoria (and therefore be allowed HRT) or whether I needed time in counselling first. The whole process would take months, at least up to half a year. Until I had that diagnosis I would not be eligible for any treatment or approved for any further waiting lists. I had walked in with low expectations, but even so, this was disappointing.

I asked if there was anything I could do to speed things up, especially considering that appointments were so tricky for me to get to, but there wasn't. Despite being told I was a 'straightforward case', it would not change anything – nobody got to skip the assessment process. Everybody would be measured in exactly the same way, with set mandatory appointments, no matter what. Therefore, whether I liked it or not, I would now be slowly assessed and sometime next year I would be approved for treatment, assuming I was deemed trans by the panel. The first part of my treatment would be the exact same HRT that I was already taking; the next part would be laser hair removal, which I also was already getting. I pointed out how bizarre it was to be measuring my suitability for something I was already doing, and had been doing for almost the entire year. Although the doctor herself was understanding of my situation, and could see the ridiculousness of it, she explained there was no way around it. It wasn't her call. Rules were rules.

My appointment worked as a depressingly strong example of trans healthcare. We're often treated as if we need to be protected. We don't get to explain what treatment we need. We have to be examined to make sure we're not just confused, or even lying. We can beg and cry and show all the evidence we have, but it rarely changes anything. Despite statistically insignificant percentages of trans people who feel any sort of regret, transition is treated as high risk. In my time as part of the trans community, I have never met anybody who started to transition and then declared that they had made a mistake and weren't trans. I did know one non-binary trans person who had intended to transition with HRT, then decided they wouldn't go that far but would keep their new pronouns. I do not know anybody who has cancelled their transition altogether, although I did know a trans woman who came out and started to transition, stopped, then promptly started again, which is a completely understandable thing to do. With so much of society making it difficult to be a trans person, it's natural to want to quit. But once you do, that's when you remember how bad dysphoria gets when it's not being treated. To pretend to be someone you're not is agony when dysphoria demands to be appeased. It's one reason that for the legion of trans people who seek out HRT, overwhelmingly they proceed to take it for the rest of their lives.

Despite how few people stop transitioning, myths about 'detransitioners' are rife. But a closer look at these cases often reveals the reason why these people stopped transitioning: cis people. Whether stunningly unsupportive family or violent members of the public, it seems that the primary reason to stop transitioning is transphobia and harassment. That's a huge difference from someone suddenly realising they're not actually trans, which is how the media often spin it. As with many things in transgender-related discourse, when it comes to people who have cancelled their transition the truth is disrespectfully warped and weaponised to create a malicious controversy where none actually exists.

Before leaving the GIC, I walked to the receptionist's window and waited to be seen as I wanted to have a word with them. An apathetic young man about my own age eventually came to the window and looked at me expectantly. I explained that the doctor I'd just seen had said I should request a note be made in my file – something to the effect of a request to bundle my appointments together when appropriate. That was the one accommodation I had been offered. When I pointed out that I lived down on the coast, the doctor told me I should make this request to make sure I didn't ever make a 500-mile round trip just for a ten-minute chat. At this the receptionist laughed in my face and shook his head. Bluntly, he stated that they didn't offer that service and everybody would have to arrive whenever their appointment slot opened up. I pleaded my case and the unique nature of my situation, but I was met with a shrug. With no other reason to hang around in the deserted waiting room, I walked out and prepared to make the morning's journey in reverse.

On the return train ride to Debi's flat, I reflected on the mixed feelings I'd been left with. I was now in the GIC system and this was progress. But it was progress towards treatment that I already had. I was essentially making an investment of time and money to save some other time and money down the line. It was absurd to think that I'd read countless hysterical hit-pieces against trans people claiming that we sought out medical care on a whim, when this was the reality. By the GIC's loose projection, I'd be granted HRT around two and a half years after initially seeing my GP about it. The idea that the NHS was irresponsibly urging people to transition was laughable. Nobody who jumped through all these hoops, and convinced this many people to let them continue, could be transitioning as a lark.

While I was still back in the North, I decided I wanted to try and visit my parents. Truthfully, I wanted to visit the family dog more than anything else, but reconciling with my parents felt like the sensible and mature thing to do while I was up there. Max was an adorable chocolate-coloured cocker spaniel who had been a combination of friend, dependant, and patient listener whenever I had stayed with my parents. When my relationship with Nicole combusted, I had spent long nights binge-watching Star Trek while Max nestled up against me. During my time at college he had bounded up the stairs every morning and leapt into bed with me, waking me up by frantically licking at my face. He'd grown used to learning what it meant whenever I dragged a suitcase down the stairs and headed out the door. On the day I left for the coast, he had whined with such sadness and love in his giant eyes that I considered calling the whole thing off. The fact I couldn't communicate how much I wanted to bundle him into my arms and take him with me caused me to shed more than a few tears over the last few months.

Once back at the flat, I sent a text message to my dad saying that Loretta and I were nearby. I mentioned that we were free for the next couple of days and we'd like to come over and visit if we could. Beating me to my next question, he offered to pick us up that evening in his car and take us directly to the house. Nervous but excited, I said that sounded great and mentally prepared myself to see my parents for the first time in almost a year.

The drive over was fairly casual in tone, as my dad listed off all the family incidents and dramas that had taken place over the last few months. Although nothing too serious had happened, with everybody at least still alive, there'd been plenty of health scares and family feuds while we were away. Otherwise we made small talk about work and other everyday topics. As always, my transition was overlooked. There were no questions about my appointment or any treatment I might have had. I imagined this was probably due more to the awkward nature of the questions than to any lack of interest.

Even for autumn the weather was especially chilly and grim. As we'd been collected surprisingly late in the day, it was pitch black when we arrived at my old family home. As we stepped inside the house, Max squealed with excitement to see the two of us and charged straight at us like a bowling ball. I met him halfway with a grin and dropped onto the floor to shower him with belly-rubs and scratches. As I got to him, he rolled to his feet and gave me a curious look. Cold dread enveloped me as I realised that he might not recognise me. I was now well into my time on HRT, and my body and scent had shifted. 'Hi Max! I've not seen you in forever!' I exclaimed, hoping that the sound of my voice would reassure him. After a brief moment, he seemed satisfied that I was indeed the same person and resumed his excitement, to my own enormous relief.

As everyone settled into the living room, I could tell something was off. My mother greeted us but wouldn't even meet my gaze. At best, she seemed strangely tense that

I was here; at worst, potentially irritated. I couldn't get a read on what was going on. It didn't feel right. I feigned a relaxed attitude and tried to repeat the small talk we'd had in the car. I chatted about how my job had been lately and how we'd visited the beach over the summer. Loretta pulled out her phone and started showing off pictures of the two of us on the pier from earlier that year. With a gesture to me, my mother joked to my dad, 'He'll never want to come back up here now,' notably using masculine pronouns for me. 'She,' I said with a smile. My mother looked to me as I corrected her, then looked away and rolled her eyes. 'I use female pronouns, remember,' I said in the gentlest tone I could manage. That was the excuse they'd been looking for to bring up my transition, and from there everything went downhill.

My mother jumped into confessing that she still didn't understand why I was transitioning. She wanted another explanation of why I was making such a big change. I ignored the judgement in her voice and tried to elaborate on how important this was to me, repeating what I had stressed the previous year. From the reaction of the two of them, it dawned on me that they hadn't made any steps towards accepting my transition. While I had been away, changing and growing into someone new, they had paused their protestation only to resume it upon me walking back in. I had expected them to have done some research or slowly processed the news; but instead, because I had been out of sight, I'd seemingly been out of mind too. While I explained how much happier I was openly living as a woman, my dad explained that I'd have to speed up my explanation because he wanted to set off soon due to the time. This perplexed me, until I realised he meant returning me and Loretta to Debi's flat so he could go to bed. At this I was floored. I thought we were coming over for a late dinner and would be staying the night in my old bedroom. Instead we'd been ferried over with the intention that we'd briefly talk and then be delivered back to the flat. Although things were going drastically different from what I'd expected, I didn't want to leave. I wanted to take the opportunity to straighten things out.

When I saw how little progress I was making, I turned the questions back on them. I asked if they had told anybody else in their lives about my transition. When I had told them about my name change early in the year, I'd specifically said they should feel free to mention it to anybody who asked about me. But they hadn't told anyone at all. They were still treating it as a secret. At this point I realised this meant their neighbours wouldn't know either, and the reason for smuggling me into the house under cover of darkness became disturbingly clear. I felt like an embarrassment again. They couldn't accept my transition because they didn't want it to be happening, despite the positive effects it was having on me. They were still more worried about how they would tell such cringe-worthy news to people I'd once known. When I explained I would happily tell anybody myself who wasn't in the loop, it seemed to inspire borderline panic as they both stressed it was still too soon.

At this point I could feel myself buckling. My composure had been slowly chipped away with every question. As I knew I was moments away from breaking down altogether, I did my best to announce that I couldn't handle it anymore and was going to leave. Without waiting for a response, I dashed out of the house. Before I'd even cleared the driveway, I already had tears running down my face. This was as far as my plan went as I then realised I had nowhere to go. I made it to a crop of nearby trees before I started to weep openly. Instinctively, I went to my phone. It was dead. Being so late in the day, I had drained the battery flat and had no way to contact anyone. Because I had misunderstood the original offer, I hadn't brought my purse and I didn't even have a coat – I had nothing. Dramatically, I decided I would have to sleep in the field. I knew there was no way I could walk back into that house, and Debi's flat would take all night to get to on foot. It wasn't just the hostile attitude that had broken me but the sheer disappointment of having my hopes and expectations completely shattered. I'd come here thinking I was returning to my place in the family but I felt like a complete fool for expecting that I was going to find acceptance. I just wanted to be back home, away from my hometown and everyone in it.

While I sat sulking in my own despair, Loretta caught up with me. She was also upset but was holding herself together much better than I was. She was disappointed and also blindsided by the sudden shift in the conversation and the revelation we weren't being invited over for a meal after all. She'd stayed behind and asked my parents not to follow me, which my dad had apparently tried to do while misgendering me in the process. Loretta offered to call her mother, as although she also didn't have her purse, she still had a phone with power. We sat and waited in the dark until we were generously rescued by Debi and her partner. I dreaded the idea of having to explain to them what had happened and was still far too upset to speak as we journeyed back. Instead, I rested my head on Loretta's shoulder and sobbed into her jacket as we drove away.

I had heard of, and personally met, parents of adult transgender children and seen first-hand that parents can grow to accept transition in time. Knowing this had fuelled a small eternal hope that my parents could be the same, one that had kept burning since my initial messy coming out. Melodramatically, I got back to Debi's flat that night and scribbled in my diary to no longer trust that spark of hope, to always doubt it and to stop holding out for the fantasy of becoming a happy, picturesque family. Friends had previously pleaded with me to be careful when it came to my parents, after seeing how upset I got every time I spoke to them. They saw me as painfully optimistic, always opening my heart and then being badly burnt by not remembering how my parents had treated me last time. I finally listened to them and made peace with the fact that I'd likely never be a daughter to my parents – not in the way that I wanted anyway. There was no happy ending coming. Instead it was time to focus fully on the new life I had forged, to make an ending somewhere else.

As a trans person it's depressingly common to feel forced into moving on from someone close to you – someone who is either unwilling or unable to give you the acceptance that you need. There is already so much baggage that comes with being trans, it's unreasonable to expect us to manage every bit of interpersonal drama as well. At some point we need to quit and do what's best for our own mental health.

The advantage of moving on was that I stopped ignoring the new parental figures I'd had under my nose this whole time. While my own mother had acted outright angry and confused when I'd started transitioning, Loretta's mother was constantly delighted. As the next few months went by, I started to grow closer to Debi as she became the caring, patient, and concerned parental figure that I'd wanted. Another GIC appointment arrived and became an excuse to stay with her yet again. The three of us went out shopping and visited the cinema together. When back at home, we'd keep in touch with regular phone calls and share the ups and downs of each other's lives. Meanwhile, Laura's mother, Jenny, also considerately took time to remind me that I was still cared about and thought of. When we returned from my first trip to the GIC, I posted a moody Facebook update about feeling lonely and rejected. The next day Jenny arrived with a delivery of flowers and a touching card, explaining that she knew I was having a hard time and wanted to show support. For the first time, I started to learn what it was like to feel like someone's daughter.

Even my work colleagues became extra supportive. Seeing that I was saving holiday days and only using them for appointments, the department manager took me aside and directly asked me to take some time off as proper holiday. He explained that he'd spoken with HR and agreed an arrangement whereby I wouldn't be penalised for taking paid 'personal days' for appointments and travel (the only condition was that I should keep an eye on my e-mails on those days); and I was to start using holiday leave *as holiday*, because they thought I deserved a break.

The other 'family' I had found was the one I was always chatting away to on my phone: my Twitter followers. By this point, some people had been listening to me chatter away about my life for years, and I had learnt all about theirs too. My followers had given me advice, comforted me while I'd cried, celebrated my victories, and shared my anger whenever another hit piece against trans people burst into the media. Many of them were trans too, and had encountered their own difficulties and missing support networks.

One reason the trans community can be so strong is that we fill in the gaps of absent friends and family, the people who bail on us when they can't handle the revelation of how secretly queer we've been all this time. I'll never really understand how some people can abandon lifelong friends, or even their own children and siblings, once they learn that these loved ones are actually trans; but I've seen it happen so many times, I've stopped being surprised.

Before the year closed, I returned to the GIC for another lengthy assessment appointment. This time it was with a therapist, someone who was specifically measuring my mental wellbeing and judging if I was trans enough to be diagnosed with gender dysphoria. I'd lost count of how many times I'd run someone through my history of childhood crying and teenage secrets, but this turned out to be the most in-depth recital yet. For 90 minutes I was grilled with personal questions about everything from what my childhood hobbies were to what my current sex life was like. As with the first appointment, I had read enough about GICs to know these invasive questions were coming, so despite how bizarrely personal they got, I wasn't taken by surprise.

At the end of my appointment, the therapist explained the next steps: I would meet with my original GIC doctor, and later a nurse, and then there would be a private meeting about me the following year. With a chuckle, he admitted that from everything I had told him, and the fact that two private doctors had already deemed me trans, it was exceedingly unlikely that anyone would deny me my diagnosis or my right to move onto treatment. At this I felt like screaming and questioning why I was still being led through this patronising process when a growing army of doctors had seen how blatantly trans I was. I wanted to dramatically point at the novel of notes he'd just taken and demand that this farce end, immediately. Nobody would bring this much upheaval to their life on a whim or by mistake. I deserved treatment. I deserved to be listened to and believed when I said I was trans. Meanwhile, the battalion of other people desperately waiting for appointments had a right to be seen, rather than time being wasted on drawn-out, pointless processes like this. Instead, I giggled softly and smiled, thanking him for his honesty. I knew protesting would be a waste of time and tremendously unwise. Throwing a tantrum at this stage could set me back. At worst I could be booted out of the process and put back to the start of the queue somewhere else. So I swallowed my pride, remained gracious, and left.

The gatekeeping and plodding pace of GICs is painfully dehumanising and part of a huge self-fulfilling problem in trans healthcare. Denying trans people the ability to take control of their own care, and treating us as passive and confused children in need of careful examination, further clogs the growing waiting lists as each person takes an unnecessarily convoluted journey through the system. Waiting times for first appointments could be slashed if trans people were simply trusted as knowing who we are and what we want. At the time of writing there are ongoing discussions about the future of GICs, with the potential for some large, sweeping changes to come. It's my hope that for many of you reading this, those changes are already implemented. Nobody deserves to have their care withheld like this.

Once back at home, I found myself becoming increasingly stressed out, which was a feeling that had been growing all year. More pressure was then piled on when one lunchtime I was suddenly informed that we were being evicted from our home. I dashed out of the office and phoned Loretta to find out what had happened. It turned out that the landlord had decided that after a year of ignoring us he wanted us gone. He was going to sell the house and couldn't do that with us living there. I was distraught. That place felt like my first real home. The idea of packing everything away and finding somewhere new within our three-month deadline was incredibly daunting. In hindsight, the eviction was a blessing in disguise. We were so happy to have our own place that until now we had been putting up with the poor condition of the house. The black mould in my bedroom was growing out of control, and the house was impossible to keep warm now that the cold weather was returning. I slept every night in an icy, wet room with disgusting spores and drenched windows. It was time to look for something new.

After a few failed attempts, Loretta found a replacement home just around the corner. It seemed like a good fit for us all and was the same price we were already paying. This felt like the result of divine intervention as we'd really struggled to find our original house. I was so desperate not to lose our chance to move, I gave the okay to put in an offer without having even seen the place. Loretta had been given a tour and assured me it was a huge improvement, but all I had was her word. She wasn't wrong. When I finally stepped inside it that weekend, after we'd been accepted and the paperwork was in progress, I was amazed at the difference. Simple comforts like carpeting and a working shower helped build the excitement for moving in and lessen the sadness of being forced out of our old home.

Christmas that year was a bit of a non-event for me, partly because we'd begun to pack away the bulk of our possessions, but mostly because I fell ill for the entire period. Between the house move, my full-time job, blogging, and the extra online writing that I was determined to keep powering on with, my body had been under a lot of stress. On my final day of work that year, it finally caved in, leaving me bedridden with flu. However, after two weeks of sleeping and eating, I was back to normal, and now it was just days until we left for our new home.

On the second week of the new year, moving day arrived. It was then that the terrible state of our old house really sunk in. Thanks to Google, we found and hired two local handymen to help us move. They were horrified at the conditions we'd been living in. When one of them asked why we'd been evicted, he was amazed to learn of the landlord's plan. He insisted that nobody would ever buy this place and that the only suitable thing to do with our former home would be to demolish it and start over. That day I also met our new landlady for the first time – a smiling and confident woman, who described us as a bunch of 'lovely ladies'. During the initial meeting, she insinuated that we'd all be sleeping in separate rooms and thus the house had just enough space for us all. I didn't correct her as I was willing to let her think for now that we were just a band of friendly young heterosexual gal pals. Of course, she did find out later how exceedingly queer we all were, and thankfully had no issue with it whatsoever. But even though everything had gone to plan, I couldn't shake off the increasingly pessimistic and grumpy mood that had settled over me. At first, I dismissed it as simply being stress from the house move, but soon that excuse wore thin even for me.

Chapter 14

REFLECTION

As the new year began, I started to contemplate everything that had just gone by. Even with all the hiccups, the last 12 months had been largely positive. But despite the things I had to celebrate, such as HRT, successfully relocating, and holding down a new job, I was still haunted by a growing grim feeling of inadequacy. Specifically, I had been experiencing endless pressure to do more, to write more articles, to learn new skills, to create more tangible results in my life, and to collect more experiences. Undeniably, I had grown and changed for the better, but these lingering negative thoughts had been snapping away at me all year with increasing ferocity. Having a creative drive can be useful, but I was pushing myself to exhaustion to placate this jabbering voice that had convinced me that I wasn't good enough at anything, wasn't doing enough, wasn't successful enough and wasn't worth enough as a person.

I felt like I was losing a vital race, except I was the only participant. I wasn't jealous (at least, not in the traditional sense) as nobody else was the target of my envy. But I was comparing myself to a phantom, the idea of who I could be if I'd transitioned a little earlier and not lost so much time. I took little joy from any of my accomplishments as I now saw them as nothing but mundane stepping stones. Steps to what, I didn't know. There was no ultimate goal or prize that I was chasing, but I had an insatiable need to fill this starving void with more productivity and keep aiming to hit an undefined measure of satisfied success. In the opening months of the year I faced up to the truth that this wasn't sustainable or remotely sensible, but I didn't know how to stop. When I wasn't working or creating something new, I felt horrible and stricken with guilt, like I was foolishly burning valuable time. This stress bled over into every aspect of my life, leaving me testy and stressed out.

Analysing what I could do to lose this feeling, I knew I had felt the most fulfilled and active when at my second Nine Worlds five months earlier. I had been on multiple panels that weekend and had met countless new people on a daily basis. It had left me feeling productive, popular, and positive. But I knew I couldn't cheerfully ignore everything that had happened that week in August. I was fooling myself if I wanted to pretend it had all been a healthy and uplifting experience. When I covered that time in an earlier chapter, there was something I neglected to mention: the fact that I also had a rather public breakdown in the middle of the convention.

The latest Nine Worlds had taken place back when I had been on HRT for six months, right in the middle of summer. Through my identity and writing, my online platform had continued to grow, which is what helped me earn the responsibility of arranging my own panel, as well as speaking on others. The majority of what I wrote online revolved around the fact I was an openly transitioning trans woman, one who both regularly talked about her experiences and offered her time to those who requested a chat or advice. I saw myself as a dependable listener, an eager vending machine of guidance and support for anybody who needed a boost. Doing so was fulfilling but it also felt important and worthwhile – a way to give back to the community and help people who were preparing for transition, too. If anybody ever expressed loneliness or feelings of doubt and depression on my Twitter timeline, I'd lean in and let them know my inbox was open and I'd be there for them. More than anything, I just wanted to help people, to provide a role that I had so often needed in my own life but rarely found. I'd been spending less and less time on myself over the last few months so that I could dedicate that time to those who wanted to talk to me instead. Mentally and emotionally, I was entirely fine with this voluntary strain as I was able to shoulder the extra baggage with ease. At least that's what I'd been telling myself anyway.

One afternoon during Nine Worlds, while resting and catching up with friends by the hotel bar, I received a message through Twitter that one of the heads of the convention wanted to speak to me. As I excused myself to leave, a friend commented that I should stay and ignore it, that I deserved this break. I waved off their protest and explained that I didn't want to leave anybody waiting, even though I wasn't quite sure what this was about. I went to the lobby and found the information desk, where two members of the convention staff were perpetually sat. I explained that my name was Mia and I'd been asked to come over. The message had actually been sent around 45-minutes ago, but I'd initially missed it as I was watching a presentation. After a moment, a woman several years older than me came over and took me aside to explain. She elaborated that they'd been trying to contact me earlier as someone they had identified as an acquaintance of mine had been distressed here at the convention. Because they'd needed someone to talk to, the convention staff had highlighted me as someone who could help them after seeing our association on Twitter and knowing I was at the convention too. With no warning, I broke down into tears.

As a result of my unexpectedly explosive reaction, the poor manager frantically assured me that everything was now fine and there was no reason to worry. Even as she told me that this acquaintance didn't need to speak to anyone anymore anyway, I collapsed back into a chair behind me and continued to weep dramatically. Luckily, as this was during a packed slot of scheduled panels, there weren't too many people around to see me sobbing inexplicably, but we were still awkwardly right in the main thoroughfare of the whole convention. To their credit, the other attendees did a good job of giving me space and letting me work through my distress. Between sobs, I messily tried to promise that this outburst wasn't the manager's fault, or anybody's fault. I barely even understood why I was crying. After being comforted and distracted by the manager's attempts to calm me down for several minutes, I started to settle and compose myself, although tears were still trickling down my face. Convincing her that I was going to be okay, I let the manager get back to her duties while I sat and tried to apply makeup to my red, puffy eyes and cover up how upset I'd just been. I reminded myself I was at my favourite convention, and it was a time to be happy and excited, to focus on friends and relaxation. Despite my attempts to get back into the swing of things, I skipped the next event and retreated back to my hotel room to rest.

That night I neglected to see friends despite our previous plans, only briefly sweeping by them to explain I wasn't feeling well and was going to lie down. I appreciated their worries but the last thing I wanted to do was talk about how I felt, especially as it might trigger another bout of crying. The good thing about being friends with a band of queer people who also have fragile and varied complicated states of mental health is that they all understand when you need to cancel plans last minute. In a group like that, most of us have been there at some point.

After picking up a pizza I had ordered in, I sat in my hotel room alone and thought about what had happened earlier. When I had been told that an acquaintance needed help, it had simultaneously sent the signal that it was time to leap into action, while my mind wailed with despair that I didn't have any more energy left to give. It had been the final feathered touch to my strained mental health, which had been overstressed and ready to snap for weeks. I was spent, completely drained and unable to take on any more responsibility. I wanted to stop, but my sense of obligation wouldn't let me refuse an opportunity to help someone.

Guiltily, I knew I'd already been warned about this. Weeks earlier, my housemates had confronted me about how much I was visibly burning myself out. They claimed I was taking on the burden of protector and stand-in parent far too often, on top of everything else I had on my plate. Often when we were supposed to be hanging out together, I'd have my nose buried in my phone, juggling multiple conversations and even forgetting to eat. Instead of listening, I had dismissed everything they said as unnecessary and an underestimation of what I could handle. I was wrong, and they'd just been proven right. Unavoidably, my body was now struggling with the pace I had been putting it through. Yet I only had myself to blame. Although the incident that afternoon should have been a moment of learning and a time to reflect and change my behaviour, I ignored it.

Once the convention was over, I went right back to normal, pushing myself beyond my limits to be available at all hours and continuing to work harder than I could manage.

If I had wrapped one half of my identity around my desire to help others, the rest of it was entombed with rage. Virtually every week there was a new documentary, editorial, or political speech that demonised trans people. My response to this was to angrily parry whatever new lies had been spewed with a counter argument of shareable social media or a hastily written blog post. The anger felt justified but also useful, and both cis and trans friends praised me for writing in such a way. Doing so netted me a slowly increasing audience of like-minded people who were equally sick of seeing trans people attacked in the media. Before long, ranting about trans issues had become the entire focus of my writing. I'd once seen my casual pop culture reviews and academic writing as my primary creative outlets, but this gradually changed until I saw trans rights as the only topic worth discussing. Although in the summer I had felt energised and driven when writing my ranting responses, at the dawn of this new year I was now exhausted and bitter about how often I had to write the exact same sentiment. Every counter-argument would sour my mood and ruin my mental health, as I subjected myself to targeted hate and dehumanising language, yet I kept going back each and every time.

I'm unsurprised to reflect on how addictively I'd fallen into those patterns, because that's what happens when your identity is attacked and debated relentlessly. My prickly replies felt like a small spark of activism, an expression of outrage and refusal, but also educational and noticeable to those in my social circle who were unaware of what had even been said. But this meagre activism didn't feel like a calling or a voluntary choice; it was a responsibility, a duty, an extra mandatory job that had to be juggled around my other obligations. In reality, it wasn't any of those things, or it shouldn't have felt like it was anyway. Trans people should have just as much a right to live in peace and comfort as everybody else. All forms of trans advocacy should be a choice, but it often feels like fighting for survival. Back then, the idea of ignoring such an attack seemed unspeakable. I would walk into work every weekday morning and smile at colleagues, laugh at jokes, and outwardly seem to be living a carefree life. But my lunchtimes, evenings, and late nights were spent writing angry essays, letters, and emails, all responding to transphobia and intolerance that I couldn't ignore.

I have to note that the advocacy I did by using my platform to speak out, online and otherwise, is obviously not comparable to the dirty and dangerous work that real trans activists do. Their labour is what earned us the recognition and legal protections that we have today, and that deserves to be respectfully acknowledged as something distinctly important.

On social media there was a regular chorus of outrage from trans activists, bloggers, and writers whenever any new piece was published, but in the rest of my life there was complete silence. The profound nature of how little I saw these attacks impact all the people in my day-to-day life at work, or in the street, struck me as bizarre and increasingly irritating. I saw the blissful happiness of my colleagues and cisgender friends as a luxury and privilege. I believed that they were only carefree through a deliberate blackout of the issues that didn't affect them. I wasn't cynical enough to think that they didn't care at all about trans issues, but their detachment granted them the freedom to ignore anything that didn't openly challenge them. It reminded me of the mind-set I'd had in my teens when I'd felt like I was the vulnerable outcast and that the only happy people around me were those who lived in ignorance or simply didn't care how others were hurting. This pessimistic view was further fuelled when I consistently saw how lonely and upset so many vulnerable members of the community became with each new public attack. This of course continued to drive me to hastily remind everyone that they were welcome to talk with me for company and support. I didn't always feel that I had the energy to help; but knowing how it felt to be alone and afraid, I considered it my duty to be there for everyone who needed it.

With hindsight, I can see that my mental health was being made worse by internalising the narrative of what I was being told in the media and what I saw around me. It was a grim joke in the community that we trans people were all switching between fatigue, depression, and furious offence. My stressed state of mind wasn't unusual – it was the communal status quo. Therefore, for months I believed that being this stressed out was no cause for alarm; evidently it was just the price for being openly trans. When I wanted to change my harmful habits, I was reminded of Holly's words two years prior: how I had a right to look after my own mental health and to stop hurting myself for the good of others. I knew she was right then and was right now. The only way to escape the cycle seemed to be to leave the community altogether, ignore the pain and problems, and focus on myself. I knew that in theory I could leave, reduce my transition to a private and quiet affair, and then look for ways to find fulfilment elsewhere. But that idea wasn't even remotely tempting. I hated the thought of finding a route to happiness that meant ignoring people I knew I could help. Likewise, I didn't want to become detached and aloof from my community. I was scared of becoming the type of writer who'd use her trans identity for opportunities while removing herself from the realities and inequalities we face. I had seen others exploit the community like this, which made me all the more afraid of falling into that trap.

I often stressed that others should feel free to back down for their own mental health but I didn't think it was suitable for me to do so, especially as a writer. Being part of the community opened my mind to the wide and varied experiences of coming under the transgender umbrella. It kept me grounded and part of something important, as well as keeping me tuned in and held to account on wider issues. I couldn't leave that behind but I couldn't continue like this either. In essence, I still wanted to help and be part of the online trans community but I wanted to reduce my endless anger and the eternal pressure that now accompanied my membership.

As an attempt to counteract how I was feeling, I made a conscious effort to become more aware of my limitations along with fostering a lighter and more optimistic worldview. In February, on my one-year anniversary of starting HRT, I wrote a blog post describing my struggle to let go of negative thought patterns and pressure. Despite my efforts, so far it wasn't working. The positive person that I was striving to be was at odds with the negative patterns that were my reality. Mia Violet, the Twitter personality and blogger, seemed confident, outspoken, in control, and respectable. But she had become my persona, an edited highlight reel lacking the uncensored truth. Mia Violet, the actual human being, was a mess. In the mirror I saw someone who was exhausted, constantly wrestling with self-doubt and having a testy temper, while constantly critiquing her own appearance and never feeling worthy of anyone's time or respect. I wanted to leave behind those old habits and become the best version of myself, but they were clinging on. With this I started to question why these harmful flaws felt so integral and important to me.

Over the following days, I wrote rambling diary entries, letting the words flow freely from my gut. I poured my deepest insecurities and doubts onto the page in an attempt to illuminate how I truly felt. I also began to meditate again, presenting myself with the open question: What did I want from life? The answer was surprisingly simple: I wanted to be happy, but I didn't consider myself worthy of happiness. Why not? Because I had terrible self-worth. Underneath all my newfound confidence and pride as a trans woman, I thought I didn't deserve any of the joy I'd found. Everything I was doing was about making myself useful to other people. I read horrible hit-pieces against the trans community, even though I didn't want to, just so I could produce educated comebacks that would raise spirits. I saw my time as wasted when used on myself; therefore, giving it all to other people was the productive thing to do. I believed they deserved it more than me by virtue of requesting it. With this realisation, it struck me how much personal growth I still needed to do. I was conscious of the fact that I was as worthwhile as everybody else, but these feelings had taken root deeply. They were the cause of the constant pressure I felt to do more and the reason I had been pushing myself so hard.

Growing up trans and going back into the closet in my teens had left me with scars and quirks, which I had developed to survive. Counselling had done a lot to dust away the worst of these issues, but I was by no means a finished product. Naively, I'd expected that starting HRT and living openly as a trans woman would magically heal the rest of these wounds automatically. With the tough parts of transition now done, I at least had a clearer mind and a less cluttered life. It had given me the space to look at the state of myself and see the things that still needed fixing. I longed to talk to Holly, knowing she was always masterful at understanding what I was feeling and knew just what to say to guide me out of the muddled mess I'd found myself in. I debated going back to counselling and finding someone new who could fill the role Holly once had. Undeniably, it was a sensible idea, but with so little free time due to work, and my constant money troubles, I couldn't afford to pay the pricey fees needed for ongoing sessions. Instead, I decided I'd try to solve this alone.

Now I had a new objective: find happiness as a trans woman and solve my lifelong self-worth issues, without sacrificing my morals, beliefs, and personal goals. It felt like the biggest obstacle of my transition, perhaps the final challenge before I could let go and enjoy the rest of my life. In the latest incarnation of my blog I wrote a new entry specifically declaring that my goal for the year was to be happy. That was it. It was a deliberately vague aspiration but was also simple and encompassing – the only thing I wanted to achieve.

Throughout my life, my mental health had radically fluctuated, but I could remember specific moments and coping methods that had got me through the most difficult and frightening times. I knew that I had to pull away from my past and really commit to getting better to get out of this slump. I felt like I already had all the tools and the experience to know what worked and what I responded to best. I just needed to reflect and pull everything together to find the solutions.

The first thing I set out to fix was how ugly and unhappy about my appearance I had felt recently. This was a constant source of stress. I knew right away that the moment I had felt most confident in my appearance was before I had even started HRT. It was back when I'd worn my gothic attire in London and allowed myself to feel proud. The fact I looked blatantly trans that weekend hadn't bothered me at all because I personally loved how I looked. I had happily told myself that the whole time, reinforcing it regularly. Yet now I had fallen into the pattern of critiquing myself instead, ignoring what I liked about myself and only focusing on the negative, sometimes masking the brutality of my comments with an awkwardly light-hearted tone. It had been like waking up every morning to a radio station telling me I was masculine and unattractive, and instead of shutting it off, I'd decided to sing along. All that nasty repetition had sunk in. I believed I was ugly because I never told myself anything else.

I conceded with fresh eyes that the disparaging comments and self-deprecating 'jokes' I aimed at myself were not actually very funny or endearing; they were bitter micro-aggressions rooted in my identity as a trans woman. If I heard these things aimed at any of my friends I would be horrified, especially if they said them about themselves. I loved my friends. I saw them all as brilliant lights and startling heroes. If they ever dared to insult themselves, I would remind them of their importance and dazzling nature, wishing they could see themselves like I saw them. So, if I could easily treat others like that, why was I so harsh and critical of myself? At first, I couldn't even answer the question but I eventually admitted that the real reason was fear. I was afraid of seeing myself as beautiful because I knew there was safety in self-enforced ugliness. By convincing myself I was always awkwardly grotesque, I was protecting myself from the potential disappointment when I saw my reflection on a bad day or if I was especially dysphoric. When I started HRT, I kept my hopes low to avoid feeling dissatisfied with my physical progress, but as a side-effect I undercut the joy I deserved to feel from the continual changes I'd made over the past year. This had snowballed from telling myself I might not become as feminine as I'd like, to eventually insisting that I looked like a masculine failure. As a solution, I promised myself I would treat myself with the same care and reverence as I treated my best friends. From now on I would be banned from uttering negative comments about myself and instead only comment if I was lifting myself up or noticing something nice.

Next, I started to think about my dysphoria – something that was much trickier to fix. I noted that whenever it flared up I always slumped off lethargically to the morning bus, wearing whatever lazy and comfortable outfit I had dragged out of my wardrobe. It felt like forever since I'd worn my smart dresses or professional pink outfits. The last few months I'd settled on jeans, worn-out pumps, and baggy plaid shirts with loose, chipped buttons. One day I felt so incredibly dysphoric and uncomfortable with myself at work that I'd gone to the ladies' room and sunk to the floor. As I sat there, hoping nobody was about to walk in but too despondent to prepare for that eventuality, I started to contemplate the unpredictably intense dysphoria I'd had lately. My positive compliments were helping, but I was still responding by rolling over and letting dysphoria wash away my self-esteem whenever it flared up. On these days I felt unworthy of my transition, despicable, and manly. In contrast, the days where I felt good about myself I always picked out a daring outfit to match my mood. That day then turned into a celebration, and inevitably I felt spectacular. It then hit me that my presentation was how I needed to fight back. My vow to never put myself down was a good start, but I needed to follow through and work on feeling good that day no matter how loathsome my reflection looked to me that morning. That started with choosing the clothes that made me feel good.

The first few times I went out in a dress, back when I lived in the flat with Loretta, I was exhausted because of the apprehension over being seen. I relied on a big floppy coat as a shield – a portable escape route. It sent a message to everyone around me that I was afraid and was doing something worthy of mockery. But the gothic dress I donned in the summer had no such safety net. It was unquestionably ostentatious and came with nowhere to hide. There was a vulnerability that came with that visibility, but rather than downplay it I pulled strength from it. I wore that borderline silly outfit with excited dignity. My body language was one of proud defiance, flaunting my refusal to comply with cisnormative expectations. This fed into my narrative that day of feeling invulnerable. It unlocked the carefree happiness I enjoyed. Had I left the hotel in the same outfit but without that inner fire and self-respect, the nervous message I'd have been putting out into the world would have heightened my sense of anxious unworthiness and fed back into my fear. It would have soured the whole experience.

Essentially, what I was realising with these memories was that there is a semiotic element to clothing. I had always known this to an extent: I'd worn dresses to present the truth about my gender, relying on them to convey the message that I was a woman. But it went deeper than that. Specific outfits told myself, as well as others, how I felt about myself that day. That message then had a dramatic effect on my mood. I'd been wearing clothes recently that said, 'I feel bland, unattractive, and uninteresting.' I'd leave the house with a commitment to that truth. Everything I then saw and experienced, I'd take as a reinforcement of that same truth, which my dysphoria found delicious as every scrap of it was belittling. Combined with my prior self-deprecating comments, I'd been training my brain to see myself as a disappointment. It was no wonder I felt so glum.

The solution was obvious: I had to cut away the safety net, banish the boring outfits, and embrace the loud, girly aesthetic that I'd been envying my entire life – the very same look that would make me a magnet for attention and only underline how different I looked from cis women. But it was time to own that, to accept that I shouldn't feel good about myself as a one-off; instead, I should leave the house every day exuding confidence and a strong sense of self-worth.

For the majority of time since coming out, I had worn soft-pink lipstick and the exact same mascara and foundation every day. Initially, this had been done so that I'd look feminine but also not to draw too much attention to myself. I was afraid anything more conspicuous could lead to harassment, as any lingering eyes would surely identify me as trans. But finally I ditched the pink and this fearful attitude, replacing it with loud, cherry-red lipstick. The comfortable shirt-dresses and check flannel shirts that I'd fallen back on for dysphoric days were exiled to the back of the wardrobe. I replaced them with colourful fit-and-flare dresses, the type of outfits that I had always saved for special occasions or the days when I'd had an audience to dazzle. Now I was just out to impress myself, to push back against my dysphoria and say, 'No. You're wrong. Look at me, I'm a woman, I'm trans, and I'm fantastic.'

Whether in my new hometown or travelling to different cities to shop or visit friends, I started to do all of it while wearing precisely the type of outgoing clothes and makeup that I'd wanted to wear all along. An important consequence of beginning to dress boldly, no matter my mood or the time of day, was that it shook away my final fears about being someone blatantly trans in public. I'd grown comfortable in feminine clothes that relied on subtle or simple looks, but my new flashy fashion eschewed any neutral colours. As it had been incredibly rare for me to wear such a showy presentation for a long stroll down the high street or a day at the beach, I'd grown used to the idea of blending in. But now, wearing just a short summery dress and carrying a pink handbag covered with plastic pearls and spikes, I naturally stood out wherever I went. My new fashion did indeed draw attention to me and caused people to comment occasionally, but not exactly in the ways I'd expected. When I was sat looking at my phone one afternoon, a young woman slowed to a stop in front of me. When I looked up, I didn't even get to say anything before she cut in and said, 'You're killing it with that lipstick. I wish I could get away with red.' A few weeks later, I was waiting for my food in the local fish and chip shop and was tapped on the shoulder. When I turned around, a woman I'd never seen before excitedly asked me where I'd bought my gold-studded heels. Other times it would be my nails that were complimented, my new dresses, or even my hair. It was liberating to realise that despite all the hate in the media, so many people didn't engage with that toxicity because they didn't believe it. I looked blatantly trans, but nobody I encountered thought any less of me for it.

In a way, what happened reminds me of the common myth about makeup. Often uttered by certain clueless men, there's the claim that makeup exists so that whoever applies it can look good for other people. In reality, makeup exists to make you feel good about yourself. It's fun. It was the same thing with my clothes. I wasn't dressing up to wow the public. I did it because I felt great when garbed in something that I knew spoke to how I really wanted to look. I wasn't dressing to drown out being trans or to downplay it either. I was dressing in a way that felt authentically me and exuded a sense of love and respect for myself. However, it's important for me to note that the feminine nature of my new everyday outfits was most significant only because it spoke to my personal tastes. It was a bonus that they also helped me defy the cultural devaluation of traditional femininity, and especially femininity in trans women, but there is nothing inherent in being a trans woman that is tied to makeup, dresses, jewellery or any other traditionally feminine fashion. I know other trans women who've found their freedom in embracing punky, abrasive fashion, stylish tomboy looks, or worn-out jeans and leather jackets. Likewise, I know trans men who rock pastel colours and impeccable makeup, but that of course doesn't invalidate the fact that they're still guys. The key to being happy with your presentation, regardless of gender, is donning the style that speaks to you, the look that makes you feel invincible. There's nothing quite like the feeling of strutting down the street with a presentation that feels perfectly in sync with everything else about you.

My effort to appreciate my appearance, and dress to match, left me feeling much happier, which was something that friends and online followers started to pick up on. I realised that I vastly preferred this new idea of being seen as someone positive and uplifting, rather than angry and always ranting. In an attempt to continue fostering this personal growth, I thought back to how self-help writing had initially helped me accept that I had 'gender identity issues' and lose lifelong shame and guilt. I wondered if that type of writing could help me now to continue this momentum, to lose the sense of pressure and break my self-worth's reliance on it. This time I wasn't looking for quick fixes or a few punchy blog posts. I wanted books, something I could dive into and lose hours on, so I went shopping.

Self-help books are criticised unfairly: perhaps it's the narcissistic nature of wanting to spend time entirely on yourself, or maybe it's the societal demonisation of emotional reflection as feminine and inane. Either way, I had never read a self-help book before, having only stepped into this genre briefly through blog posts and online essays back when I broke up with Nicole. But I had always found the idea alluring. There was something comforting about the idea of listening to somebody else's experiences and expertise, then letting them guide you on how to apply that knowledge to your own life. As I started to browse what was on offer, I felt excited and ready to learn.

Over the following weeks I flew through book after book of affirming advice. All of them were written by women, which wasn't a conscious choice at first but a 'side-effect' of what appealed to me. The self-help books by male authors often seemed rooted in business advice or practical applications for getting a raise, leading a team, or starting a company. I specifically wanted to move away from lofty ambitions and just accept who I already was, with a few tweaks here and there. I soon learnt there was a word for this type of outlook: self-love. Unlike a lot of self-help books, those centred on self-love encouraged the belief that you didn't need a radical personality shift or a new, strict, disciplined routine to be fulfilled; you were already pretty damn perfect to begin with and just needed to learn to acknowledge that. This felt much more in line with what I'd been doing lately, and more likely to help since so much of my stress was rooted in insecurity. My transition itself already felt like the ultimate form of self-love – by definition, I was embracing what felt natural to me and shedding the uncomfortable parts of myself I had acquired through survival and fear. It seemed only natural to continue down this road and learn new behaviours by accepting who I was.

The books that connected with me generally preached something that took me by surprise: that being happy was difficult. In my distrustful and misanthropic teens, I'd settled on the exact opposite belief: that being happy was easy as it just took willing ignorance. But I was wrong. Sadness is the easy emotion. If you turn on any 24-hour news network, it'll only take a few minutes to feel depressed. Even 30 seconds on a mainstream news website will surely offer a selection of harrowing headlines. The media remind us how much death, hate, terror and greed are in the world. But it's easy to forget that it's also filled with light, life, love, and hope. Being happy despite everything is difficult. To be happy you have to realise that you deserve a break, and that you're no use to anybody if you've burnt yourself out. Even if you see every second of your time as painfully precious, relaxing and letting yourself feel happily distracted is never a wasted investment, because your body and mind require that rest and recharging in order to get back to work later.

This belief in happiness as an ongoing effort, and not purely a side-effect of outside factors, really resonated with me. I realised that in the past I'd been seeing my anger as a tool – something that would protect me and could be wielded to highlight injustices and the lack of trans rights in society. But every time I wrote something fuelled by outrage, I regretted it due to the lasting impact on my mental health. Worse still, I just seemed to be depressing people by underlining what they already knew. It was always painfully demanding to shackle that anger after letting it loose. So, I made the conscious decision to stop cultivating it. I still spoke out against what I saw as cultural and societal injustice against trans people but I understood when to step back, respect my limits, and let somebody else tag in. I no longer dwelled on every single bit of trans-related news, forcing myself to read insidious editorials or watch patronising documentaries. I also stopped speaking about each one at length when I knew I was just preaching to those who already agreed and had already heard what I had to say. Instead, I decided I'd pour energy into what I was good at: lifting people in the community up and helping to heal the damage. I wanted to remind those who were struggling that we could still find happiness and strength in the face of overwhelming opposition.

Soon my writing fully shifted to an optimistic tone, to match my new perspective on life. I now saw my earlier dismissal of happiness as ignorant. It had been a lazy and juvenile snub. Finding happiness didn't mean actively ignoring what was happening in the world, it meant understanding boundaries, realistic limitations, and the importance of looking after yourself. As the weeks went by, I still invited people to message me if they wanted to talk or needed help, and I reached out to them to check in, too, but I also knew when it was time to clock off and look after myself. In doing so, the pressure to push myself relented, I felt that I was now doing what I could within my limits, and that was enough.

Taking part in the trans community now felt less like stepping onto a battlefield and more like being part of a big supportive family. I wasn't logging into social media to absorb whatever new hit-piece had been written; I was checking in with siblings. This was my new 'activism'. It wasn't as loud or noticeable, but it was effective and personal for those it reached. It was a role that suited me much better than what I'd been doing before and it also seemed more useful to the community.

As a result of my efforts, my self-worth drastically improved at last and brought clarity to my previous behaviour. Undeniably, I had been living my life by looking back at the past. I was still lamenting the things I had lost by not transitioning earlier, focusing on all the things I could have done or mistakes I may never have made. I'd even wondered about how much better I'd look physically had I started HRT before testosterone had done more damage. Meanwhile, I'd been looking at the future with dread. The idea of getting older with so many things left undone had motivated me to ignore what I was already doing and to look at the next upcoming challenge. I'd seen the future as a reason to invalidate the present. As HRT still had work to do, I didn't feel like a finished person, just a work in progress. But my recent stint of self-improvement rightly revealed that only the present moment existed. The past was gone forever. No amount of mourning or speculation would ever change what had happened. The future didn't exist – not in any tangible sense – and I couldn't reliably predict it. The present moment was the only time that warranted energy as it was the only thing I had the ability to alter. Finally, I was able to see that pushing on and living in the face of so many difficulties in our society was itself a triumph. Even if I was never able to successfully complete any of the projects I was working on, it didn't mean I'd 'failed' anyone; I'd already succeeded just by showing up.

I'd always resisted the stereotype that transitioning turns you into a new person entirely, but the more time passed, and the more effort I put into improving my mental health alongside transition, the harder I found it to relate to who I used to be. My short temper, something I had struggled to keep in check, evaporated altogether. New friends laughed at the concept of me getting angry and explained they couldn't even imagine it – in time, neither could I.

Altogether my worldview had become the exact opposite of what it used to be. When I looked back at old photos of myself, I couldn't even connect to who I used to be. With a glum face and dead eyes, it was like looking at a stranger. It was hard to believe that a sense of secret shame and numb apathy had once been my everything. I now felt like I was turning into the person I'd always wanted to be, shedding the remains of the gloomy, pessimistic armour I had worn to protect myself. I didn't need to carry that negativity anymore as I finally liked myself. My online persona was no longer a mask. I had finally become that resilient and light-hearted woman that I wanted to be.

My transformation is a reminder that transition isn't something that can take place automatically. It's tempting to think of it as something that happens on its own once you get hold of HRT and a new wardrobe, but it takes work. It's true that chemical changes do play a part, but they won't wipe away all your toxic beliefs about yourself or the earlier trauma from growing up in hiding – not without your help. When people ask me how I rebooted so much of my personality, I explain that it happened because I wanted it. I reflected on the things I didn't like and the parts of me that I knew were poisonous. In my case, it was my anger and my deflated self-worth. I had to willingly explore where they came from and understand the way that I was relying on them to cover my vulnerabilities. Only then was I able to actually uproot them and become someone new.

Despite everything I have just said, it would be irresponsible for me not to take a moment to touch on the importance of antidepressants. I've talked about the things that I did to improve my mental health here, not just because they were significant and tied to my transition, but so that my experience might help others who want to do the same. But self-help books, meditation, and critical thinking are not substitutes for medical help or a treatment for depression. They may very well help but they can't replace medicinal intervention when that's what's required. Lots of people close to me have wrestled with depression, and during the times I was struggling I did consider the possibility that I, too, had depression. I promised myself I would go to see my GP if I began to feel that I was a danger to myself or if my mental health slipped outside of my control. In the early days of my transition I considered asking for antidepressants when my dysphoria was at its worst but I held back out of fear that it might derail my transition. But I know many people who did go to their local surgery, started antidepressants, and didn't encounter any second-guessing or delays from the GIC. Ultimately, it's something you need to decide for yourself, but I'd always advise talking to a doctor if you genuinely believe you need that kind of help.

Thanks to the trans community, and those I met by being associated with it, that year I became more popular than I'd ever been in my life. At conventions, and even GIC appointments, I got used to checking my phone and seeing a message from someone who'd spotted me and wanted to say hi, grab a coffee, or even take a selfie together. I now had a growing network of friends spread across the entire country, who knew me via my ramblings on social media or the articles I'd had published on the Internet. I wasn't exactly famous but I now meant something to a lot of people and they meant something to me in return. Where I'd originally panicked about the idea of how I was going to get to and from the GIC when my first appointment arrived, I found myself getting offers from friends who generously wanted to give me a lift there, or even offer a bed to sleep in closer to the clinic. It was like being part of a giant, loving family – one that always had my back.

As the final month of summer began, it was time to visit Nine Worlds again. This was my third time attending – two years since that first influential visit and one year since I'd broken down in the lobby from stress and exhaustion. Coincidentally, it also aligned with having spent 18 months on HRT. On the first day, I picked up a pink and black dress to wear, something bold and overly fancy to compliment my new scarlet hair colour. I then finished it off with my increasingly trademark pair of gaudy, rose-coloured sunglasses. Parting painted red lips into a melodramatic pout and pulling down my glasses with my pink-painted fingernails, I snapped a silly selfie. Scrolling through my phone, I found the photo I'd been looking for: an ancient one from years earlier, where I stood with shaggy brown hair and a scratchy messy beard. It was strange to remember that only a few years had passed by between this and the photo I'd just taken. As I thought my followers might get a kick out of it, I put the two photos side by side and sent it off to Twitter, adding a note that if I could go from this shaggy dirt-bag to a goofy, red-haired girl, then there was hope for everybody. I then shut my phone and headed off for an afternoon of watching panels and catching up with friends.

Later, when I got back to my hotel room, I checked my phone to find a flood of interactions with the photo. I'd got dozens and dozens of messages from newly out trans people of all ages, many thanking me for posting the photo and explaining that it gave them some reassurance and hope that they could change too. Knowing that I was helping people by sharing my story was incredibly heart-warming. It reinforced my belief that continuing to cultivate a more positive presentation was the best way to use my platform, as well as supporting my own mental health.

Chapter 15

CHANGES

With a new grip on my life, I knew it was time to mop up some important things that I had been ignoring. The first of these was the medical side of my transition. When I first started HRT, I had my hormone levels tested every three months. By getting my levels checked I was able to see that my testosterone and oestrogen were where they should be, and also that my liver wasn't about to explode. Granted, I was quite fuzzy on the details when it came to my liver, but I just trusted that the doctor knew what he was looking for and would catch any problems before anything bad happened. After my levels had settled at the nine-month mark, my doctor recommended we change to testing every six months instead. However, as my local clinic was still kindly offering blood tests every quarter as a precaution, I took the opportunity to find out what my chemical situation was (not good, as it turned out).

Just before Christmas my levels had been slipping, but now they were a disaster. My oestrogen level had been slashed, free-falling all the way out of female range, while my testosterone had spiked and made a run towards the low threshold of male levels. At first I dismissed the poor results as something to deal with later – this was ironic considering how I had reacted towards my first test results back in the beginning. When I saw my hormone levels for the very first time after starting HRT the previous year, I frantically got in touch with Kate Adair, a long-time friend and knowledgeable trans advocate. I hadn't understood what the numbers meant and was worried that neglecting to steer them into an absolutely perfect range might sabotage my progress. Kate rightly assured me that my levels were just fine, as well as reminding me that they would fluctuate up and down. There was no reason to panic as each test only provided a brief snapshot from that one moment anyway. Just as she said, during my first year of HRT my levels did jump up and down, and over time I became much more blasé about them. I learnt to trust that I'd be needlessly stressing myself out by examining the numbers too closely. I just had to make sure they were in a very loose range. How I felt was more important than if I'd lost or gained a few dozen points. However, my latest blood test suggested that my levels had slumped right into a ditch, well outside even the most liberal target. Realising they weren't going to recover without some help, I made an appointment with my private doctor to talk about the results.

Although I'd originally seen an online doctor for HRT, I'd changed along the way to a London-based private clinic. I'd done this for one reason: fear of losing my precious hormones. When I was given my prescription by the online doctor, that service had only recently become available. My worry was that soon they'd be shut down. I heard whispers about investigations being instigated, and anger in the NHS that a new doctor had strode onto the scene and dispensed HRT without a traditional and rigid assessment process. My solution had been to begin seeing a private doctor in person, who after just two appointments handed me a prescription to continue my HRT routine under his guidance instead. I was setting off to see him for what would be the final time, to ask for his help in reaction to my radically altered levels.

My doctor took a look at my high testosterone and low oestrogen numbers and immediately started talking about solutions. I had dreaded that his answer would be to do nothing – the strategy I'd already tried – but instead he was satisfied that change was warranted. His solution was spironolactone, a drug I had heard many stories about. In the USA, spiro is the go-to method of lowering testosterone in trans women. Administered in tablet form, spiro is inexpensive and effective. It also came with a laundry list of side-effects and health risks. Although that might have once given me pause, at this stage I would have snorted plutonium if a professional said it would help get my transition back on track.

Spiro turned out to be wonderful. Although it tasted like chalk and dissolved into disgusting mush upon touching my tongue, its effects were undeniable. Once I'd settled into the routine of taking it every morning, I felt fantastic. It was like being back to normal: light and tranquil, in tune with the depth of my emotions, and able to think freely. I hadn't realised at the time, but with rising testosterone I'd fallen into a similar foggy state of mind to the one I'd inhabited before HRT. I'd been getting stressed much more easily, while complex emotions tangled into a frustrating mess. I often focused on hormones because they were what caused the physical changes to my body; it was easy to forget that they were just as important for my mental health too. I've spoken with many trans men who've talked of a paralysing lethargy when their testosterone levels fell, and now I'd experienced what running on low oestrogen did for me. Clearly, on their own testosterone and oestrogen are not universally 'good' or 'bad' – everyone, no matter what their gender, has both in their system to some degree – but trans people face profound effects when they're out of alignment with their identity.

Since starting HRT, my emotional state had seen such a blanket improvement that I'd entirely forgotten the severity of what dysphoria had done to me in the past. The idea of spending days in bed from intense apathy and self-loathing felt bizarrely dramatic, but that's exactly what I had done on a regular basis when I was still waiting to get my hands on HRT. Yet since starting hormonal transition, my dysphoric episodes had been entirely manageable. They still left me with the occasional nasty thought about myself, but they never told me anything that I wasn't able to power through with a little pep talk.

One of the best parts of starting spiro was that breast growth rapidly resumed and continued for months. I soon finally filled out my bra and had a noticeable chest. It was as if my body was playing catch-up. But something I hadn't missed quite as much that also came roaring back was mood swings. At the end of summer, I decided to attend the launch party for 'The Nopebook', a website I had recently been writing for. The party was taking place in London, meaning I could have travelled home afterwards, but instead I decided to stay overnight in a cheap hotel. After checking in, I decided I would grab a quick shower before the party, but to my horror I hadn't packed any of my favourite shampoo or conditioner. Frantically, I searched the hotel bathroom and found that all they had was a thick green sludge described as a shampoo, conditioner, and body wash combo. The idea of using such a bargain throwaway product on my poor sensitive tresses caused me to crumble to the floor and weep. As someone with very limited finances, I was always cutting corners with my purchases but I never sacrificed quality when it came to my hair. After minutes of cursing my clumsy nature for forgetting something as vital as shampoo, I started to see how ridiculous it was to cry with despair over haircare products. In fact, it was quite funny. Without even getting up, I then began to laugh about how much of a diva I was being, even while I still had tears in my eyes. In the end I used the dubious bottle of goop, and although it did leave my hair quite dried-out and frizzy, I had a lovely time at the party. Other 'sensible' things I cried about after changing my dose included not feeling pretty enough one morning, feeling sorry for all the dogs in the world that didn't have owners, and remembering how good the ending to *Mad Men* was.

It would be convenient if I had an excuse or simple reason for why my levels suddenly inverted, but the truth is that it can simply happen for no reason. Medical transition is often part-science and part-improvisation. Altering doses and tablets is sometimes necessary just to keep on track. Across my friendship group of trans women, many of us are on radically different types of HRT, and even those on the same type have varying degrees of dosage. What our bodies need to bring us to the right range is usually very personal and difficult to predict, even with evidence. When I had my first blood test after starting spiro, I was relieved to find that it had indeed crushed my testosterone down to its lowest-ever level.

When I returned to the GIC for my fifth appointment, I was told that I'd been diagnosed with gender dysphoria and therefore was finally eligible for HRT on the NHS. This was a huge relief as it meant I no longer had to find the money for pricey visits to a private doctor; now my prescription would be dispensed by my local GP, with the GIC providing guidance when needed. As I was happy with my new dose, I talked the endocrinologist into agreeing to have me stay on spiro. Although she advised against it, I found the side-effects entirely acceptable, considering how great an impact it was having on both my body and mental health.

Another thing I had been ignoring was the impending end of my job contract. With weeks left until its conclusion, it was with mixed feelings that I got the news it wouldn't be renewed. Sympathetically, my manager explained that he'd love to keep me there, enjoying my presence around the office and appreciating my work, but my contract and job role had been very specifically created to last for a limited time only. The intention was originally that the experience would be mutually beneficial to me and the company, and I'd move on to bigger things. I'd actually forgotten that the position I was working in was originally intended as a graduate role, something for someone fresh out of university. Over time it had evolved and my list of responsibilities had ballooned. I'd made friends in other departments and had been given the freedom to help them with their own projects. Apparently, my manager tried to nudge HR into extending the contract so I could continue as I was, but they explained that there was no flexibility in the contract for that. If I was going to stay, I'd first have to leave the company, and then re-apply for a new role.

I would have stayed forever if they'd let me. The low pay didn't bother me given that I'd settled in as a full member of the team and didn't want to leave them behind. But I also knew I'd hit the ceiling on what the job could provide for me. I was comfortable there but bored. Therefore, I decided to turn my disappointment into an opportunity and consider a career change. IT had never been where I'd wanted to end up anyway. I'd been very lucky in how things had worked out, but the job was supposed to just be a safe place to transition in. It was never meant to be where I forged my career.

While browsing for job openings, I came across a position that was radically different to anything I'd ever done. It involved working on the front desk in a building that was open to the public. As well as troubleshooting problems and helping anyone who wandered in with questions, it also required supervising assistants, periodically wandering around to help with odd jobs, and being one of two people responsible for the entire building of an evening. It was an incredibly sociable job. Years earlier, I had considered myself far too shy, awkward, and trans for any role like it. I had spent the last year sat behind a desk at the back of an office, but now I felt curiously confident and self-assured enough to consider applying. The only downside of the job was the hours – they were notably less than the full-time week I'd been working in my current role. If I ended up being given the job, I'd have to ramp up the freelance writing I'd been doing to cover the missing salary.

The more I thought about the role, the more the challenge appealed to me. I pictured myself typing away in a frenzy every morning, then rushing off to help visitors all evening. I would then arrive home at night, collapse into bed, and begin the whole thing over again the next day. That was too enticing a challenge to turn down. I put in an application where I openly talked about being transgender, explaining that my experience within the community had honed my interpersonal skills and given me awareness of the importance of sensitivity and patience. Something in my application must have ticked the boxes they were looking for, as I was shortly invited for an interview.

The day of the interview, I had mixed feelings about the job. I was now second-guessing if it was really for me or if I should try and head back to an office. I knew that if I woke up feeling dysphoric and uncomfortable, then I'd still have to doll myself up and be prepared to deal with the public all afternoon. Was that something I could handle? I wasn't sure. Regardless, I knew that I shouldn't skip the interview – if nothing else, it would be experience. Similar to my last interview, I sat before a panel who bounced between different questions while I did my best to answer honestly (and tell them what I thought they wanted to hear). Towards the end I was asked what event in my life I wished I'd done differently. Frantically, I tried to think of some impressive or wise realisation that I could link back to an event in my life. My mind went blank. All I could think of was my transition. 'Coming out as transgender,' I said, not quite sure where I was about to go with this. I slowly explained that I had learnt a lot in the last three years, and that with this knowledge there are things I know I should have done better. I elaborated, drawing from times where I'd acted hastily and out of insecurity and fear, where I wished I had been more decisive and aware of my actions in a wider context. I wasn't sure if it was a good answer but I wagered it was probably one they didn't hear very often.

I was riding home on the bus that afternoon when I was called and offered the job. I accepted, keeping my hesitation and indecision to myself. In the weeks leading up to my start date, I bounced between excitement and dread. Despite my apprehension, once I actually started I realised I was right at home. The entire team were full of smiles and had a sense of humour I could relate to, while the job itself was perfect for me. I spent my days helping people out and finding all sorts of tasks to do. Surprisingly, I found the social aspect of the job my favourite part: being able to talk to others meant that I never grew restless or bored. If anyone was uncomfortable or unhappy with being served by a trans woman, they never said anything. I also used the job as an excuse to dress up, wearing my big, bold dresses and continuing to let my personality shine through my clothes. Occasionally, someone would pass through who rocked a stereotypically queer presentation, visibly messing with gender norms and often with brightly dyed hair. If we caught each other's gaze, we'd frequently share a knowing smile or a little look of acknowledgement. These moments always warmed my heart; it was like receiving an unspoken high-five or a secret message of support.

The only part of my new job I disliked was the fact that I had to travel home at night. Pre-transition I had almost always worn headphones when out of the house, but I learnt very quickly that I didn't feel safe doing so this late anymore. Being perceived as a woman travelling alone in the dark left me feeling vulnerable and exposed. I always kept my headphones stuffed in my bag and walked in silence, to stay aware of my surroundings. I learnt that my neighbourhood had a whole different side to it at night, which I had rarely seen. My first week was particularly eventful, too. When drunken men spilled onto the street ahead of me, coming out of a non-descript building that I had never understood the purpose of, I slowed my walking speed to a crawl. I followed silently behind them and waited for them to branch into a direction I didn't have to follow. Another night I was confronted by an agitated woman who begged me for money to get home. As I passed her a handful of change, she struck up conversation and asked me my name. I didn't feel that I had any choice other than to play along. Thankfully, after telling me that my name was lovely, she reassured me that if I ever needed help then she and her friends would 'take good care of me', whatever that meant. She then wished me well and stumbled away into the night. The next day as I hopped off the bus, two idling men in a dark doorway paused their conversation to ask how I was doing. I smiled in response and hurried away, with no intention of finding out where that conversation was going to lead. My solution was to rapidly learn the safest route back home, cutting through a residential area and avoiding the local pubs. I then spent my first few weeks briskly power-walking through my neighbourhood and hoping I could get to my front door without any extra attention.

As I settled into the job, I found that I couldn't decide between marching down the brightly lit route, where I could see anyone coming but they could also see me, or creeping through the shadows like Batman to get home unnoticed. Eventually, I decided to take the more public route, thinking that if anything did happen I'd want it to be in the light where at least other people could see. But even when I was surrounded by other people, it didn't deter every creepy encounter. One evening I had stepped into a takeaway to grab some food on my way home. Having waited a while for my order, I collected my food from the counter, and then a middle-aged man wished me a happy evening. Instinctively, I flashed him a smile and said 'Thanks!' as I passed by his table on my way out. At this he asked why I was 'shooting off' so quickly and where was I going. When I explained I was heading home to eat, he invited me to stay with him instead. I shook my head, saying that people were waiting for me to bring home their food. However, he still insisted that I should stay, blaming how late it was for why eating with him was a more enticing offer. Nervously laughing, I said that I needed to go and bolted mid-conversation amidst more of his assurances that we could have a nice time together. What had made me especially uncomfortable was the casual way in which he seemed to think he was so entitled to my time and attention. I'd remained polite because I didn't trust what he might say if I firmly told him to back off. Mainly I was thankful that my food had been ready before his, so he didn't have an excuse to follow me out. Although it wasn't the vibe I got from his tone or body language, it's possible he was trying to be friendly and was oblivious to how he was coming across. But the fact remained that I had no idea what his intentions were. I had to prepare myself for the worst outcome to remain safe.

The scariest night came when I ended up being followed. While walking up a quiet road close to home, I spotted a man staggering slowly towards me. Something about him put me on edge. As I was about to pass him, he stopped. As I walked by, he remained still and watched me. I then turned my head as I pretended to flick my hair free from beneath my hood, which allowed me to see him turn around and begin to follow me. After a few seconds, where helpfully the only thing I could think of was 'Oh dear', I saw another man crossing the road towards me. 'Sorry to bother you, babe!' he called out while gesturing with a gangly arm. 'That's okay. Hi,' I said without thinking. I knew I had made a ridiculous mistake by stopping to address him back. When he reached me, he had to awkwardly bend his body just to reach my eye level. 'Have you got any money, babe?' he said. I should have said no, but worrying about what he might say if I did, I fished into my bag for my change. I didn't want to pull out my purse in front of him, so instead I awkwardly fumbled with both hands in my handbag while he stared on expectantly in silence. 'Oh, I have a bit, here you go,' I said. At this point I was now worried he was going to notice that I was trans. I had no idea what would happen if he figured that out. 'That's great, thank you. Sometimes it's fate people meet, y'know? I think it's fate we were here at the same time. But you don't have any more do you? I just really need it, that's all,' he said. The comment he made about 'fate' disturbed me more than the request for extra money. Now I felt like I was being very politely mugged. 'Maybe? I'll have a look,' I replied. I dove back into my bag and created another awkward few seconds of rummaging. After plucking up my last few coins, I dropped them into his palm. 'It's fate, babe. Thank you. I needed this,' he said. With that, I took a step back and turned to leave, calling, 'Okay. Bye!' I hurried off and only then realised that during the whole exchange I had completely forgotten about the other guy, the one who had possibly turned round to follow me. I didn't dare look over my shoulder again but I hoped that he'd been forced to wander away while I'd been accosted by Mr Fate. Luckily, I made it home without any other incidents. I wasn't in a rush to risk it again next time, but with no alternative route to get home I had to accept that I was going to roll that dice every single night.

The flip side of travelling home at night was travelling to work in the middle of the day. I'd left behind my sleepy comrades on the morning bus route and now travelled amongst an entirely new set of people. I worked out that if I left extra early I had time to go via the city centre and get some shopping in before I arrived for work in the afternoon. In my first week, as I strolled down to the shops, I was catcalled from a nearby bench by a man my dad's age. 'Show us your tits, love!' he shouted unimaginatively, to laugher from his friend. In that moment, I considered spinning on my heels and shouting back a refusal but of course, I didn't dare to actually do so. The horrible reality is that many attacks on trans women are done by men seeking to violently reassert masculinity, often after feeling humiliated for simply noticing us, before realising that we're trans. We're women, but the media has spent decades convincing people we're deceitful men (which does make them complicit in this violence). That whole fallacy needs to be ripped out of our culture, but for now it's still disturbingly prevalent. As a trans woman it would be extraordinarily dangerous to deliberately provoke someone, especially the type of man who is happy to yell lewd demands at women in the middle of the day.

Being catcalled made my skin crawl, but in a patronising and demeaning way it also validated something I'd been thinking about. Although I felt extremely guilty and gross for pulling a positive realisation from misogynistic harassment, it was a sign that I was increasingly being seen as a woman with minimal effort on my part. No longer did I have to carefully apply foundation, mascara, and lipstick before stepping outside. Simply heading out of the house in jeans and a flattering t-shirt was seemingly enough to provoke the correct pronouns from strangers, with all the positive and negative baggage that they came with.

Perhaps it was the leftovers of my low expectations, or still wanting to protect myself from getting too excited, but for weeks I was consistently ecstatic every time I was referred to as 'this lady' or 'that girl' by someone who'd already heard my voice or had a close look at my bare, makeup-free face. For instance, when I rolled into a taxi one morning, having called one because I'd overslept for my Saturday morning shift, the driver asked: 'What route would you prefer, lovely?' I was thrilled to have been correctly gendered but winced when I saw his eyes linger on me in the mirror while I responded. I was convinced that my voice had drawn him to take a better look at me, which had then caused him to change his mind when he saw how I really looked. Yet, at the end of the journey he wished me a nice day and again ended by calling me 'lovely'. I realised I'd fallen into that paranoid line of thinking in self-defence. He'd been looking at me just because I was talking, but I'd scrambled to find the worst explanation for a mundane action. I then reminded myself that it didn't matter if I was misgendered; I knew who I was and liked how I looked. It was fine to enjoy being correctly gendered, but I was only wasting my energy by thinking about how I might receive the wrong pronouns.

On the subject of my voice, it's appropriate to take a moment to talk about it. As a result of what my body went through in my teens, I have a deeper and more masculine-sounding voice than is traditional for a woman. I know of exercises to move my resting pitch and train myself to talk in a more traditionally feminine manner, but I decided early on that I didn't have enough energy or inclination for such a routine. The way I saw it was that my voice was nothing to be ashamed of; it was a natural effect of being a trans woman who was transitioning at this age. It didn't make me feel dysphoric, so to allow myself to feel ashamed or embarrassed by it would be to play into the social demonisation of trans women. There were moments across my transition when I knew it had got me misgendered, but that wasn't enough to push me to undertake the exhausting effort of changing it. Instead, I settled on a softer and higher tone of voice, which felt comfortable and natural, without straining myself to reach something outside of my range.

My goal with my voice, and the rest of my appearance, was not to be mistaken as cisgender, but to be accepted and respected as female, regardless of being trans. I was grateful that I didn't feel at risk by being recognised as transgender – a result of the hard work of trans activists over the last few decades. I didn't see a reason to hide it. Of course, not every trans person is as lucky or privileged in that sense. What dysphoria demands is personal and varied, and I entirely support whatever anyone decides to do to find their own comfort and happiness.

When I went for my yearly flu jab in the autumn, I returned to the chemists that had misgendered me almost two years earlier during my eye test, yet the attendant effortlessly gendered me as female while handing me over to a colleague. More than anything, this candid exchange was the catalyst to change my expectations. It hit me that I no longer had to try to brace myself for misgendering, I didn't have to. I hadn't been considered male by anybody in months. I still believed that I looked notably trans, but clearly hormones had changed my body enough that strangers no longer saw my gender as a confusing question mark, or as potentially male.

I was in a cheap hotel on a short excursion to see friends when the impact of how much I had changed really hit. I stepped out of the bathroom, having just had a shower, and in a long, full-length mirror I saw my body reflected back. Inevitably, I was reminded of the time I saw my reflection in the flat I had shared with Loretta, when dysphoria had sucker punched the pride and happiness I felt. I took a moment to look at its new shape. Years ago I had felt striking disappointment and a violent disconnect between expectation and reality. Now my dysphoria was reduced to a light shower of momentary bemusement. Running my hands over my body, I found my muscle memory was still catching up. Where my hands expected angles, I now found soft curves. Meanwhile, my face was rounder and perkier; I didn't look as tired or gaunt as I had in the past. But there had been more than just surface changes. My eyes held an energetic light to them that they'd always lacked. There was life in me now. My body was not that of a cis woman – it never would be. Eternally, it would hold signs of the way I was born and the first puberty I had endured. But it was still a woman's body. It was a body I now loved. It was mine, and there was nothing wrong with it. The internal voice that used to growl in my ear that I would never be good enough was now silent.

Together, the chemical changes to my body and mind, as well as the tangible alterations I had made to my life, had left me feeling complete. Now I was the one in control, rather than my dysphoria or other people's ideas of who I should be. I continued to try to pass on this goodwill, regularly using social media to write affirmative reminders and share the little tricks and thought exercises that had helped me remain resilient and cheery. When a hashtag went around intended for people to share the names of trans people they admired, I was touched to see so many people name me as one of them, putting me alongside people I had respected and looked up to since even before I had decided to transition. Some people even said that I was an outright inspiration to them, that my frequent upbeat attitude and encouraging messages helped assure them that transition could be something happy and freeing. Although I'd strangely got used to overwhelmingly kind messages like that, it was seeing so many in a row that made me realise I'd become the very type of person I idolised back in my teens. I was a happy and proud trans woman, a visible example of what transition can bring, and someone doing their best to pass on advice. But I also knew I wanted to do things differently with that responsibility. I could say the things that I'd always needed to hear back in my younger years. Instead of spreading the fear and pessimism that had frightened and guilted me into believing I wasn't trans, I could share the opposite message.

The next day I tweeted out a new thread of light-hearted advice, one aimed directly at people who were still struggling to accept that they were trans enough. I explained that the term 'transgender' is not one that's closely guarded or reserved for those of us who are most certain; it belongs to anybody who suspects they might not be cisgender. I went on to assure people that it is okay to question or doubt your gender for your own personal reasons; you don't need to be miserable, you don't need to hate your body, and you certainly don't need to have a history of stereotypical 'signs' in your childhood. Sometimes transition is just about giving yourself a tune-up and an upgrade. Nobody has to prove that they deserve to transition and come out as transgender. There is no test to pass and no permission needed. Furthermore, transition doesn't have to be secretive and shameful; it can be noisy and exciting. There's absolutely nothing wrong with being transgender and nobody should feel they have to hide away in a bedroom. I knew that as long as I had any sort of platform I'd be doing my best to keep passing on that message. Because regardless of how inferior or inadequate someone feels, if they want to transition for any reason, then they are trans enough.

CONCLUSION

Recently, as Christmas was approaching once again, I found myself in Central London on a Saturday night. I was alone. With time to kill before my train was due to leave in another two hours, I'd taken a walk and was sat on a short wall, enjoying the atmosphere. Dozens of people were passing by every minute, each one looking busy, anxious, or excited, embroiled in their own story. I started to contemplate how much had changed for me over the last few years. I'd become unrecognisable from the person I used to be – inside and out – but a lot had happened to get me here. I thought about the years of jealousy and repression, of lost time swallowed by dysphoria, how my transition had forced me to re-evaluate long-held truths about who I was. But this last year in particular had an air of circular completion to it. Events from earlier in my life had been echoed back but with simple and satisfying conclusions, the endings that I'd always wanted. Even now I was sat just as I had been years ago, when I'd been atop that wall and contemplated quitting transition. Inevitably, I had accepted that day that I had to continue and see it through. And I had. Now I didn't see the women around me with envy, or as dreadful reminders of the years of hardship that lay between me and them.

Likewise, the men no longer reminded me that everybody saw me as no different to them, because they no longer did. Now I was simply another woman enjoying the night air and lost in my thoughts. With a calm certainty, I realised that this quiet and private moment was the end.

It was hard to tell when this part of my life really began. My transition date was murky to pin down, especially as I'd gained, lost, and rediscovered the revelation that I was trans along the way. But my transition had never really been about hormones, clothes, or my body; it had been about that feeling deep in my gut, the one that had reminded me that so much of my life didn't feel right; the same part of me that had told me I wasn't trans enough, wasn't woman enough, wasn't loud enough, and just wasn't good enough. Being uncomfortable and uneasy with myself had been such an inherent part of my personality, I could trace it back to my earliest memories and right on through to recent years. That feeling morphed and changed as time passed, but it had never left. It was even still there when I began HRT, a reminder that I still wasn't who I wanted to be. But regardless of when it started, I knew this chapter was finishing because I was finally free of it. My life no longer felt steered and defined by my worst qualities, or my failure to live up to the standards that had been set both by those around me and by myself in my moments of self-loathing and fear. The last three years I had thought about little other than my desire to transition and the things I didn't like about myself. But now I had become someone I truly loved. I was free to move forward without that conflict and stress, to discover the next part of my life, unburdened and happy.

Of course, I'm never going to leave that part of my life entirely behind. I am a trans woman and I'll always wear that status with pride and speak out for trans rights at every opportunity, but it's liberating to know that my evolving identity no longer takes up so much of my headspace. I no longer waste time thinking about the validity of who I am, what others think of me, or how I'm going to untangle the next logistical mess that comes from being trans. I'm at peace.

Even things with my parents have changed. After a year of very little contact, I reached out and expressed my hope that we could put everything that's happened behind us and start over. They responded and echoed the same sentiment; we all shared a desire to move forward and focus on the future. As a result, I was invited over for dinner with them. Even though I was a little nervous about what might happen, I happily accepted and took the opportunity. Amazingly we then got along better than we ever have in my entire life. That evening I could see that they were both making an effort to respect my transition, but not through guilt or shame. They were embracing my new identity so that they could reacquaint with their daughter, and seemed excited by who I'd grown into. Meanwhile, I was able to talk to them with honesty and without restraint for the first time in my life, forming a real connection with them. Afterwards, my dad took me aside and admitted that he was delighted by how upbeat I'd become. He explained that in previous years he'd been stressed and worried about why I was so frustrated and disinterested in everything, but now it was clear what I'd always needed to do. I conceded that I must have been difficult to live with back then, to which he cut in and said that it didn't matter now. I agreed, and reiterated that I wanted to look forward too. I could easily dwell on what went wrong, or even hold a grudge for how badly my coming out went, but I'd gain nothing from it. Instead, through acceptance and forgiveness we've become a family again.

While talking about our future recently, Loretta surprised me with a proposal, asking me to marry her with a gorgeous ring and a handful of flowers. I leapt towards her into a hug, frantically repeating 'Yes' over and over. I'm sure you won't be surprised to learn I did cry, of course. After all that we've been through, and the ways that I've changed, I'm ready and thrilled about the idea of being a bride and starting a whole new story together. In the past, we had talked about marriage but always dismissed it as something for after my transition, when things had settled and I'd potentially grown happier with my appearance. It had always felt like an eternity away, yet here I am looking at wedding venues and daydreaming of what it'll be like to invite all our friends to celebrate with us. What felt like an impossibility for years has finally happened, and I couldn't be happier.

I hope in some way this book has been enlightening, or at the very least entertaining, as a single account of one trans woman's experience with gender across her life. Everything from my childhood, to my awkward teens, to my time in counselling, illustrates why I find the common misconception that trans people transition on a whim such a laughably silly one. It took a lot of effort to accept that I was trans enough to be transgender, and choosing to transition was a whole other conundrum altogether.

Transition is often presented in the media like it's something we decide over lunch, after thinking we'd like to shake up our lives. I've read boring opinion pieces from celebrities who, for some unfathomable reason, have decided it's their turn to chip in on us, especially trans women. They often talk about us as if we picked our gender from a catalogue, trying it on for the first time. We're treated as tourists in our gender, visitors who have decided to holiday somewhere new, then put down some roots. But these people regularly insist we'll always be foreigners in these lands, never knowing what it was like to be born here, or to grow up surrounded by these people and expectations. But as you can see from my own story, I never fitted in where I started; I always belonged here. I'd never argue I had the same upbringing as the cis girls around me, but I certainly didn't have the experience of the cis boys either. My teenage years were a special nightmare, decorated with self-hate and a constant hollow need to be someone I couldn't be. As a young adult, I dragged myself through life in a haze, bored and empty. It was only after I started to transition that my life suddenly gained colour, I finally connected to my emotions and learnt to like myself as a full person. I became who I'd always wanted to be and stopped being what other people were trying to make me into.

If there's a closing message I'd like to impart, I suppose it would be to the cisgender readers: Please try to respect and understand the diversity, depth, and validity of our lives. Listen to the stories that trans people tell, understand we're complex human beings and not politicised concepts. Ultimately, we're just trying to live the only way that we can, by being true to who we are. Trans or cis, that's the only way any of us can be happy, by listening to that feeling in our gut that already knows what we need to do.

It's tempting to let the book close on a purely positive note, but that would be irresponsible of me. I have to stress again that transphobia is still epidemic in the media, and in our society. There's a reason why in this book I've had to anonymise things like where I've worked. With the abuse that I can get online, I don't trust that making that information public would end well. But that said, I've been lucky enough to carve out a relatively safe life for myself down here through generous help, the privilege of my education and skin colour, and a lot of luck. Though I live payslip to payslip, the majority of us in the trans community don't even have as much security and stability as that. Don't be fooled by glitzy award shows into thinking that the trans community isn't one dealing with rampant poverty.

Meanwhile, although it's been a relief to realise I'm now regularly seen as female by strangers, that's because I've been lucky with the effects of HRT. I don't believe I look cisgender, but the changes I have got certainly contribute significantly, along with the fact that my tastes in clothing and accessories skew towards traditional femininity. Essentially, I now unintentionally benefit from cisnormativity. But every trans person deserves to have their gender respected and not be the victim of incorrect presumptions, regardless of their appearance. Expecting all trans people to follow a similar path, or come equipped with obvious visual clues, is a mistake, yet it's one repeated endlessly. It creates a deeply problematic hierarchy, one that is doubled-down on in the media where those who look like they could be cisgender are presented as the poster children for being transgender. But instead of celebrating this limited line-up we should be questioning why as a society we're still depending on aesthetics and standards of conventional beauty to endorse someone's gender. Not all of us want to transition with HRT, conform to expectations with our clothing and hair, or even have a gender on a male/female spectrum to begin with. Until everybody who identifies as transgender feels included and protected, then we've only got selective acceptance for the privileged.

If you're cisgender and reading this, then you're especially in a position to help fight for our rights. You can talk to friends and family, boost and donate to trans people and groups in need (I personally recommend Mermaids, the charity for trans children), and ensure you counter any transphobia that you might come across in your day-to-day life. It really will make a huge difference to the lives of the trans people you come across, and help the continuing campaign to build a more tolerant society. Now is the time to prove that at a defining point in history, when a marginalised group was under attack and struggling for their rights, you stepped up and helped.

As for anyone reading this who thinks that they might need to transition, I'll end on a similar note to the one that the book began on: If you want to come out as transgender because you feel that you're not cisgender, then that's your right to do so, regardless. It will be easy to doubt yourself, to question whether you're making the right choice, but I assure you that if you have these feelings then they are well worth exploring and seeing through. Always remember that you deserve to be whoever you want to be, and what your transition entails is entirely up to you and nobody else. Being transgender is complicated, confusing, scary, and sometimes downright weird, but it's also funny, invigorating, and empowering. If you're ever feeling lonely, afraid, or overwhelmed by all of this, I implore you to head online and look for others to talk to. The trans community is a welcoming place, and there is a place here for you. We've got your back.

RESOURCES

RECOMMENDED BY THE PUBLISHER

Albert Kennedy Trust – AKT provides support for LGBT young people who need supported accommodation that is safe. It is a targeted service that provides housing support for LGBT people only: www.akt.org.uk

Gendered Intelligence – specialises in supporting young trans people aged 8–25, as well as delivering trans youth programmes, support for parents and carers, professional development and trans awareness training for all sectors.

200a Pentonville Road
London
N1 9JP
0207 832 5848
www.genderedintelligence.co.uk

GIRES – resources and e-learning for professionals who wish to improve their knowledge on transgender issues and how to support trans people: https://www.gires.org.uk

LGBT Foundation – offers a variety of support such as counselling, telephone support, events and workshops.

5 Richmond Street
Manchester M1 3HF
info@lgbt.foundation
0345 330 3030
http://lgbt.foundation

Mermaids UK – supports transgender children and their parents and will offer support to community groups and schools working with transgender children.

Suite 5
High Street House
2 the High Street
Yeadon
Leeds LS19 7PP
0344 334 0550
info@mermaidsuk.org.uk
www.mermaidsuk.org.uk

Mind Line Trans + support phoneline – currently open two nights a week (Monday and Friday) from 8pm until midnight: 0300 330 5468

http://bristolmind.org.uk/help-and-counselling/mindline-transplus

Press for Change – an organisation which supports transgender people in enforcing the law in terms of their rights and supports institutions to adhere to the law in supporting trans people: www.pfc.org.uk

Samaritans – suicide prevention. Phone: 116 123. Email: jo@samaritans.org. Local centres can be found on their website: www.samaritans.org

Stonewall – Stonewall's website provides information with regards to support that can be obtained locally by them. The website also provides information relating to rights for trans people, reporting hate crime and how to obtain support: www.stonewall.org.uk/help-advice

True Vision – provides a hate crime reporting service through their website if young people are not confident in phoning the police: www.report-it.org.uk/report_a_hate_crime